NAME DROPPING?

NAME DROPPING?

A No-Nonsense Guide to
the Use of Names
in Everyday Language

PHILIP GOODEN

A&C Black • London

First published 2006
A & C Black Publishers Limited
38 Soho Square
London W1D 3HB
www.acblack.com

© 2006 Philip Gooden

ISBN-10: 0-7136-7588-8
ISBN-13: 978-0-7136-7588-7

A CIP catalogue record for this book is available from the British Library.

This book is produced using paper that is made from wood grown in
managed, sustainable forests. It is natural, renewable and recyclable. The
logging and manufacturing processes conform to the environmental
regulations of the country of origin.

Typeset by RefineCatch Limited, Bungay, Suffolk
Printed and bound in Great Britain by The Bath Press, Bath

INTRODUCTION

'What's in a name?' asks Juliet as she stands on the balcony talking to the night air and agonising about the hostility between Romeo's family and hers. Although Juliet comes to the conclusion that names do not, or should not, matter much, most people would say that names are very significant indeed. If they were not, then – to take a couple of examples – no one would ever be given a nickname nor would companies spend time and money coming up with titles for new products. In other words, a name is not an arbitrary collection of syllables but reflects some inner quality or attribute of that which it names – or so we often think. From here the process spreads outwards whenever the name taken from a person, place or product is used to characterise something else.

Expressions derived from people and places can be wide-ranging and even contradictory in their implications. Politicians are pleased to be called *Churchillian* and may go out of their way to court the comparison, but which aspect of Churchill are we talking about? Is it his speech-making or his inspirational leadership, is it his capacity for drink or his well-known bouts of depression? Writers are *Dickensian* if they throw a grotesque character or two into the mix, but the expression is just as frequently used to describe a grimy, real-life scene straight out of the 19th century while, paradoxically, it can also mean 'sentimental' or conjure up the image of a cosy, old-fashioned Christmas. Epithets such as *Thatcherite* or *Blairite* or *Bushite* (interesting that these particular leaders all have that snappy '-ite' suffix, which can have a pejorative ring to it, as opposed to the softer '-esque' or the more neutral-sounding '-ist' or '-ian') are bandied about, whether in approval and disapproval. And *Hamlet-like*? Does that apply to a person who's heroic, or gloomy and isolated, or someone who simply can't make up his mind?

Generally speaking, the more widely a term is used, the more extensive (and vague) are its borders. Yet, though expressions that carry only one or two senses may belong in the specialist realm, other comparatively narrow terms have found a place in daily language. Film buffs will talk happily about *Cronenbergian* or *Bunuelesque*, while *Hitchcockian* is much more widely understood. How many people, out of the hundreds of thousands who might use *Svengali-like*, know the Victorian novel it came from – or need to know its derivation, since the term is so thoroughly embedded in the language?

This book arose out of the question: what exactly are expressions such as *Kafkaesque* or *Orwellian* or *Monroe-esque* trying to pin down? If they refer to such terms at all, dictionaries tend to define them in a circular fashion as 'in the style of Bloggs ... the politician ... writer ... artist, etc.' But what do the words actually *mean*? *Name Dropping* provides some answers, even if these aren't definitive in some cases, because the reader may well disagree on exactly what shades of meaning are conveyed by, say, *Bothamesque* or *Mozartian*. In addition, the book provides a kind of snapshot of where we are now. *Jordanesque* – from the model not the country – didn't exist a handful of years ago. Nor did *Beckhamesque*. Some names endure, others come and go. How many people are going to understand *Blimpish* a few years from now? When I started writing this book, Kenneth Clarke was a big if ageing beast in the political jungle and David Cameron was a gleam in the eye of a few Tory hopefuls: but here are the Cameroons with their *Cameronian* sound-bites and where are the *Clarkeites*?

Name Dropping defines hundreds of words deriving from famous and notorious individuals and quite a few from places as well. Using examples from the media and other sources, the book shows how these terms are employed, sometimes casually, sometimes with great care. There's a commentary on each expression together with a 'Pretentiousness Index', which gives some idea of how familiar or obscure the word is, and how you might be judged if you were using the word in an everyday context, whether to describe, to clarify, or simply to show off your knowledge. Finally, there is an index in which terms are grouped under headings like *Arts* and *Politics*.

What's in a name...?

Philip Gooden

A

ADONIS-LIKE

like the figure of Adonis in Greek mythology;

'youthful and beautiful', 'perfectly formed':

> 'When he [the young Sean Connery] modelled there were always lots of
> girls in the classes because they were attracted by his Adonis-like physique.
> He was a great inspiration for any artist and was amazing to paint and
> draw.' (quoted, Daily Telegraph)

In the myth Adonis was loved by both Aphrodite (Venus to the Romans)
and Persephone, queen of the underworld. When Adonis was killed by
a boar, Zeus, king of the gods, agreed that he could spend six months in
the underworld and, reborn, the summer months above ground with
Aphrodite. The Adonis myth is probably symbolic of the annual cycle of
growth and decay. *Adonis-like* suggests great male beauty and a perfect
physique. There is also a hint of untouchability to the term, since Adonis
is somehow innocent of all the female attention lavished on him.

PRETENTIOUSNESS INDEX *!*

AHAB-LIKE

in the style of Captain Ahab, a character in Herman Melville's novel
***Moby Dick* (published 1851);**

'furious', 'obsessive', 'fighting to the death':

> The fish the Arsenal goalie had found himself locked in Ahab-like combat
> with was a 28lb carp. (Guardian)

In Melville's famous novel, Captain Ahab pursues a white whale that
has bitten off his leg during an earlier expedition. Ahab's quest, which
ends in his own destruction as well as the whale's, is obsessive to the
point of madness. Properly used, *Ahab-like* combines ideas of
vengeance, mania and struggle-to-the-death – or it may just describe a
fish that is difficult to land, as in the *Guardian* quote.

PRETENTIOUSNESS INDEX *!*

ALAMO-LIKE

connected to the defence of the Alamo mission in Texas during the War of Independence against Mexico in 1836;

'fighting against the odds', 'defiant', 'brave but doomed':

No one can predict what will happen after the first ball is struck on Friday but any exhortations are unlikely to be couched in Alamo-like terms. (Guardian)

The story of the Alamo is a key part of early US history and long ago entered the realms of myth. In the 1830s Texas was a province of Mexico, which had itself won freedom from Spain little more than a decade earlier. The defenders of the Alamo numbered only a few hundred while their attackers were several thousand strong. The mission was overrun and almost all the defenders killed – including such legendary frontiersmen as Davy Crockett and Jim Bowie – but the 'defeat' was the prelude to a final victory for Texas at the battle of San Jacinto with its famous battle-cry 'Remember the Alamo!' *Alamo-like* suggests defiance on the part of the fledgling state and country and in particular recalls the words of commander William Travis, who declared that he would never surrender or retreat. Legend also has it that Travis drew a line in the sand, inviting those of the garrison who wished to stay and fight to step across it.

PRETENTIOUSNESS INDEX **Nil** BUT THIS IS PRINCIPALLY A US REFERENCE.

ALICE-IN-WONDERLAND

reminiscent of Lewis Carroll's story *Alice's Adventures in Wonderland* (published 1865);

'surreal', 'illogical', 'dream-like', 'topsy-turvy':

The officials who try to explain the Council's Alice-in-Wonderland policies are mostly decent, well-meaning human beings who do so with hand-wringing and many martyred grimaces. (The Times)

Alice's adventures in Wonderland, after she pursues the White Rabbit down a rabbit hole, form the basis of what is probably the most quirkily popular book in English. There is a logic to what happens to her, although it is not the logic of the everyday, waking world but rather of one that grows 'curiouser and curiouser', in Alice's own words. The expression *Alice-in-Wonderland* is frequently applied in exasperation to procedures or rules – particularly bureaucratic ones – that seem to defy comprehension or common sense.

PRETENTIOUSNESS INDEX **Nil**

AMAZONIAN

connected to the Amazons, a mythological nation of women warriors;

'strong but feminine', 'self-reliant':

That vulnerable woman is an Amazonian princess with incredible strength, bracelets that deflect bullets, and a golden lasso that forces its trapped victims to tell the truth. (Observer)

Ancient Greek mythology claimed that the Amazon women lived near the Black Sea. Their dedication to fighting was such that they supposedly cut off their right breasts so as to be able to wield their bows more easily. *Amazonian*, quite widely used to describe any physically imposing female figure, particularly in sport, suggests a strapping style of beauty without implying masculinity.

PRETENTIOUSNESS INDEX **Nil**

APOLLONIAN

like the Greek god Apollo;

'harmonious', 'handsome', 'beautiful':

He [Alexander the Great's image] is the Apollonian profile, brow sliding to axe-blade nosetip without hitch, beardless cheeks, huge eyes, small mouth with pleated lips. (Guardian)

Apollo was a multi-tasking god, with responsibilities ranging from the sun to poetry to medicine. He is sometimes seen as the representative of harmony and control, as opposed to the over-the-top excitements suggested by *Dionysian* (see entry). He is also a byword for beauty, and it's in this sense that *Apollo* and *Apollonian* are most often used.

PRETENTIOUSNESS INDEX *!*

ARCADIAN

from the region of Arcadia in ancient Greece;

'rural', 'innocent':

For those of us who have been unashamed fans since its first season, this year's Big Brother *has been the best and most bizarre, though the days of Anna the lesbian nun and Nasty Nick seem almost Arcadian now.* (The Times)

The inhabitants of Arcadia in the central Peloponnese claimed to be the oldest in Greece and their way of life was traditionally rural. In art and literature this became idealised with images of pastoral innocence, accompanied by music and dancing, and Arcadia turned into a pagan or non-religious equivalent of Eden. *Arcadian* therefore harks back to a region/time of lost content, and its overtones of innocence may even be used in a dumbed-down way to recall the early days of *Big Brother* (see example).

PRETENTIOUSNESS INDEX *!*

ARTHURIAN

connected to Arthur, the legendary king who is supposed to have reigned over part of Britain during the fifth century AD, following the Roman occupation;

'romantic and mysterious', 'legendary', 'courtly', 'chivalrous':

> *Another local legend – with Arthurian overtones – relates to a knight, Sir Guy, who was sheltering in the ruins when a wizard approached and led him up a winding stair into a hall where a hundred marble knights and their horses lay.* (Daily Telegraph)

A general with the Latin name of Artorius is first mentioned in the seventh century as having led the Britons in a series of battles against Saxon invaders. But the legend of King Arthur didn't really take off until the medieval period, and it is in English and French texts of that time that the stories start to accumulate: of the Holy Grail, of Lancelot and Guinevere, Arthur's queen, of Camelot and the sword called Excalibur and the Round Table. The medieval interest in chivalry and knightly behaviour and their association with Christianity found a focus in these legends – for example, Edward III created a version of the Round Table at Windsor in the middle of the 14th century. The suggestiveness and mystery of the *Arthurian* stories are part of their appeal and one legend even claims that Arthur is not dead but merely sleeping until his kingdom should need him again. Obviously that day has not yet arrived. *Arthurian* is therefore a very vague term, more to do with literature and legend than history, and carrying almost whatever noble and magical sense the user wants to give it.

PRETENTIOUSNESS INDEX **Nil**

ATTLEEAN

in the style of Clement Attlee (1883–1967) or the government of which he was Prime Minister (1945–51);

'reticent', 'unobtrusive but effective':

Neither clean-cut executive decisions nor Attleean taciturnity are Tony's style, but he would still be well advised to make his mind up quick.

(Guardian)

Clement Attlee was head of the post-war Labour government that was elected in 1945 and defeated the Conservatives under Winston Churchill. A modest man – he said of himself 'I have none of the qualities which create publicity' – he nevertheless led an administration that produced domestic reform on a wide scale, particularly in welfare. On a personal level, Attlee is remembered for his self-effacing manner while, historically speaking, his government was quietly reformist.

PRETENTIOUSNESS INDEX **Nil** BUT THIS IS SOMETHING OF A SPECIALIST TERM FOR POLITICAL HISTORIANS.

AUGEAN

connected to Augeas, king of an ancient Greek state, and always used with reference to his legendary stables;

'filthy', 'laborious':

But a dreadful stint as a live-in domestic for an ancient couple in Chelsea soon put her straight [...] She was never off duty, and the agreed three-hours-a-day turned into an Augean marathon. (Independent)

The task of cleaning out the Augean stables was one of the 12 labours of Hercules. Augeas's stables, full of cattle, had never been cleaned. Hercules accomplished the task by diverting a river so that it flowed straight through them. *Augean* is used to emphasise a job that requires extensive cleaning and clearing, either literally or metaphorically. It's more usual in this second application, and frequently suggests that a clean-up is necessary on moral grounds.

PRETENTIOUSNESS INDEX *!*

AUGUSTAN

in the style of the Roman emperor Augustus (63 BC–14 AD) or of the era dominated by him;

'imperial', 'peaceful and ordered':

'While neo-conservatives may yearn for a new Augustan age based on unfettered US power, most Americans still see strategic advantages in international co-operation.' (quoted, Daily Telegraph)

Gaius Octavius, who took the title of Augustus when he became emperor, was a nephew of Julius Caesar and later became his adopted son. The period of his rule marked the end of a century of civil war and turmoil in Rome and her territories, and represented a high point in the history of the Roman Empire. The term *Augustan* harks backs to an era of peace enforced by a supreme power and crops up occasionally now to describe US dominance of world affairs. The word is also used to characterise the literature of the time, which celebrated Roman values and virtues in the writing of poets such as Virgil.

PRETENTIOUSNESS INDEX *!*

AUSTENESQUE

typical of the style or themes favoured by novelist Jane Austen (1775–1817);

'ironic', 'witty', 'comic', 'highly observant', 'romantic':

> *His name is practically Darcy, for goodness sake, and even without the letter swap, he sounds like a romantic hero of Austenesque proportions.*

(Observer)

It is hard to sum up Jane Austen or *Austenesque* in a handful of adjectives. She has her own flavour, easy to recognise, hard to analyse. Novels like *Pride and Prejudice* (1813) or *Emma* (1816) combine a Cinderella-style fairy tale, in which the neglected or apparently undeserving heroine finally achieves happiness, with some of the most hard-headed social observation ever committed to paper. For all her awareness of human weakness and stupidity, and of social pressures, Jane Austen still produces happy endings. Depending on the angle from which she's regarded, she is an arch-romantic or an arch-realist. *Austenesque* is not found very often, perhaps because the word is slightly cumbersome.

PRETENTIOUSNESS INDEX *!*

B

BABYLONIAN

connected to the ancient city of Babylon in Mesopotamia;

'decadent', 'luxurious':

'To get to that other place I would do drugs; there is this kind of Babylonian village that exists in this city. I am happy it does exist, but it is not where you want to end up.' (quoted, Observer)

Babylon was the city of exile for the Old Testament Jews in the sixth century BC. The city was a byword for luxury and corruption, and it provides an eye-catching addition to sex-and-scandal books with titles such as *Hollywood Babylon* or *Washington Babylon* or, more ironically perhaps, a book on the British film industry titled *Shepperton Babylon*. The adjective *Babylonian* suggests a kind of baroque corruption and decadence, while the noun *Babylon* is Rastafarian slang for white society or for the police.

PRETENTIOUSNESS INDEX **!!**

BACCHANALIAN

in the style of the riots and revelry associated with the Roman god Bacchus;

'wild', 'orgiastic':

This bacchanalian rite of passage is so ubiquitous in recent American cinema that the crazy final party in Risky Business can safely stand for all of them. (Guardian)

Bacchus was the Roman form of the Greek god Dionysus, associated with fertility and uninhibited creativity as well as wine. Bacchus is more usually linked only with drink (and having a good time), while the noun *Bacchanalia* and adjective *bacchanalian* are fairly literary terms describing an unrestrained celebration.

PRETENTIOUSNESS INDEX **!**

(see also *Dionysian*)

BACONIAN[1]

in the style of Elizabethan writer and philosopher Francis Bacon (1561–1626);

'ornately written', '(describing) a person who believes that Shakespeare's works were actually written by Francis Bacon':

> *The attention Shakespeare's words have accrued through the centuries resembles the attention the Holy Book has had. He has been bowdlerised, annihilated by Baconians and Marlovians, decoded and glossed.* (Guardian)

Rather like the Kennedy assassination or the attempt to prove that the moon landings were faked in the Nevada desert, there's something about Shakespeare that drives people crazy. This was especially true in the 19th century, when assorted 'scholars' and fanatics grew desperate to prove that someone else – anyone else – wrote the plays. A favourite candidate was Francis Bacon. In part this was based on the belief that Shakespeare's background was too humble and obscure for such brilliant creativity. How could a lower-class provincial from Stratford know so much about the world of kings and courtiers? Convinced *Baconians* also thought they had found internal evidence within the texts, including codes, showing that their man was the author. The contemporary attempt to 'prove' that Shakespeare was really a Catholic sometimes seems to have echoes of Baconianism about it.

PRETENTIOUSNESS INDEX *!*

BACONIAN[2]

typical of the style of the painter Francis Bacon (1909–92);

'powerful', 'visceral', 'nightmarish':

> *Younger painters in Britain today either try to reinvent Freudian and Baconian figurative violence or go the opposite way...* (Guardian)

Francis Bacon, born in Ireland to English parents, was arguably the most important British painter of the second half of the 20th century. In his pictures of alienation and anguish – 'Three Studies for Figures at the Base of a Crucifixion', a series of 'screaming' popes based on paintings by Velazquez – grotesque figures distort or melt as if labouring under intolerable inner pressure, often against backgrounds that are minimal and restrained. Bacon forged a kind of art that confronts the viewer with the suggestion of some ghastly truth. *Baconian* may also refer to the louche life of the artist who enjoyed drink, gambling and gay sex in industrial quantities, if some of the stories are to be believed.

PRETENTIOUSNESS INDEX *!*

BALKAN

characteristic of the area of south-east Europe sometimes known as the Balkan peninsula;

'unstable', 'quarrelsome', 'prone to division and bloodshed':

The pact that brings England, Wales, Scotland and the two Irelands together for Lions tours is really a Balkan peace. (Daily Telegraph)

The wars that followed the break-up of the former Yugoslavia in the early 1990s focused the world's attention on this historically fluid region and revived the use of *Balkan,* although formal or diplomatic contexts are likely to prefer a more neutral geographical description. The boundaries of the region are shifting and contested but it generally includes countries such as Greece, Albania and Serbia. Much of this territory was under the control of the old Ottoman Empire and it has, historically, been positioned on the fault-line between the cultures of Europe and the Near East. The process of Balkanisation is one of splitting up into hostile groups or small states. Although *Balkan* may have a romantic resonance if it recalls the days of exotic 19th-century travel, any contemporary application is likely to be negative, as in the *Telegraph* quote above (a *Balkan* peace is always on the verge of breaking down).

PRETENTIOUSNESS INDEX **Nil**

BANQUO-LIKE

like (the ghost of) Banquo, a character in Shakespeare's *Macbeth*;

'haunting', 'relentless':

The grisly topic follows us everywhere. We take refuge in the glittering restaurants around Strasbourg cathedral, but it appears, Banquo-like, at our tables, shaking its gory locks at us as we fondle our foie. (Daily Telegraph)

In Shakespeare's play, Macbeth has Banquo killed by hired assassins because he suspects that the Scottish nobleman knows too much, specifically that he has already murdered his way to the throne. At a feast to celebrate his coronation, Macbeth twice sees the spectre of Banquo covered in blood and shaking his 'gory locks'. The sight, which is visible to no one else, terrifies him. *Banquo-like* suggests the persistent return of something disturbing and particularly unwelcome at what would otherwise be a pleasurable moment.

PRETENTIOUSNESS INDEX *!*

BARBIE-DOLL

like the US doll known for its long hair and clothes and accessories;

'glamorous', 'pliable', 'empty-headed':

> *She has a long, blonde Barbie-doll hairstyle that puts the sex into the 1950s beehive, sphinx-like eyes lined with make-up, and pouting lips.*
>
> (Daily Telegraph)

When used about a real woman, *Barbie-doll* hovers somewhere between compliment and insult. Compliment because it suggests sexual attractiveness, albeit of a male fantasy kind, and insult when the associations with the original doll are foremost, so that the expression combines the bimbo with the clothes-horse.

PRETENTIOUSNESS INDEX **Nil**

BARDIC

in the style of a 'minstrel-poet'; in the style of Shakespeare;

'describing a national, public poet/dramatist', 'Shakespearean':

> *The basic joke is that an old Shakespearean ham, Edward Lionheart, having been robbed of a coveted award, decides to murder seven critics in appropriately Bardic style.* (Guardian)

In a specialist sense a bard may be a poet recognised by the Welsh Eisteddfod. But *the Bard*, spelled with a capital *B*, was a coyly romantic way of referring to Shakespeare in the 19th century and later periods, comparable to toe-curling descriptions like 'the Swan of Avon'. The adjective *Bardic* is likely to be found now only in an ironic or hammy context, as in the *Guardian* quote.

PRETENTIOUSNESS INDEX *!!*

BASIL FAWLTY-LIKE

in the style of Basil Fawlty, the hotel owner played by John Cleese in the TV series *Fawlty Towers*;

'manic', 'inept', 'snobbish':

In a pamphlet for the Centre for Policy Studies he developed his theme, deriding the Tory effort as Basil Fawlty-like because they were told, 'Don't mention tax and the economy', once the party's greatest strengths. (The Times)

Supposedly based on a hotel where the Monty Python team stayed when they were filming in Torquay, *Fawlty Towers*, first aired in 1975, justifiably became one of the most popular BBC programmes of all time. In large part this was because of Cleese's interpretation of Basil Fawlty, by turns timorous, fawning and bullying, and guaranteed to put his foot in it. The episodes were tightly constructed farces, and the *Times* quote above is a reference to a classic of the first series when Fawlty, fazed by the arrival of a group of German tourists, repeatedly instructs his staff not to mention the war before himself performing a Hitler-style walk in front of his guests.

PRETENTIOUSNESS INDEX **Nil**

BATEMANESQUE

in the style of the drawings or cartoons of H(enry) M(ayo) Bateman (1887–1970);

'behaving incongruously', 'provoking outrage because of a *faux pas*':

First, Jeremy Paxman called Health Secretary John Reid an 'attack dog'. Then the Leader of the Commons, Peter Hain, described Michael Howard as an 'attack mongrel'. Yet these weedy insults have provoked uproar and outrage on an almost Batemanesque scale. (Daily Telegraph)

Henry Mayo Bateman was an artist whose work appeared in magazines such as *Punch* and *Tatler*. He specialised in large-scale cartoons showing the results of social gaffes and *faux pas*, with titles like 'The cad who threw a snowball at St Moritz' or 'The man who dared to feel sea-sick on the Queen Mary'. The innocent or hapless figure who makes the 'blunder' is surrounded by outraged or guffawing spectators. Bateman's world is a fairly cosy and conventional one, dependent on widely recognised social norms, but *Batemanesque* may still be used to describe the social shock or amusement when someone behaves in public in an inappropriate way. That said, this is a reference not likely to be understood by many people now.

PRETENTIOUSNESS INDEX *!*

BEARDSLEY-ESQUE

in the style of writer and artist Aubrey Beardsley (1872–98);

'decadent', 'elongated', 'stylised':

Tall, slim and somewhat Beardsley-esque, he was a distinctive figure.

(The Times)

Aubrey Beardsley, who died of consumption at the age of 26, was a key figure in the *fin-de-siècle* movement of the 1890s. His brilliantly accomplished drawings, with their whipcord-like use of line and artful deployment of black and white contrasts, embodied the then-fashionable ideas of decadence. Popular all over again in the 1960s, when his erotic drawings were widely seen for the first time, Beardsley's cartoons adorned countless student walls. *Beardsley-esque* is also used to describe a certain male physical style/appearance, thin and elegant with a hint of the perverse.

PRETENTIOUSNESS INDEX *!*

BECKETTIAN

connected to the Irish-born novelist and playwright Samuel Beckett (1906–89);

'absurd', 'despairing but comic':

> *She invites me to sit beside her in the stalls, facing the empty stage – a set-up which, combined with her cool resistance to the business at hand, induces the strangely Beckettian feeling that I am still waiting for the real Isabella Rossellini to turn up.* (Observer)

Samuel Beckett was a leading figure in what became known as the Theatre of the Absurd, a type of drama that was fashionable in the decades following World War Two and which, with its disjointed dialogue and humorously surreal 'plots', pointed to the meaninglessness of life. Beckett's best-known play is *Waiting for Godot* (1955), in which two tramps pass the time waiting for a figure who never materialises, and this is the reference in the *Observer* quote above.

PRETENTIOUSNESS INDEX *!*

BECKHAMESQUE

in the style of footballer David Beckham (1975–);

'supremely skilled at football', 'at the centre of media attention', 'extravagant':

> *Cabin in the Sky's prices [for tree-houses] start at £3,000 for a basic platform with waterproofing. Or you could always have a Beckhamesque extravaganza – if your garden is big enough and your pockets deep.*

(Observer)

It may seem slightly unfair to choose a quotation that emphasises David Beckham's spending power or lavish tastes, since the footballer's position as one of the most celebrated Englishmen in the world was initially earned through his prowess on the field. Captain of the England national team and currently playing for Real Madrid, Beckham has achieved superstar status and the scrutiny that goes with it. His hair styles, his dress sense, his tattoos, his off-the-field antics, above all his marriage to ex-Posh Spice Victoria – everything is media fodder, to be characterised as *Beckhamesque*. Together, the Beckhams have finessed their global celebrity into a highly lucrative brand.

PRETENTIOUSNESS INDEX **Nil**

BECKY SHARP-LIKE

similar to the character of Becky Sharp in the satirical novel *Vanity Fair* (1847) by William Thackeray (1811–63);

'go-getting', 'unscrupulous':

Budge began her working life as a housemaid in pre-war Berwickshire and reached the climax of her Becky Sharp-like career with her marriage in 1975 to the lobotomised heir of one of Scotland's great titles. (Guardian)

Becky Sharp is the original bad girl of Victorian literature. From an obscure background, Becky rises through society using sex and deviousness to make herself secure and comfortable. In fact, she's no worse – and a lot more attractive – than most of the male characters. The *Becky Sharp-like* comparison suggests a mix of sex and ambition.

PRETENTIOUSNESS INDEX *!*

BERGMANESQUE

characteristic of the style or themes favoured by Swedish film director Ingmar Bergman (1918–);

'chilly', 'austere', 'pessimistic', 'intimate':

Apparently resentful of the acclaim accorded to his comedies – the 'early, funny ones' – he [Woody Allen] decided to immerse himself in the cold Bergmanesque bath of serious dramas such as September and Another Woman, which won him no new friends and alienated most of the old ones.
(Independent)

When art-house cinema started to establish a foothold in the Britain of the early 1960s, it was often associated with the films of Ingmar Bergman, such as *The Seventh Seal* or *Wild Strawberries*. The frequently dour and earnest style of Bergman's film-making fitted most people's perception of Scandinavian culture, and was about as far removed as possible from the traditional Hollywood product. The *Independent* quote above refers to Woody Allen, probably the US director most consciously turning out 'art-house' films.

PRETENTIOUSNESS INDEX *!*

BETJEMANESQUE

typical of the style or themes of poet John Betjeman (1906–84);

'suburban', 'melancholy', 'lyrical':

> *Gerrards Cross is a Betjemanesque small town in the heart of affluent Buckinghamshire commuterland, its entrance off the main A40 through a gateway flanked by beechwoods in full fig, and a velvet expanse of village green.* (The Times)

John Betjeman's poetry reached an unusually wide audience, helped by the welcome return of familiar devices like rhyme as well as by the reassuring range of his subject matter, although the lyricism and cosiness is often undercut by melancholy and wistfulness. Towards the end of his life Betjeman became even better known as a TV personality than as a poet. His teddy-bear looks, his championing of then-unfashionable Victorian architecture, his love affair with suburbia and the provinces, all confirmed him as an authentic English eccentric. A conveniently vague term, *Betjemanesque* tends to conjure up images of girls in tennis outfits, gardens in Surrey and neglected churches that turn out to be 'gems'.

PRETENTIOUSNESS INDEX *!*

BEVANITE

describing the beliefs of Labour MP Aneurin (Nye) Bevan (1897–1960) or one of his followers;

'old-style socialist', 'passionately left-wing':

> *A committed Bevanite, he embraced many Left-wing causes, including the Movement for Colonial Freedom and the Campaign for Nuclear Disarmament.* (Daily Telegraph)

Bevan was the standard-bearer for what was seen as the 'old left' long before the advent of Tony Blair. A former miner, Bevan became MP for Ebbw Vale (the Welsh mining constituency later held by one of Bevan's most devoted followers, Michael Foot). Bevan's greatest monument was the establishment of the National Health Service in 1946. The term *Bevanite* describes a dead or dying breed of politician, light years away from the spin and media savvy of new Labour.

BIG BROTHERISH

in the style of the fictional character of Big Brother, head of the Party in George Orwell's novel *1984* (published 1949);

'all-powerful', 'all-seeing and all-knowing', 'sinister':

Is such meddling another step towards a Big Brotherish editing of literature and history? (The Times)

Long before Big Brother gave his name to a TV series, he was a character in Orwell's classic satire on totalitarianism. Whether Big Brother really exists even within the confines of the novel or whether he is merely the imagined figurehead of the Party is never made clear. In part, Orwell based BB – 'black-haired, black-moustachio'd, full of power and mysterious calm' – on the Russian dictator Joseph Stalin, whose avuncular 'Uncle Joe' image was belied by his extreme ruthlessness. In current usage, *Big Brotherish* is a standard accusation levelled against government, providing a sinister alternative to the expression 'nanny state'. Television's *Big Brother*, which features an all-seeing (but unseen) authority figure on whose whims the housemates or victims become childishly dependent, is an accurate reflection of one aspect of Orwell's novel. (It's interesting to note that *Room 101*, another long-running TV show, also derives from *1984*, in which the room with that number is the place of ultimate torture.) The specific reference in the *Times* quote above is to the rewriting of history in Orwell's *1984* so that everything that happens conforms to the Party's outlook and predictions.

PRETENTIOUSNESS INDEX **Nil** THIS IS A VERY WIDELY FOUND TERM, AND I DOUBT WHETHER ONE IN A THOUSAND USERS RECALLS ITS ORIGINS IN GEORGE ORWELL'S NOVEL, SO THOROUGHLY HAS IT BEEN ABSORBED INTO EVERYDAY ENGLISH.

(see also *Orwellian* and *Stalinesque*)

BIRTIST

typical of the style or approach of John Birt (1944–), a former Director-General of the BBC;

'bureaucratic', 'reformist', 'modernising':

The longest and most gruelling section is devoted to the way he 'stream-lined' the BBC for the 21st century. In these pages all is for the best in the best of all Birtist worlds.   (Daily Telegraph)

John Birt began his broadcasting career with Granada and London Weekend Television, becoming Director-General of the BBC in 1992. He introduced reforms in the organisation, including an internal market whereby different sectors competed against each other. Birt's changes were unpopular within and beyond the BBC, and he was regarded as a soulless bureaucrat tampering with a national institution, although some argued that the corporation had to adapt to face a digital, multi-channel future that was very different from the old days of a handful of terrestrial TV channels. After stepping down from the BBC in 2000, Birt was given a peerage and appointed by Tony Blair as a personal advisor. Birt may be admired in some quarters but he has never been liked – his brief for 'Blue Skies' thinking in government was widely mocked – and any application of the term *Birtist* is likely to be critical.

PRETENTIOUSNESS INDEX **Nil**

BLAIRITE

typical of the style, policies and politics of Prime Minister Tony Blair (1953–) or describing one of his supporters;

'modernising', 'addicted to spin', 'opportunist', 'deceitful', 'informal', 'telegenic':

Mr Cameron beats Mr Brown on the Blairite assets of likeability (by 52 to 46 per cent) and charisma (by 44 to 29 per cent), but is behind him on all other measures.   (The Times)

Of all the British Prime Ministers of the last 40 years, only Margaret Thatcher and Tony Blair have provoked such widely differing personal and political assessments, not merely inside their own parties but in the country at large. It is no coincidence that both oversaw substantial modernisation, even revolution, in the parties they dominated, and that both won three election victories in a row and have together notched up more than two decades in Downing Street. Tony Blair realised that Labour, after years of unelectability, had to align itself with post-Thatcherite British politics; soon after being elected leader in 1994 he rebranded his party as New Labour, ditching the old shibboleths such as a commitment to nationalisation and proclaiming a new rigour in areas like law and order where Labour had traditionally been perceived as weak. Blair was lucky in inheriting a relatively strong economy from the outgoing Tories and having in Gordon Brown a Chancellor of the Exchequer who extolled prudence and good management. He was also received, almost rapturously in some quarters, as a new and youthful face – the youngest Prime Minister for nearly two centuries – after years of Tory sleaze and decline under John Major. As long as things went well, Blair was hailed as the saviour of the Labour Party and, to a certain extent, of the country. But the rot always sets in after a few years: the early suspicions of Blair as a leader more interested in style than substance, as a control-freak and (from the perspective of the left) a traitor to true socialism, have spread with the result that *Blairite* is now more generally employed as a term of abuse than praise. Fairly or not, the term has shifted from suggesting modernisation and freshness to conveying a slickness and lack of principle, and Blair is attacked for everything from his closeness to George W. Bush to the behaviour of his wife Cherie. And though even his enemies would concede that he is highly skilled at presentation, they merely use that as another stick to beat him with.

PRETENTIOUSNESS INDEX **Nil**

BLAKEAN

in the style of poet and painter William Blake (1757–1827);

'visionary', 'unconventional', 'paradoxical':

Sartre takes refuge instead in Blakean aphorisms. 'To be faithful is to be unfaithful to everything.' 'The absence of God is more divine than God.'

(Independent)

Blake was a unique figure in English poetry, and one who was thought mad by some of his contemporaries. From an early age he experienced visions, once telling his mother that he had seen 'a tree filled with angels'. An anti-authority figure, he was charged in 1803 with uttering 'treasonable expressions' but acquitted. The *Independent* quotation, however, focuses on another *Blakean* feature: his taste for riddling or paradoxical aphorisms such as 'The tigers of wrath are wiser than the horses of instruction.'

PRETENTIOUSNESS INDEX *!*

BLIMPISH

in the style of Colonel Blimp, a creation of the political cartoonist David Low (1891–1963);

'stuffy', 'reactionary':

If it were me – and I am not sure if this is too Colonel Blimpish – I would encourage every university course to include aspects of wooding, or if not, of boat-handling, lobster-potting, or any other de-alienating activity.

(Daily Telegraph)

The idea of Colonel Blimp came to cartoonist David Low in the early 1930s. He was inspired by, among other things, the sense of an existing word (a *blimp* being a gas-filled balloon) and a military man's letter to the newspapers which, objecting to the mechanisation of the cavalry, insisted that soldiers ought to wear spurs in their tanks. Blimp, a corpulent, walrus-moustached figure, was the mouthpiece for spluttering patriotism and stuffy views. At first a satirical figure, he later came to be regarded quite fondly as embodying a kind of Britishness. However, *Blimpish* now has almost entirely negative associations.

PRETENTIOUSNESS INDEX **Nil**

BLOFELD-STYLE

like Ernst Stavro Blofeld, the arch-villain in Ian Fleming's James Bond novels and films;

'ultra-villainous', 'diabolically ingenious':

Perhaps [TV] controllers could save time and embarrassment by installing Blofeld-style trapdoors in their offices. (Independent)

Every superhero needs an arch-enemy who is almost as indestructible as he is. Blofeld, head of the terrorist organisation SPECTRE, has this role in the Bond stories, even if he actually appears more frequently in the films than the novels (six times as against three). In the early films like *From Russia with Love* his face wasn't shown but only his hands stroking a white Angora cat. The part later became a valuable cameo role, played by such distinctive actors as Donald Pleasence and the wonderfully camp Charles Gray. Blofeld had the habit, in the films at least, of rounding on unsuspecting subordinates and despatching them through trapdoors, etc.

PRETENTIOUSNESS INDEX **Nil**

(see also *Bondish*)

BLOOMSBURY-ISH

connected to the group of artists and writers who met originally at the house in Gordon Square, Bloomsbury, belonging to sisters Vanessa and Virginia Stephen (later Woolf);

'bohemian', 'dedicated to art and friendship', 'earnest', 'elitist':

This was established as the location of a Bloomsbury-ish bohemian community of yore, with lavish bar, magnificent library and a printing press long since fallen into disuse. (Guardian)

The Bloomsbury group, an informal association without rules, first gathered in Gordon Square in the early years of the 20th century (when the Bloomsbury district was neither fashionable nor expensive). The group was dedicated to friendships and aesthetics, and included several influential figures such as economist Maynard Keynes and historian Lytton Strachey as well as Virginia Woolf and E.M. Forster. Many of the Bloomsburyites felt they were rebelling against Victorian social, sexual and artistic conventions, and the terms *Bloomsbury* and *Bloomsbury-ish* came to stand for a vaguely progressive, art-for-art's-sake outlook. Often identified with privilege and elitism, *Bloomsbury* tends now to be used in its historical/cultural context. It remains a convenient way of pigeon-holing a bohemian group or person although, like *Bohemian* (see entry), the expression can look a bit musty.

PRETENTIOUSNESS INDEX *!*

(see also *Forsterian*)

BLYTONESQUE

in the style of or typical of the subject matter of children's writer Enid Blyton (1897–1968);

'child-like', 'old-fashioned', 'innocent':

Major Bruce Shand, a bluff Army type, once said that he felt he had given his children an 'even run' – his two daughters and one son had emerged from their Blytonesque childhood of ponies, bicycles, small furry pets and long hot summer hols as rounded, easy going, no-nonsense human beings.
(Daily Telegraph)

Enid Blyton enjoyed the kind of literary success with children that her contemporary Agatha Christie achieved with adults and, for all that the latter's stories are to do with murder and human wickedness, both writers evoke a lost England of hot summers, sleepy villages and middle-class adventuring. In Blyton's case, of course, the adventurers were children, as in her *Famous Five* and *Secret Seven* books as well as the school stories in the *Malory Towers* series. Enid Blyton also created Noddy and the rest of the gang for younger readers. Children's books and tastes have changed radically, but *Blytonesque* isn't a particularly disparaging term. At most it registers the naive, slightly saccharine innocence of her world.

PRETENTIOUSNESS INDEX *!*

BOADICEAN

reminiscent of Boadicea (or Boudicca), female leader of a revolt against the Roman occupation of Britain;

'warlike', 'powerful and domineering':

So farewell Hamilton, old bean. Farewell Christine, battleaxe of Boadicean proportions. (Daily Telegraph)

Boadicea was the widow of the king of the Iceni tribe in eastern England. When the Romans reneged on a treaty, Boadicea led a revolt against them in 61 AD and sacked Colchester and London. After her defeat by the Roman governor of Britain, she died, possibly as a result of taking poison. England obviously doesn't know what to do with its heroines, since the adjective *Boadicean* tends to be found in humorous contexts, signifying a woman who is large, intimidating and strident – a dragon or a battleaxe. For all that, there may be a tinge of affection in the use of the expression.

PRETENTIOUSNESS INDEX *!*

BOHEMIAN

connected to the old kingdom of Bohemia, now part of the Czech Republic;

'artistic', 'unconventional':

And yet, significantly, when the group requires a bohemian backdrop for their latest album cover they insist on holding the photo-shoot at Newcombe's squalid little apartment, in the hope that its seedy glamour will rub off on them. (Guardian)

A *Bohemian* was originally an inhabitant of Bohemia, later a gypsy (since they were supposed to come from there) and so a vagabond or a person leading an 'irregular' life. The use of *Bohemian* to suggest an artist (writer, painter, etc.) goes back almost two centuries, and implies that a person with artistic leanings is likely to enjoy an unconventional existence, rejecting social norms. This is essentially a 19th-century expression, spilling over into the 20th century, and it is perhaps surprising that the term is still widely used since plenty of people lead *bohemian* lives without bothering about the 'artistic' bit.

PRETENTIOUSNESS INDEX *!*

(see also *Bloomsbury-ish* and *Fitzrovian*)

BONDISH

in the manner of James Bond, the secret agent created by novelist Ian Fleming (1908–64);

'glamorous', 'suave', 'ruthless':

In the cold light of day, however, it's hard to deny that the 1960s Connery films were the most Bondish of all, and that among them the most potent cocktail has always been Goldfinger. (Daily Telegraph)

It's hardly necessary to identify or explain James Bond, 007, secret agent extraordinaire. *Bondish* (also *Bond-esque*) might apply to a range of personal attributes and tastes (from 'worldly' to 'patriotic' to 'womanising') or, in the films, to the quality of the villains or even the appearance of the girls. In the *Telegraph* quote above it's not clear whether *Bondish* applies to the films themselves, in which case it's a circular reference, or to the original novels. Bond aficionados are clear about the distinction between the books and the films, which, particularly in the Roger Moore years, became a playground where high-camp met high-tech. The early Sean Connery versions are generally regarded as being more faithful to the spirit of Ian Fleming.

PRETENTIOUSNESS INDEX **Nil**

(see also *Blofeld-style*)

BORGESIAN

characteristic of the style or themes favoured by Argentinian writer Jorge Luis Borges (1899–1986);

'mirror-like', 'esoteric', 'labyrinthine':

The air of unreality thickens when the hapless teacher is mysteriously charged with performing a series of assassinations to save her. A sinister Borgesian game uncoils whose denouement is cleverly obscured until the final pages. (Observer)

Born in Buenos Aires, where he eventually became director of the National Library, Borges is most famous for short stories that play games with reality and identity. They are eerie and compressed, so that it often seems as though an entire novel has been condensed into a few pages. Sometimes presented as detective-style puzzles, they have a dream-like, bookish atmosphere reminiscent of G.K. Chesterton, of whom Borges was an admirer. Borges's status as a sage was heightened by the blindness that afflicted the closing years of his life, and *Borgesian* connotes a riddling wisdom.

PRETENTIOUSNESS INDEX !

BOSCH-LIKE

in the style of a picture by the Flemish painter Hieronymus Bosch (c.1450–1516);

'grotesque', 'horrifying', 'hellish':

> *Last year Saatchi paid half a million pounds for Jake and Dinos Chapman's Hell, a tableau depicting Bosch-like tortures enacted by thousands of tiny model Nazi soldiers.* (Guardian)

Hieronymus Bosch, about whom little is known, still provides a benchmark for artistic depictions of hell. Bosch's images of tormented human beings, nightmarish animals and strange implements set against a dark, flickering landscape look oddly contemporary. This is the reason why the output of currently fashionable artists such as the Chapman brothers (see quote) can be compared to the work of a man six centuries after his death.

PRETENTIOUSNESS INDEX !

BOSWELLIAN

showing the style or attitudes of Scottish writer and biographer James Boswell (1740–95);

1) 'devoted', 'painstaking':

> *If the Boswellian labour of indexing all his works had failed to prick my conscience, this lady's passing remark had done the trick. Get a life!*
> (Alexander Waugh, *Fathers and Sons*)

2) 'frank', 'disarmingly honest, especially about oneself':

> *The second is Brandreth's positively Boswellian candour about his own gaffes and humiliations – and they were many – while he learned the Westminster ropes.* (Guardian)

One of the key meetings in the history of English literature took place on 16th May 1763 when James Boswell encountered Samuel Johnson for the first time. Boswell, the ambitious son of a Scottish judge, had long been angling for an introduction to Dr Johnson, arguably the most celebrated literary figure of the day. The meeting did not go well at first, with Johnson being rude about the younger man's Scottishness and Boswell being too eager to ingratiate himself with the great sage. Nevertheless, a strong friendship developed between the two and over the next 20 years Boswell gathered material for his classic *Life of Samuel Johnson*, which eventually appeared in 1791. Boswell was absolutely dedicated to the task and to the man who had inspired him, and one meaning of *Boswellian* suggests this faithful discipleship. But the Scot was a complex, moody character with an energetic sex life, which was reflected in his letters and journals. These weren't published in his lifetime but their frankness, about himself as much as anyone else, also gives the sense of 'candid' to *Boswellian*.

PRETENTIOUSNESS INDEX **Nil**

(see also *Johnsonian*)

BOTHAMESQUE

typical of the style of playing or personality of England cricketer Ian Botham (1955–);

'all-rounder', 'colourful', 'assertive':

The Queenslanders in the crowd will pile on the pressure – whereas Flintoff had the Bothamesque ability to quell their XXXX-induced cockiness.

(Guardian)

Ian Botham was the dominant player of his era and remains famous for what seemed to be the almost single-handed victory of England over Australia in the 1981 Test series. Despite the almost inevitable run-ins with the tabloids, Botham is still a very popular figure, one who has forged a new career in television and charity work. *Bothamesque*, however, is likely to suggest a swaggering assurance combined with save-the-day skills.

PRETENTIOUSNESS INDEX **Nil**

BRANSONESQUE

connected to or in the style of businessman, entrepreneur and balloonist Richard Branson (1950–);

'dashing', 'enterprising', 'very rich':

What kind of elected president are you going to impose on us? A clapped-out politician deprived of political power: Thatcher, Major, Jenkins, Owen, Ashdown, Kinnock, even Blair? Or a populist Bransonesque president, selling Britain to the world? (Observer)

Richard Branson is Britain's best-known billionaire – and probably Britain's best-known beard too – and one who, despite his wealth, has managed to retain a reputation for hipness and informality, even a kind of super-ordinariness. His ballooning exploits have kept him in the public eye and he takes care to link himself with the launch of each latest Virgin enterprise. Branson, combining an approachable image with a 'can-do' attitude, used to be regularly touted as the kind of person who might be elected president of the country if the monarchy ever disappeared – hence the *Observer* comment above.

PRETENTIOUSNESS INDEX **Nil**

BRECHTIAN

connected to the writings or the theories of German playwright Bertolt Brecht (1898–1956);

'radical', 'politically committed', 'stylised':

> *[The film* Manderlay*] is more focused than* Dogville *but has similar ideas and, shot in the same Brechtian style, on a bare sound stage with minimal props, feels like an unnecessary near-remake.* (Independent)

Bertolt Brecht, author of *The Threepenny Opera* (1928) and *Mother Courage* (1941), forged a style of drama which stressed that what the audience was watching was a piece of theatre rather than an attempt to create the illusion of reality. To this end, the traditional apparatus of sets was dispensed with, and the plays were often composed of short scenes and included song and dance. *Brechtian* can describe this style of drama presentation, but it generally carries the additional sense of 'politically committed' or 'propagandist', since Brecht was closely associated with the East German Communist Party.

PRETENTIOUSNESS INDEX *!*

BRIDESHEAD

typical of the style or content of Evelyn Waugh's novel *Brideshead Revisited* (published 1945);

'lavish', 'aristocratic', 'snobbish', 'nostalgic':

> *So, while an open-top 1930s Jaguar SS100 capable of 125mph may be perfect for reliving that Brideshead life that you never quite had, it doesn't half rattle the fillings.* (Daily Telegraph)

Evelyn Waugh's novel was written in the closing stages of World War Two and marked a departure from his earlier satirical work. With its focus on the history of an old, aristocratic Catholic family and its loving evocation of pre-war life at Oxford and in country houses, *Brideshead Revisited* was an antidote to the austerity of the war years. Waugh wrote it with serious intent as a study of 'the operation of divine grace on a group of diverse but closely connected characters', but the book is remembered for its languid air of luxury, an impression helped by the famous TV adaptation of the 1980s. *Brideshead* therefore is shorthand for a lost and lavish way of life.

PRETENTIOUSNESS INDEX *!*

BROBDINGNAGIAN

connected to the imaginary land of Brobdingnag in Jonathan Swift's satirical novel *Gulliver's Travels* (1726);

'on a large scale', 'gigantic':

Jefferson, a Brobdingnagian 6ft 10in tall, made a career-best 165 last week against Nottinghamshire. (Daily Telegraph)

Brobdingnag is the second of the imaginary countries visited by Gulliver the traveller. Where the first, Lilliput, had been occupied by miniature people, Brobdingnag is full of giants, who literally look down on Gulliver as their physical and moral inferior. Although *Lilliputian* (see entry) suggests insignificance and pettiness as well as referring to something small, the counterpart expression *Brobdingnagian* tends to be no more than a striking way of describing a person or object of large or unnatural size.

PRETENTIOUSNESS INDEX *!*

(see also *Swiftian*)

BRONTEAN

in the style of the novels produced by the Brontë sisters, Emily, Charlotte and Anne;

'secluded', 'brooding', 'ruggedly romantic':

The familiar Brontean figures are present and correct: clever, frustrated girls, strong-minded but powerless women, enigmatic men, precocious children. (Daily Telegraph)

With the passing years, the legend surrounding the Brontë sisters has grown to be as potent as anything in their two best-known books,

Emily's *Wuthering Heights* (1847) and Charlotte's *Jane Eyre* (1847). The sisters' upbringing in a parsonage in the Yorkshire town of Howarth, their intense and introverted creative lives, the pseudonymous publication of their first novels, even their early deaths, all have contributed to what is probably the archetypal image of romantic authorship. *Brontean* has a range of applications: from suggesting a kind of suppressed feminism to being used to describe the bleak but exhilarating moorland that surrounds their home.

PRETENTIOUSNESS INDEX *!*

(see also *Heathcliffian*)

BROWNITE

connected to Gordon Brown (1951–), Labour MP and Chancellor of the Exchequer;

'prudent', 'dour', 'economically competent':

> *If the content weren't enough – Brownite talk about redistribution and equality for all – the e-mail is dark brown on light brown except for the bottom of the page which is, er, light brown on dark brown.* (The Times)

Gordon Brown, the son of a Scottish clergyman, has been Chancellor of the Exchequer since Labour's return to power in 1997, giving him the record for the longest continuous period of service in that office. During an extended period of low inflation and high employment, Brown is generally credited for his 'prudent' management of the economy, so dispelling the perception that Labour is incompetent in this area. He has been helped by his dour, serious approach and his evident mastery of economic minutiae. Since he is considered to be more in keeping with Labour tradition than Blair, *Brownite* (also *Brownian*) may indicate a less than wholehearted New Labour outlook; it may point to an earnest, unsmiling approach to politics; or it can suggest a certain dullness and obsession with policy detail.

PRETENTIOUSNESS INDEX **Nil**

(see also *Blairite*)

BRUMMELLESQUE

in the style of 'Beau' Brummell (1778–1840), arbiter of taste;

'stylish', 'decisive in influencing taste':

> *And even now, when chain shops have obliterated its originality, to walk*

down the King's Road is the nearest thing I know in London to going on holiday. It still has an echo of that Brummellesque buzz. (Daily Telegraph)

George Brummell was famous for his wit, his dress sense and his friendship with the Prince Regent (later George IV). He died impoverished in France but his name is a byword for dashing good taste.

<small>PRETENTIOUSNESS INDEX</small> *!!*

BRUTUS-LIKE

with the character of Marcus Junius Brutus (85–42 BC), assassin of Julius Caesar and a principal conspirator in Shakespeare's play of the same name;

'noble', 'honourable', 'treacherous':

Some I remembered and cherished from their first appearance in the paper, such as Andrew Rawnsley's description of Sir Geoffrey Howe's Brutus-like assassination of Margaret Thatcher. (Guardian)

The main image of Brutus comes to us through Shakespeare's play *Julius Caesar*, where he is presented as an idealistic but naive figure, one who joins the anti-Caesar conspiracy in the belief that he is acting selflessly in the interests of the Roman Republic. This is where the 'noble' aspect of his character comes in, but in practice all that anyone remembers of him is that Caesar, seeing Brutus advancing on him with dagger drawn, is supposed to have said 'Et tu, Brute?' ('You as well, Brutus?') and given up the fight against his murderers. Unfairly or not, *Brutus-like* suggests a treacherous individual, one who will turn ruthlessly on former friends or allies. This interpretation was reinforced by the story circulating in Rome that Brutus was in fact an illegitimate son of Caesar.

<small>PRETENTIOUSNESS INDEX</small> *!*

BUCHANESQUE

reminiscent of the style or themes of novelist John Buchan (1875–1940);

'rugged', 'thrilling':

The head coach Andy Robinson did not care if the script lacked any hint of Buchanesque suspense; a sequence of four straight defeats is over and his rebuilding plans can proceed against Scotland next Saturday with fewer vultures circling the drawing-board. (Guardian)

John Buchan produced over a hundred works of fiction, biography, poetry, etc., combining a literary career with strenuous public service (ending as governor-general of Canada). However, he is remembered today for his adventure thrillers, specifically *The Thirty-nine Steps* (1915), *Greenmantle* (1916) and *The Three Hostages* (1924). Forerunners of the James Bond stories in their straightforward patriotism, though much more gallant in their attitude, Buchan's tales start in the smoking-rooms of clubs where gentlemen-adventurers gather before setting off for various corners of the world during what was the high point of the British Empire. A slightly dated reference, *Buchanesque* might suggest anything from 'clubbish' to 'imperial' to 'boyishly adventurous', but it tends to be used as a synonym for 'thrilling'.

PRETENTIOUSNESS INDEX *!*

BUDDHIST-STYLE

connected to the teachings of the founder of Buddhism, Siddhartha Gautama (c.563–c.483 BC);

'detached', 'tranquil', 'not materialistic', 'spiritually pure', 'seeking enlightenment':

Presiding over the haggling hordes, Mrs Maxwell finally managed a Buddhist-style detachment from her worldly goods. (The Times)

Whatever the complexities of the teachings of Buddha, the popular image of him in the West is of a seated, meditative figure, the emblem of remote tranquillity. Unless the term is used in a specifically religious context, *Buddhist-style* is likely to refer only to someone who manages to remain serene against the odds or someone who sets no store by material possessions.

PRETENTIOUSNESS INDEX **Nil**

BUNTERESQUE

in the style of Billy Bunter, fictional creation of Frank Richards;

'fat', 'greedy':

The chemistry intensified; Vorderman slimmed down and turned herself from a maths frump into a vamp seen at film premieres, while Whiteley became more Bunteresque. (The Times)

Billy Bunter was the 'fat owl of the Remove' of Greyfriars School in the boarding school stories that ran in the *Magnet* comic between 1908 and 1940. Frank Richards – real name Charles Hamilton (1876–1961) – created the archetypal fat schoolboy in the days when obesity and greed were comic targets rather than an excuse for government intervention. While the adjective *Bunteresque* (or *Bunter-like*) may be mocking, it carries a faint overtone of affection too.

<small>PRETENTIOUSNESS INDEX</small> *!*

BUNUELESQUE

in the style of or typical of the themes favoured by Spanish film director Luis Buñuel (1900–83);

'surreal', 'perverse', 'subversive':

Assailed by Bunuelesque S & M fantasies of bedding her hunk on a mountain of garbage, she finds herself generating industrial amounts of rubbish to lure him inside her kitchen. (Guardian)

Luis Buñuel's first film, *Un Chien Andalou* (1928), was co-directed with the surrealist artist Salvador Dali (see *Daliesque*). It opened with a notorious image of an eyeball being slit; Buñuel announced early on his desire to surprise and shock. The reference in the *Guardian* quote above is to one of his most popular films, *Belle de Jour* (1967), in which a bourgeois housewife relieves her boredom and lives out her fantasies by working afternoons in a brothel.

<small>PRETENTIOUSNESS INDEX</small> *!*

BUNYANESQUE

in the style of John Bunyan (1628–88), author of *The Pilgrim's Progress*;

'plain and vigorous', 'embarking on a pilgrimage', 'journeying':

The M25 is a circle that goes nowhere [...] A walk that becomes a Bunyanesque pilgrimage, a way of reimagining London from its scattered ruins. (Guardian)

The Pilgrim's Progress (published in two parts, 1678/1684) famously recounts the story of Christian who sets out on a journey to the Celestial City. Bunyan's allegory has remained popular ever since, and any quest that involves setbacks but has some higher, spiritual purpose may be described as *Bunyanesque*.

<small>PRETENTIOUSNESS INDEX</small> *!*

BUSHITE

typical of the style, personality or politics of the 43rd US President, George W. Bush (1946–);

'tax-cutting', 'asserting the national interest', 'hard-edged', 'stumbling in speech', 'folksy':

> *This president, who flew away on Monday to fundraisers in the west while the hurricane blew away entire towns in coastal Mississippi, is very much his father's son when it comes to the kinds of emergencies that used to call forth immediate White House action before its Bushite captivity.* (Guardian)

George W. Bush is the most controversial President of the United States since, well, since his predecessor, Bill Clinton. But whereas Clinton had the good fortune to preside over a relatively prosperous and tranquil stretch of US history, Bush's presidency will forever be defined by the Twin Towers attacks and the nebulous 'War on Terror' that followed, together with the invasions of Afghanistan and Iraq. I suspect that *Bushite* tends to be used pejoratively – there's something dismissive in the very sound of the word. But the qualities in Bush that set many people's teeth on edge – his simple formulations, his gung-ho approach to solving world problems, his religiose talk, his smirk – are also the things that appeal to those others who see in the President a straight-talking, God-fearing kind of guy. So *Bushite* is almost meaningless unless or until it is defined by its context.

PRETENTIOUSNESS INDEX **Nil**

BUTSKELLITE

adjective formed from *Butskellism* and combining the names of two British post-war politicians, the Conservative Cabinet minister R(ichard) A(usten) Butler (1902–82) and the Labour Party leader Hugh Gaitskell (1906–63);

'middle of the road', 'socially liberal':

> *In the fifties, however, sociology was more fashionable than ever, boosted by two other developments: the growth of mass marketing and the Butskellite consensus.* (Dominic Sandbrook, *Never Had It So Good*)

During the 1950s the policies of the Conservative and Labour parties seemed set to converge, particularly in the social field. There was little disagreement over the benefits of the welfare state, the need for full employment and so on. In particular R.A. Butler, who had overseen the 1944 Education Act, which provided free secondary education for all children, embodied the 'one-nation' Toryism that was, sadly, discredited in the 1980s. Hugh Gaitskell, leader of the Opposition, was also a moderate figure during a period in which the two principal parties scarcely bothered about establishing clear blue water between themselves. This lack of difference was apparent enough for the terms *Butskellism* and *Butskellite* to be coined.

PRETENTIOUSNESS INDEX *!*

(see also *Gaitskellite*)

BYRONIC

connected to the life or writings of poet Lord (George Gordon) Byron (1788–1824);

'dashing', 'romantic but dangerous', 'rebellious', 'dazzling', 'witty':

A world of mystery, horror and passion unravels as Jane [Eyre] falls for the strange Byronic figure of her employer whose mad Creole wife is hidden away upstairs. (Observer)

Lord Byron was a dominating, almost mythical figure in the culture of early 19th-century England and beyond. He enjoyed a hectic life as a poet and letter-writer, seducer and traveller, dying prematurely (from fever) even as he hoped to participate in the Greek War of Independence against Turkey. The spell he cast over women, and men, was famous throughout Europe. His separation from his wife Annabella after only a few months of marriage sparked a dynamite trail of rumours as to its cause, and anything from homosexuality to incest to satanism was grist to the rumour-mill. (And it seems likely that Byron did have an affair with his half-sister Augusta.) The heroes of some early 19th-century novels, such as Rochester in *Jane Eyre* or Heathcliff in *Wuthering Heights*, have a defiantly *Byronic* edge. Anyway, *Byronic* may describe a look – slightly dishevelled but always flowingly 'poetic' – as much as an attitude of careless rebellion and highhanded masculinity. It's perhaps ironic that the term is least likely to be used to refer to his poetry.

PRETENTIOUSNESS INDEX **Nil**

BYZANTINE

connected to the city of Byzantium (later Constantinople and now Istanbul);

'very intricate', 'labyrinthine', 'devious':

But the system of government in New Orleans is byzantine in its complexity, with different levees answering to different authorities, and corruption and incompetence legendary. (Sunday Times)

Originally founded as a Greek colony, Byzantium was renamed by the Roman emperor Constantine in the fourth century AD and became the capital of the Roman Empire in the east. The empire declined but the pre-eminence of the city lasted for another thousand years. The Byzantine political and bureaucratic system was highly structured and complicated, and *byzantine* has been used ever since to signify any processes, particularly governmental ones, that are very complex. There's usually a hint of criticism in the term, with the implication that deviousness and sometimes dishonesty are involved.

PRETENTIOUSNESS INDEX *!*

C

CALIBAN-LIKE

similar to the character of Caliban in Shakespeare's play *The Tempest*;

'savage', 'instinctive', 'child-like':

American architect John Cassavetes, disgusted with life in the States, takes his daughter (Molly Ringwald) to live on a Greek island where the only other inhabitant is a Caliban-like shepherd (an exuberant Raul Julia). (Observer)

In Shakespeare's strange and final play Caliban is one of the occupants of an island ruled by the magician Prospero. The offspring of a witch, Caliban is characterised as a 'savage and deformed slave' and kept under control by Prospero. There's something brutish about Caliban but something child-like as well. Shakespeare gives him some of the most poetic lines in the play and he is a more sympathetic figure than the civilised villains.

PRETENTIOUSNESS INDEX *!*

(see also *Prospero-like* and *Miranda-like*)

CALIGULAN

in the style of Caligula (12–41 AD), Roman emperor between 37 and 41 AD;

'vicious', 'sexually depraved':

For £150 an hour she offers men the chance to develop themselves into 'sex gourmets' – lovers with such an instinctive feel for pleasure centres that Caligulan nights and astronomical laundry bills await. (Observer)

Even among the ranks of the more debauched Roman emperors, Caligula stands out for his arbitrary cruelties. (He once wished that the Roman people had a single neck so that he might kill them with one blow.) The reference to *Caligulan* nights in the *Observer* quote is based on his reputation for sexual excess. A real *Caligulan* night would probably be an uncomfortable experience, but perhaps the writer is thinking of the soft-porn film *Caligula* made in 1979 and subsequently disowned by just about everyone involved with it.

PRETENTIOUSNESS INDEX *!!*

CALVINIST

reflecting the beliefs or manner of theologian John Calvin (1509–64) or describing one of his followers;

'strict', 'dour', 'emphasising sin':

> *'Despite what people may think about a Calvinist upbringing, I don't think my father was stern,' he says.*   (Daily Telegraph)

The best-known of Calvin's doctrines is probably his belief that certain individuals were predestined for salvation. He stressed the sinfulness of man in his unredeemed state and the pre-eminence of biblical authority. But *Calvinist* is now used as shorthand for a rather forbidding and authoritarian outlook both in life and in religion.

PRETENTIOUSNESS INDEX **Nil**

CAMERONIAN

characteristic of the style or attitudes of David Cameron (1966–), elected leader of the Conservative Party in 2005;

'bringing a new style', 'youthful':

> *If this season's bestseller is a book entitled* Is It Just Me Or Is Everything Shit? *[...] the time seems right for a national emotional shift of Cameronian proportions.*   (Spectator)

After three election defeats in a row, and as many leaders, the Conservative Party finally plumped for a new leader in what they hoped was the Blairite mould in December 2005. Some commentators labelled his supporters Cameroonians (or Cameroons) while his policies are, of course, *Cameronian*. But what exactly does that mean? No one seems to know. At the moment *Cameronian* simply implies something that is fresh, buzzy, new, happening, blah-blah…

PRETENTIOUSNESS INDEX **Nil**

CANDIDE-LIKE

with the manner or outlook of Candide, the central figure in Voltaire's satirical novel of the same name;

'innocent', 'trusting', 'naive':

Like Björk in Dancer in the Dark, Barry is an innocent. He is a Candide-like figure whose suffering is in proportion to his honesty. (Daily Telegraph)

Candide is a wide-eyed innocent who, under the guidance of his tutor Dr Pangloss, endures a variety of misfortunes with philosophical optimism ('Optimism' is the alternative title to the book, first published in 1759). *Candide-like* isn't a pejorative or dismissive term; if anything there is a trace of pity or admiration in it for an optimism that is resiliently maintained in the teeth of the evidence.

PRETENTIOUSNESS INDEX *!*

(see also *Panglossian*)

CANUTE-LIKE

connected to King Canute (c.994–1035) and the story of the incoming tide;

'presumptuous', 'futile':

But I can't help feeling that its general secretary, Brendan Barber, is taking a Canute-like stance over this issue – with similar foreknowledge that his actions are futile. (Daily Telegraph)

The Danish-born Canute (or more correctly Cnut) was king of England from 1016 until his death in 1035. There are two versions of the Canute-ordering-the-waves-to-turn-back story. In the first version the king, as a Christian convert, wanted to show his obsequious courtiers that the power of an earthly ruler was limited, since he could no more control the forces of nature than they could. In the second but 'inaccurate' version, Canute is depicted as a foolish, arrogant figure commanding the incoming tide to withdraw. The story may not be true in the first place but it seems a little hard that a demonstration of the limits of a king's power should turn Canute into a byword for obstinacy and stupidity, which is what *Canute-like* usually suggests. In particular, the expression is applied to those who naively believe they can turn back some sweeping process of change in human affairs.

PRETENTIOUSNESS INDEX **Nil**

CAPRAESQUE

in the style or recalling the themes of US film director Frank Capra (1897–1991);

'populist', 'sentimental':

It's a clever premise, bringing together populist notions of an Ealingesque or Capraesque kind in which the little man is pitted against the big, anonymous organisation, together with larger ones about causation, accidents and the nature of a divine order. (Observer)

Capra's best-known film is the often-shown *It's a Wonderful Life* (1947), in which a Christmas-time angel demonstrates to a suicidal James Stewart that his life really has made a difference to the small town where he lives. In another representative film, *Mr Smith Goes to Washington* (1939), a hick young senator – James Stewart again – fights big government corruption in the Senate. The term *Capraesque*, therefore, nails down a schmaltzy upholding of American values and a celebration of small-town life.

PRETENTIOUSNESS INDEX *!*

CARTERESQUE

typical of the style or policies followed by the 39th US President, Jimmy Carter (1924–);

'idealistic', 'homespun', 'do-gooding':

Another Carteresque proposal could be introduced very quickly. He imposed strict regulations to force car manufacturers to improve the miles per gallon achieved by every car. (Independent)

Jimmy Carter, President of the United States from 1976 to 1980, had the bad luck to preside over a period when inflation was running high at home and American power was challenged or snubbed abroad. His time in office saw the Soviet invasion of Afghanistan in 1979 and it ended ignominiously with the Iran hostage crisis, in which around 100 US diplomats were imprisoned within their own embassy in Tehran for 444 days (they were released only when Ronald Reagan was inaugurated as President). Carter attempted to project a folksy image – wearing sweaters when he broadcast to the nation, walking with his wife Rosalynn to the White House after his inauguration rather than travelling by motorcade – but he never succeeded in being a true man of the people and his pious, sometimes preachy tone tended to irritate. He early identified environmental problems, which were largely forgotten in the glitter and triumphalism of the Reagan era. As sometimes happens with political figures who are perceived as failures in office, Carter's reputation has grown in the years since he lost power (he was awarded the Nobel Peace Prize in 2002), although there are some who have always thought he should have received more credit as President.

PRETENTIOUSNESS INDEX **Nil**

CASSANDRA-LIKE

in the style of Cassandra, daughter of the king of Troy, who foretold the destruction of the city;

'doom-laden':

> *Braver hypochondriacs may have stood up from their pub seat and pointed at you, shouting Cassandra-like warnings of imminent financial meltdown amidst all this fiscal devil-may-care jollity.* (Guardian)

The mythical figure of Cassandra never delivered a cheerful prophecy, foreseeing only the ruin of her own city of Troy. She was also doomed not to be believed. So being a *Cassandra* or *Cassandra-like* is to be both gloomy about the future and, generally, ignored. People tend to forget that Cassandra was right.

PRETENTIOUSNESS INDEX **Nil**

CASSIUS-LIKE

similar to Gaius Cassius, one of the leaders of the conspiracy against Julius Caesar and a character in Shakespeare's play of the same name;

'conspiratorial', 'devious', 'treacherous', 'lean':

> *Meanwhile, back in the office, Cassius-like underlings will be waiting to grab your job while you are still stocking up on giant Toblerones in the Gatwick duty-free.* (Observer)

Our impression of Cassius comes almost entirely through Shakespeare's *Julius Caesar*, in which he is depicted as a manipulative and envious figure, and the principal organiser of the assassination. Caesar describes him as 'lean and hungry', his bodily shape suggesting his dangerous ambition, and he is generally seen as the most unscrupulous of the conspirators. As the *Observer* quote above indicates, there's a back-stabbing quality to someone who is *Cassius-like*.

PRETENTIOUSNESS INDEX *!*

(see also *Brutus-like*)

CHANDLERESQUE

in the style of Raymond Chandler (1888–1959), US writer of detective novels;

'hard-boiled', 'flip and witty':

> *The heroic motivation to protect women unites all three main characters, as does their gruff Forties-style voiceover, a hard-boiled staccato that occasionally risks a note of Chandleresque humour: 'He was as expert as a palsy victim performing surgery with a pipe wrench.'* (Independent)

Beginning with *The Big Sleep* (1939), Chandler introduced Philip Marlowe, the original private-detective-as-knight-errant, of whom his creator said 'Down these mean streets a man must go who is not himself mean, who is neither tarnished nor afraid.' *Chandleresque*, however, tends to refer less to Marlowe than to the milieu of the author's books – the mean streets of 1940s Los Angeles – or to his writing style, with its throwaway one-liners and elaborate images.

PRETENTIOUSNESS INDEX **Nil**

CHAPLINESQUE

in the style of comic actor and director Charlie Chaplin (1889–1977);

'accident-prone', 'skilled in slapstick', 'tramp-like', 'poignant':

> *Lloyd had seen a version of Atkinson's Chaplinesque prat-faller Mr Bean in their earliest student theatrical revues.* (Guardian)

Few people now could name any of Chaplin's films, except perhaps *The Great Dictator* (1940) in which he satirised Hitler; it is as an image or a series of attitudes that he is remembered: playing the forlorn tramp, the accident-prone little man. The majority of Chaplin's pictures were made before the arrival of sound, and he left an indelible impression with his woebegone features, the pathos of his situations and (occasionally) his acts of revenge on those who'd done him down. *Chaplinesque* may refer to any clown-like mime that is meant to stir pity but it's more likely to describe moments of slapstick, as in the *Guardian* quote above.

PRETENTIOUSNESS INDEX **Nil**

CHAUCERIAN

in the style of medieval poet Geoffrey Chaucer (c.1345–1400);

'humane', 'bawdy', 'humorous':

Our marshalling as 'pilgrims' – a Chaucerian lollipop man was a nice touch – was the most effective part of the evening. (The Times)

Chaucerian denotes not so much a style of writing as an approach to life. Large areas of Chaucer's own life are blank or shadowy, but the persona that comes down to us through his writings is comic and sympathetic. He is most famous for the extended sequence of stories, *The Canterbury Tales*, in which a group of pilgrims on the way to Canterbury in the Middle Ages agree to tell stories to pass the time on the journey. Some stories are romantic, some are a bit dull, but the best-known are probably the bawdy ones such as *The Miller's Tale* or *The Reeve's Tale*, with their mixture of bed-hopping, mistaken identity and farting. It's from these tales that Chaucer gets his reputation as a slightly risqué writer but one who almost always seems in humorous sympathy with his creations.

PRETENTIOUSNESS INDEX **Nil**

CHAUVINIST

like the French patriot and soldier Nicolas Chauvin (and later an abusive shortening of *male chauvinist*);

'fanatical', 'unthinkingly patriotic':

As members of an upper class whose time is up, he and Bond treat foreigners as objects of suspicion and disdain [...] none is to be trusted, all speak funny and each, in turn, is to be vanquished by 007's patriotic British steel. Bond's Britishness is Fleming's – stoic, right-wing and chauvinist. (Observer)

Nicolas Chauvin, a devoted follower of Napoleon, was wounded many times while serving in the army. Somewhat unfairly perhaps, he was then caricatured in several plays of the post-Napoleonic period, which poked fun at Chauvin's extreme dedication to the emperor and his country. He became the archetype of the unthinking patriot.

PRETENTIOUSNESS INDEX **Nil**

CHEKHOVIAN

typical of the style or themes favoured by Russian writer and dramatist Anton Chekhov (1860–1904);

'elegiac', 'subtly observed':

It took nearly two years for Brian Friel to complete this unsatisfying, Chekhovian-bound tragicomedy about the mid-1970s decline of a family of Catholic gentry in Donegal. (Evening Standard)

Chekhov's short stories are regarded as masterpieces of the genre, but he is best known for four plays written towards the end of his brief life, including *The Three Sisters* (1901) and *The Cherry Orchard* (1904). Set in pre-revolutionary Russia and focusing on the lives of the provincial gentry, these tragicomedies deal with boredom, decline and frustration. Any story or drama that is understated, autumnal or shows a wry sympathy with the fading upper classes is likely to be labelled *Chekhovian*.

<small>PRETENTIOUSNESS INDEX</small> *!*

CHESTERTONIAN

characteristic of the style, themes or approach of the writer G(ilbert) K(eith) Chesterton (1874–1936);

'vigorous', 'patriotic', 'whimsical', 'paradoxical':

> *Chestertonian Englishness is founded on an apprehension of alien threats, which are built into its very heart.* (Guardian)

Journalist, novelist, poet, literary critic and Catholic apologist, G.K. Chesterton wrote a great deal, but his best-known work remains the series of Father Brown detective stories, about a mild-seeming Catholic priest who solves mysteries with logic and a dash of spirituality. In other writings Chesterton championed the 'little man' against the state and celebrated the virtues of an older, half-buried England. Chesterton's patriotism was idiosyncratic – for example, he campaigned against the Boer War – and has more than a touch of Merrie England about it. His fondness for paradox and for fantastic puzzles, often labelled *Chestertonian*, was useful both in his detective stories and his religious and social writings.

<small>PRETENTIOUSNESS INDEX</small> *!*

CHRISTIE-LIKE

typical of the style, subjects or plots of mystery-writer Agatha Christie (1890–1976);

'cosy', 'mysterious', 'suspenseful', 'ingenious':

> *The race for the Fulham job has taken another Agatha Christie-like twist with the news that Chris Coleman is not out of the running at all.*
>
> (Guardian)

Fortunately, the days of knocking Agatha Christie seem to be over – not that adverse criticism ever made any difference to her extraordinary success – and she is newly appreciated more than 30 years after her death as a supreme exponent of the traditional whodunnit. Dame Agatha will always be identified with the 'cosy' corner of detective fiction, an England of sunny villages and mansion blocks, retired colonels and ladies of the manor. Christie's ingenuity may have tailed off in her later novels but in classics such as *The Murder of Roger Ackroyd* (1926) and *Murder on the Orient Express* (1934) she rewrote the rules of the game. Readers came to expect last-minute surprises, twists in the tale, hence the *Guardian* reference above.

PRETENTIOUSNESS INDEX **Nil**

(see also *Poirot-esque*)

CHURCHILLIAN

typical of the style, rhetoric or leadership of politician, writer and statesman Winston Churchill (1874–1965);

'maverick', 'legendary', 'commanding', 'inspirational':

Two who are still alive [of ten Great Britons in AOL poll] are Baroness Thatcher and Dame Ellen MacArthur, whose achievements are very different but who both embody some kind of Churchillian British grit, one sinking the enemy and the other staying afloat. (The Times)

Winston Churchill was born at the height of the Victorian age and, as grandson to the Duke of Marlborough, into a position of supreme privilege. After a military career, including a period as a correspondent during the Boer War, he pursued a political career that saw him briefly as Home Secretary and later as Chancellor of the Exchequer in the latter half of the 1920s. For all that, Churchill's public life before World War Two has sometimes been described as a failure, and he famously spent the 1930s in the political wilderness, warning of the danger of Fascism in Europe but lacking the power to do anything about it. It was then that he gained the reputation as a maverick outsider. When the threat posed by Nazism became plain even to the most blinkered, Churchill was vindicated. He became Prime Minister in 1940, at the head of a coalition government. Churchill remains famous for his sonorous oratory, and phrases from the wartime speeches that crystallised Britain's will to resist are embedded in the popular consciousness. Whenever a contemporary leader appeals to the nation, particularly in time of war or danger, it's likely that the term *Churchillian* will be applied, and many politicians go out of their way to court the comparison. But Churchill was also a man of wide abilities outside politics: images of him painting or writing are nearly as familiar as those of him giving speeches or inspecting troops or touring London during the Blitz. He remains as famous for his witticisms as his cigars and drinking ('I have taken more out of alcohol than alcohol has taken out of me'), as well as his moods of depression, which he christened the 'black dog'. There was a Renaissance quality to him, which the term *Churchillian* also suggests.

PRETENTIOUSNESS INDEX **Nil**

CICERONIAN

in the style of the Roman orator and politician Marcus Tullius Cicero (106–43 BC);

'formal', 'eloquent':

In the early 1960s, America's public rhetoric – from John F Kennedy's Ciceronian inaugural ('Ask not what your country can do for you, but what you can do for your country') to Martin Luther King's 'I have a dream' speech – was rather old-fashioned.   (Guardian)

Cicero emerged from a relatively obscure background to become one of the most influential and famous figures in the Roman Republic. A persuasive speaker in the law-courts and the Senate, he also ensured that his speeches were preserved for posterity by arranging their publication. The *Ciceronian* style is formal, elevated and powerful – and, when applied to a present-day speaker, perhaps consciously old-fashioned (see quote).

PRETENTIOUSNESS INDEX *!*

CINDERELLA

like the character or situation of Cinderella in the fairy tale;

'used to drudgery', 'neglected', 'ultimately successful':

Some are terrific, some blinkered by political concerns, but all get ground down and spat out from this Cinderella service.   (Spectator)

Everyone knows that Cinders did go to the ball, courtesy of her fairy godmother, where she won the heart of Prince Charming and wound up living happily ever after with him. But it is generally the grim, overlooked aspect of her life as a kitchen drudge that is evoked in the use of *Cinderella* to describe a group, institution or service that is low in the pecking order, and whose work or reputation is the opposite of glamorous, the opposite in fact of everything that is usually meant by 'fairy-tale'.

PRETENTIOUSNESS INDEX **Nil**

CIRCEAN

like the witch Circe in the *Odyssey*;

'enchanting but dangerous', 'transforming':

> *Is it not possible that Cruise is the one who has fallen under Holmes' Circean spell, and not the other way around?*　(Guardian)

Circe was a beautiful sorceress who transformed men into beasts. She turned Odysseus's crew into pigs, and Odysseus escaped the same fate only because he was forewarned. In the myth Odysseus and Circe eventually became lovers. *Circean* suggests a power that is seductive but dangerous and even degrading in its effects.

PRETENTIOUSNESS INDEX *!*

CLARKEITE

in the style of or describing a follower of Conservative politician Kenneth Clarke (1940–);

'blokish', 'robust', 'pro-Europe':

> *But Europe [...] is always with us – and, whatever befalls the constitution and the euro, there's no reason to believe, after 15 years of failing to do so, that the Tories will suddenly find a form of words both the Clarkeite and sceptic wings of the party will support convincingly.*　(Daily Telegraph)

Ken Clarke, one of the few survivors from the Edward Heath Conservative government of the early 1970s, seems to have had his day now that he has finally abandoned any hopes of becoming leader of his party. Under Margaret Thatcher and John Major, he was Health Secretary and Chancellor of the Exchequer. Generally more popular with the public than he ever was with most of his party, Clarke – a jazz-loving, Hush-Puppy-wearing bird-watcher – is seen as a regular bloke, one who speaks his mind without bothering too much about political spin. However, in the media use of the term, *Clarkeite* generally refers to his pro-European stance and his belief that Britain should switch currencies by abandoning the pound in favour of the euro. Seems like ancient history now.

PRETENTIOUSNESS INDEX *!*

CLAUDIUS-LIKE

similar to the character of Claudius, king of Denmark in Shakespeare's *Hamlet*;

'hypocritical', 'blustering', 'murderous':

> *His contempt for his mother's Claudius-like lover – a foul-mouthed, bully-*
> *ing coach-fleet operator superbly played by Denis Quilley – is hilarious.*
>
> (Daily Telegraph)

In Shakespeare's famous tragedy, Claudius kills his brother in order to lay hands on the Danish throne and on his brother's wife. He spends the play fending off his nephew Hamlet's attempts to unmask him. Shakespeare shows us that Claudius has a conscience, even if he's unable to act on it, and he can come across as a not totally unsympathetic character. However, *Claudius-like* tends to suggest deceit covering itself with a show of bonhomie.

PRETENTIOUSNESS INDEX *!*

CLINTONIAN

connected to the 42nd US President, Bill Clinton (1946–);

'charismatic', 'slick', 'deceitful':

> *For eight years I have tried not to tell outright lies, but there have been some*
> *Clintonian evasions and prissy parsing.*   (Guardian)

During his term of office (1992–2000) Bill Clinton divided American opinion more than any recent US President – until the arrival of his successor George W. Bush, that is. To his supporters in the Democratic Party and elsewhere Clinton was a consummate politician, a brilliantly empathetic speaker, an authentic hero risen from a working-class background – the 'first black President' in one of the more over-the-top descriptions. These are the positive associations of the term *Clintonian*. His many detractors agreed that he was the consummate politician, but to them he was a representative of all that was most hated about the legacy of the 1960s: a draft-dodging, pot-smoking, morally dubious opportunist. The Lewinsky scandal almost brought Bill Clinton down. He survived, just, impeachment charges of perjury but his evasive performance under questioning and his admission that he had misled the American people, together with evidence of other, barely suppressed scandals, turned *Clintonian* into a word of near-abuse. In particular, Clinton's legalistic hair-splitting as he tried to defend himself seemed demeaning both to him and the office he held. So, with the expression *Clintonian*, you pays your money...

PRETENTIOUSNESS INDEX **Nil**

(see also *Lewinsky-like*)

CLOUSEAUESQUE

in the style of the fictitious French police inspector Jacques Clouseau, played by Peter Sellers in *The Pink Panther* (1963) and subsequent films;

'bumbling', 'accident-prone':

Warner calls her smart, gripping analysis of the gin debate a 'tragicomedy', and if the tragedy lies in the brutal conditions that decided so many Londoners to drink themselves to death, the comedy can be found in the clueless, Clouseauesque legislative measures brought in to combat the problem. (Guardian)

The Pink Panther of the title was a diamond but all that anyone remembered from the first film was Peter Sellers' disastrous policeman, constantly enduring pratfalls on his way to mess up another investigation. *The Pink Panther* spawned half a dozen sequels – one of them produced after Sellers' death and using out-takes from earlier films – and the word *Clouseauesque* entered the language to signify bumbling incompetence, usually in relation to the police or the law.

PRETENTIOUSNESS INDEX *!*

COLOSSEUM-STYLE

in the style of the entertainments provided at the Roman amphitheatre or arena known as the Colosseum;

'savage', 'bloody and brutal', 'under public gaze':

This is politics as entertainment, Colosseum-style: sensitivities are mauled and reputations torn to shreds as public figures confront their electorate, confess mistakes, are caught out. (Observer)

There had been theatres of wood and stone on the same site east of the Roman forum before the building of the most famous of them all was begun by Vespasian (emperor 70–79 AD). Gladiator fights, contests with wild beasts, even mini sea-fights (the arena could be flooded), were staged for public pleasure. Blood-letting, spectacle and a dash of sadism are suggested by *Colosseum-style* entertainments, of which *Big Brother* and its clones are probably the closest descendants.

PRETENTIOUSNESS INDEX *!*

CONFUCIAN

connected to the Chinese philosopher Confucius (551–479 BC) and his teachings;

'wise', 'revered', 'ancient', 'preaching order and harmony':

An ambitious concept car, the Alas, even promised the very Confucian aim that it would 'harmonise the relationship between sky, earth and human beings' – all down to the design of the headlamps and the radiator grill.

(Observer)

Confucius's sayings and teachings, like those of the Greek philosopher Socrates, were recorded by his disciples, and out of this grew a complex belief system that formed the moral basis of Chinese social and political life during the next two and a half millennia. Confucius emphasised the importance of justice and ethics, as well as respect for one's elders and ancestors. *Confucian* is sometimes used in the West as shorthand for 'sage' or simply to evoke a vague sense of oriental, even mystical wisdom.

PRETENTIOUSNESS INDEX **Nil**

CONRADIAN

typical of the style or themes of novelist Joseph Conrad (1857–1924);

'exotic', 'connected to the sea and adventure':

With its Conradian journey to the edge of civilisation, the movie is all about Jackson's questing verve as a director. (Daily Telegraph)

Polish-born but a naturalised British citizen, Joseph Conrad is forever associated with sea stories such as *Lord Jim* and *The Shadow Line*, which were inspired by his career as a sailor. But Conrad's range is much wider than the straightforward sea yarn, and he is rightly considered one of the greatest novelists of the early 20th century, a writer who in novels like *The Secret Agent* (1907) or *Nostromo* (1904) tackled such essentially modern themes as terrorism and alienation. Outside the refined context of literary criticism, however, *Conradian* may mean not much more than 'exotic', 'adventurous'.

PRETENTIOUSNESS INDEX *!*

CONSTABLE-LIKE

reminiscent of the style or subject of landscape paintings by John Constable (1776–1837);

'pastoral', 'tranquil', 'idyllic':

> *When I arrived at Nigel Rowe's farm near Dedham, only the weather was Constable-like.* (Guardian)

Arguably the most popular English painter on the strength of two or three iconic images such as *The Haywain* or *Dedham Vale*, Constable still gives us an idealised picture of English rural life nearly two centuries after his death, a landscape where the sun is always shining and the sheep safely grazing. The views may be the result of artifice, whether at the hand of the farmer or the painter, but they look natural. Constable was interested in the effects of light, the movement of clouds, the harmonious blending of nature with the human presence, and all of this contributes to his deep appeal.

PRETENTIOUSNESS INDEX *!*

CORBUSIAN

in the style of Swiss-born architect and designer Charles-Édouard Jeanneret, known as le Corbusier (1887–1965);

'modernist', 'plain', 'rational':

> *Perhaps Bengtsson was also thinking of those Swedish public housing projects of the 1950s and 60s, rational Corbusian open-plan machines for living, with their underfloor heating and fitted kitchens.* (Guardian)

Le Corbusier was highly influential in the design of urban building in the middle of the 20th century, particularly for the public housing schemes that emerged in the wake of World War Two. He was one of the first not merely to take account of the impact of the automobile but to celebrate that impact, and his buildings make heavy use of overtly 'modern' components like glass, steel and concrete. Reacting against the cluttered, unhealthy disorder of urban dwellings at the end of the previous century, le Corbusier is identified with high-rise blocks of geometric design and with clear, unadorned exteriors and interiors. Le Corbusier's modernism attracted criticism – in an early manifesto he declared that a 'house is a machine for living in' and in the 1920s he proposed knocking down a large area of Paris – and now seems, ironically, rather dated. However his surviving buildings are, like the furniture he designed, regarded as classics.

PRETENTIOUSNESS INDEX *!*

CORDELIA-LIKE

similar to the character of Cordelia in Shakespeare's play *King Lear*;

'truth-telling', 'honest', 'devoted':

> *But too many narrative strands are left trailing [...] and O'Brien fails to show what it is about Jamie that draws Emer back to him with a Cordelia-like fidelity.* (Guardian)

In Shakespeare's tragedy, the ageing King Lear decides to apportion his kingdom of Britain among his three daughters. He challenges them to say which of them loves him most, and while two (Goneril and Regan) reply with conventional flattery, his favourite and the youngest, Cordelia, replies that she loves him only 'according to my bond'. Cordelia also points out the inconsistency in her sisters' speeches: why are they already married if they are giving all their love to their father, as they claim? When she marries, she says, she will share her love between husband and father. Lear flies into a rage and banishes Cordelia. Later, when he has been rejected by the two 'loving' daughters, it is Cordelia who comes to his aid, showing that she is his only true daughter. *Cordelia-like* can thus suggest an uncomfortably honest attitude but, more often, it describes a faithful devotion shown by a daughter to a father.

PRETENTIOUSNESS INDEX *!*

(see also *Lear-like*)

CORIOLANUS-LIKE

in the style of Coriolanus, principal character of Shakespeare's play of the same name;

'scornful', 'arrogant':

> *Despite vaulting ambition, Coriolanus-like, he will not bend to please the people.* (Guardian)

Coriolanus was a real-life figure in the fifth century BC, but he is known now – though, it has to be said, not much known – as the title character of one of Shakespeare's later dramas. He was a Roman general and aristocrat who, banished from his own city, led an enemy army to its gates. In practice, references to Coriolanus boil down to his hatred and contempt for the (Roman) mob, the 'mutable, rank-scented many' as he describes them. So *Coriolanus-like* tends to refer to a patrician distaste for ordinary people and a refusal to hide it.

PRETENTIOUSNESS INDEX *!!*

COWARDIAN

typical of the style or themes of dramatist and composer Noel Coward (1899–1973);

'quick-fire', 'gossipy', 'sophisticated':

> *But always, the progression of their emotional lives is filtered through sub-Cowardian staccato dialogue that makes for uncomfortable and frustrating listening.* (Guardian)

Cowardian often recalls the clipped and subtly comic dialogue of plays such as *Private Lives* (1933) or the inimitable way he delivered his own songs, whether jokey or wistful. Noel Coward, whose own social world stretched from the royal to the louche, fell out of fashion during the 1960s 'kitchen sink' period of English drama but before his death the great technical artistry of his plays – another *Cowardian* feature – began to be appreciated once more.

PRETENTIOUSNESS INDEX *!*

CROESUS-LIKE

like Croesus, the king of ancient Lydia;

'fabulously wealthy', 'having unlimited and valuable assets':

> *The Croesus-like resources of owner Roman Abramovich is Chelsea's good fortune.* (Daily Telegraph)

Unlike Midas but also associated with extreme riches (see *Midas-like*), Croesus was a real figure, the last king of Lydia (in what is now south-west Turkey). He conquered various Greek city-states and his wealth was legendary, but he was defeated in turn when he attacked the Persians under their king Cyrus. 'Rich as Croesus' is a proverbial saying, and *Croesus-like* hints at exotic, uncountable sources of wealth.

PRETENTIOUSNESS INDEX **Nil**

CROMWELLIAN

typical of the approach or policies of Oliver Cromwell (1599–1658);

'puritanical', 'severe':

> *In an age of almost Cromwellian righteousness, there has been more agonising over his bed-hopping, his failed marriage and his seeming reluctance to ever grow up than how Ian Bell might play his slider in Birmingham this week.* (Observer)

Oliver Cromwell, victor of the Civil War and Lord Protector of England from 1653 until his death, is associated with the execution of Charles I, the brutality of his treatment of the Irish, and Puritan beliefs and attitudes in general. *Cromwellian* is most often used in negative contrast to the more relaxed periods of monarchy that came either side of his rule. Fairly or not, the term equates with 'kill-joy'.

PRETENTIOUSNESS INDEX **!**

CRONENBERGIAN

typical of the style or themes favoured by Canadian-born film director David Cronenberg (1943–);

'perverse', 'chilly', 'transgressive':

> *[Helmut] Newton was a photographer who never saw the point of not overstating the obvious: in one infamous shoot [...] the women sported medical corsets and braces as Cronenbergian sexual accessories.* (Observer)

A distinctive director, David Cronenberg is identified with films that confront bodily disease and decay while using the overall approach of the horror movie, as in *Rabid* (1977) or *The Fly* (1986). Another strand in Cronenberg's work is a kinked sexuality, as in *Dead Ringers* (1988) or *Crash* (1996), and it is these films, with their combining of flesh and steel, that are the reference point in the *Observer* quote above. *Cronenbergian* may suggest a mixture of attraction/repulsion in both the film-maker and his followers.

PRETENTIOUSNESS INDEX **!!**

CRUSOE-LIKE

in the style of Robinson Crusoe, the fictional character created by Daniel Defoe (1660–1731) in the novel of the same name;

'solitary', 'remote', 'self-reliant', 'grizzled':

> *'The Galapagos is hanging on by its fingernails,' said Godfrey Merlin, a Robinson Crusoe-like figure with matted hair, a wild beard and deeply burned skin.* (Daily Telegraph)

Defoe's famous story, first published in 1719, was based on the real-life adventures of Alexander Selkirk, who survived four years alone on a desert island. (Selkirk asked to be put ashore, believing that his ship was likely to sink.) *Crusoe-like* is a term with several applications, describing either an individual and his appearance (see quote) or a person who lives cut off from the rest of the world, by choice or otherwise. It can also be used to describe an exotic desert-island-type setting, so that the solitariness from which Crusoe suffered becomes a selling-point in a crowded globe.

PRETENTIOUSNESS INDEX **Nil**

CYCLOPEAN

in Greek and Roman mythology, connected to an imagined race of giants who had a single eye in the middle of their foreheads;

'one-eyed', 'on a massive scale':

> *[The road] turns a corner, enters a gateway and runs between stone walls of truly cyclopean masonry.* (Daily Telegraph)

The Cyclops supposedly lived in what is now Sicily and were most famously encountered by Ulysses as he returned home from the siege of Troy. *Cyclopean* might be used as a rather elaborate way of describing someone with only one eye but, more often, it is applied to a prehistoric Greek style of building that used very large and irregular stones.

PRETENTIOUSNESS INDEX *!*

D

DALEK-LIKE

in the style of the Daleks, the aliens featured in the BBC TV series *Dr Who*;

'robotic', 'speaking in a staccato voice':

> *'She never said a nice word to me, neither did my dad. All that came out of my dad's Dalek-like mouth was orders, orders, orders …'* (quoted, Guardian)

When it comes to British audiences and their taste for aliens, even Steven Spielberg's ET can hardly match the Daleks in popularity. The fact that ET is cuddly and cute while the Daleks are viciously destructive may say something about the British taste for out-and-out villains. The Daleks, conceived by writer Terry Nation for the second series of *Dr Who* in 1963 and surviving into the relaunch of the programme in 2005, are slimy mutants who encase themselves in pepper-pot-like shells. Apart from their desire to conquer the universe, probably their most distinctive feature is the rasping, one-note voice. But none of this really needs describing. Generations of schoolchildren have grown up with cries of 'Exterminate!' and 'You will obey' ringing in their ears. Much loved as the Daleks are, it's interesting to note that the expression *Dalek-like* is fairly frequently applied to those in authority who are perceived as not-quite-human because of their tendency to parrot stock phrases and instructions.

PRETENTIOUSNESS INDEX **Nil**

DALIESQUE

typical of the style or subject matter of Spanish painter Salvador Dali (1904–89);

'bizarre', 'surreal', 'dream-like':

> *What staging trickery there is is limited to some moments of Alice in Wonderland loveliness (a smiling, speaking clock; dishes of food rising up*

through the floorboards) and a smattering of Daliesque oddness (a talking chair, a doorknob with moving eyebrows and a Yorkshire accent). (Guardian)

Salvador Dali was and is the best-known of the artists connected to the surrealist movement. He was arguably the most astute in a commercial sense, with a genius for self-promotion and knowing just how far to take his provocations. Among his trademark images are giant, floppy watches and elephants on stilt-like legs, all set against a barren landscape. *Daliesque* may refer to a specific image or to the calculated sense of strangeness that pervades his pictures, even if their very popularity has made them less disturbing.

PRETENTIOUSNESS INDEX *!*

DAMASCENE

connected to Damascus, capital of Syria; frequently linked to the idea of 'conversion';

(in the sense used in the example) 'sudden'; 'revelatory':

But there is no sudden Damascene conversion to adulthood. Harry defends himself for being both a party prince and a caring prince. (The Times)

Damascene can describe the elaborate, wavy pattern used for centuries to decorate metalwork and fabrics, but is most often connected to the conversion of Saul of Tarsus. Saul, a persecutor of the early Christians, was on the road to Damascus when 'suddenly there shined round about him a light from heaven, and he fell to the earth, and heard a voice saying unto him, "Saul, Saul, why persecutest thou me?" ' (Acts 9:3–4). Saul subsequently became Paul. Any abrupt and life-changing experience, particularly one in which the past is reassessed (and generally regretted), can be described as *Damascene*.

PRETENTIOUSNESS INDEX *!*

DAMOCLEAN

from Damocles, a legendary flatterer in ancient Syracuse; always used with reference to the story of the sword of Damocles;

'perilous':

Let us take an example from the dark, Damoclean times hanging over us – terrorism. (Guardian)

In the legend, Damocles complimented Dionysius, the absolute ruler of the Sicilian city of Syracuse in the third century BC, by calling him the most fortunate of men. In response, Dionysius invited Damocles to a banquet at which a sword was suspended over the place where the flatterer was to sit. The sword, intended to show the fragility of fortune, was hanging by a single horsehair. Damocles survived, and probably kept his mouth shut afterwards. *Damoclean* has come to describe any impending disaster.

PRETENTIOUSNESS INDEX **Nil**

DAN BROWN-STYLE

in the style of the thrillers produced by Dan Brown, particularly *The Da Vinci Code* (2003);

'best-selling', 'fast-moving', 'conspiratorial', 'involving codes and ciphers':

> *As the swashbuckling master-of-disguise, he takes on a Dan Brown-style conspiracy to restore the French monarchy, in the process rescuing and bedding femme fatale Kristin Scott Thomas.* (Observer)

Dan Brown's books are obviously going to be used as a benchmark for a certain style of thriller for a long time to come. The ingredients were there in earlier novels such as *Angels and Demons* (2000) but were brought to a peak in the super-selling *Da Vinci Code*: high-level skulduggery, secret societies, breathless plotting and a crossword-like obsession with unravelling keys and codes. Brown is adept at blurring the lines between fact, speculation and fiction – a useful defence against the criticism that *The Da Vinci Code* in particular has provoked from the Catholic Church.

PRETENTIOUSNESS INDEX **Nil**

DANTEAN

in the style of medieval Florentine writer Dante Alighieri (1265–1321);

'hellish', 'heavenly', 'visionary':

> *First appointment to an academic position in an American university is (unlike Britain) a low hurdle. The high hurdle comes seven years later, with the tenure decision. It usually happens around the Dantean middle-age of 35.* (Guardian)

Dante's greatest achievement is the *Divine Comedy* (*Divina Commedia*) divided into three parts, 'Inferno', 'Purgatory' and 'Paradise', the realms through which, as narrator, Dante is conducted. *Dantean* (also *Dante-esque*) is most likely to suggest a panoramic vision of the after-life, specifically the sufferings of hell. The reference to 'Dantean middle-age' in the *Guardian* quote above is to the 'Inferno', which begins 'In the middle of life's journey, I found myself in a dark wood'.

PRETENTIOUSNESS INDEX *!*

DARCY-TYPE

like Fitzwilliam Darcy, the hero of Jane Austen's *Pride and Prejudice* (1813);

'romantic and aristocratic', 'dashing':

He looked dashing in his DJ and his brooding dark looks made him seem like a Darcy-type character. (Independent on Sunday)

Like most of Jane Austen's novels, *Pride and Prejudice* is a version of the Cinderella story, in which the neglected/socially inferior/not-so-pretty heroine gets her hands on the male lead in the closing pages after various vicissitudes. It is probably because of the many film and television versions of *Pride and Prejudice* that Darcy has become the archetypal romantic hero: temperamental and craggily handsome. The film interpretations of Darcy from Laurence Olivier in 1940 to Matthew MacFadyen in 2005 have certainly helped, although most people's image is probably coloured by Colin Firth's role in the television adaptation and, in particular, the scene (not in the book) where he emerged in a dripping-wet shirt from a dip in a convenient lake.

PRETENTIOUSNESS INDEX *!*

DARWINIAN

characteristic of the attitude, beliefs or writings of naturalist Charles Darwin (1809–82) or describing one of his followers;

'believing in natural evolution', 'natural', 'ruthless':

But, naturally, men still need accessories – not because we are particularly interested in them but because we are hairy-chested creatures who want to come top in the Darwinian struggle for mates and power. (The Times)

Nearly two centuries after his birth, Charles Darwin's writings remain controversial, not only among the specialists who dispute some of his findings while agreeing with his general principles but among those who reject him altogether. Darwin argued against 'intelligent' design in nature, maintaining that those members of species that survived and bred were able to do so because of some mutation or advantage originally bestowed on them by chance. This, and his implicit treatment of mankind as one kind of animal among many, was part of a revolution in human understanding. In *On the Origin of Species by Means of Natural Selection* (1859), Darwin talked of the inevitability of a 'struggle for existence' among all living things – either because more are born than can survive on the resources available or because of harsh physical conditions that lead to premature death for some – but he did not coin the expression 'survival of the fittest'. Nevertheless, Darwinism has come to be identified with a sometimes ruthless struggle for survival, one in which the weakest go to the wall. And, fairly or not, *Darwinian* is generally used a shorthand term for a strippeddown, unsentimental attitude to life and, as such, the expression may contain a hint of criticism.

PRETENTIOUSNESS INDEX **Nil**

DELPHIC

in the style of the ancient oracle at Delphi in central Greece;

'ambiguous', 'obscurely prophetic':

In London last Friday Federal Reserve chairman Alan Greenspan delivered one of his Delphic utterances, and one translation suggested he thought American imports and exports were not defying the laws of supply and demand after all. (Daily Telegraph)

The Delphic oracle was operated by the priests of the god Apollo who interpreted the utterances of a priestess seated on a tripod in a state of 'divine ecstasy'. The oracle was consulted on questions of law and religion to which, unsurprisingly, the priests could give sensible answers. But when it came to predicting the future, the oracle became riddling and ambiguous, so that a prophecy might be valid whatever happened. It's in this sense that *Delphic* is used now, with an emphasis on the baffling quality of such pronouncements.

PRETENTIOUSNESS INDEX *!*

(see also *Sibylline*)

DEMILLEAN

in the style of Hollywood director Cecil B. DeMille (1881–1959);

'showy', 'epic', 'spectacular':

> *Throughout the fifties and sixties, the studios kept up a steady stream of biblical epics and DeMillean spectaculars, on the logic that whatever TV did, Hollywood had to do the opposite.* (Tom Shone, *Blockbuster*)

DeMille had a long career in Hollywood, directing his first film in 1913 and his last in 1956. He's remembered today for his biblical epics like *Samson and Delilah* (1949) and *The Ten Commandments* (1956), with Charlton Heston playing Moses. DeMille mixed piety and showmanship with a dash of tasteful decadence (he is supposed to have spent three weeks on the Golden Calf orgy in *Ten Commandments* – and also to have claimed that he was providing an orgy that even Sunday-school children could watch). DeMille specialised in big crowd scenes and lavish effects, like Samson pulling down the temple on his enemies or Moses parting the Red Sea, and his influence can be seen in other directors' films such as *Ben Hur* (1959) and *Gladiator* (2000).

PRETENTIOUSNESS INDEX *!*

DIANA-LIKE

with the looks, style or appeal of Diana, Princess of Wales (1961–97);

'charismatic', 'stylish', 'iconic':

> *But Suu Kyi herself has resisted this Diana-like cult of personality – and pointed out that the struggle is not hers but her people's.* (Observer)

Even before her tragically premature death in a Paris underpass, Diana was an iconic figure: a fashion-plate, a campaigner for high-profile causes, a royal divorcee. Her death transformed her, for a time anyway, into a secular saint. All the scepticism and bad-mouthing she'd received from the media and the public was swept away in a near-pathological display of grief. Only some years after the event is it possible to refer to her in a relatively objective way and to see her as a fairly ordinary and attractive woman. *Diana-like* is one of those comparisons that can be admiring or critical, depending on context.

PRETENTIOUSNESS INDEX **Nil**

DICKENSIAN

in the style of or typical of the themes favoured by novelist Charles Dickens (1812–70);

1) 'sentimental', 'squalid', 'Christmassy', 'heart-rending':

My left hand clutched the witness box until its knuckles went white. I sketched a tragic, Dickensian picture of family trauma and personal degradation. (Independent)

2) 'sprawling', 'comically inventive':

As well as having a plot of Dickensian implausibility the whole thing is on Dickensian scale, with dozens of characters, but the story rattles along amusingly. (Spectator)

Dickensian is one of those terms with such a range of meanings, some of them contradictory, that it usually needs some additional definition from its context. On the one hand, there is the relatively realistic Dickens who depicted the lives of the London underclass. On the other, there is the sentimentalist who set out to make readers weep. Then there is the frequent association of the author with Christmas – stagecoaches rolling past snow-covered cottages, roaring log fires in inn parlours – even though that season tends to be rather grimly presented in his writing (for example, the Christmas scene early in *Great Expectations*). And there is the use of *Dickensian* to mean 'life-enhancing', 'full of invention', as in the second of the quotes above. Of all the terms associated with writers, only *Shakespearean* and *Orwellian* have a similar breadth.

PRETENTIOUSNESS INDEX **Nil** BUT THE TERM IS SO WIDE-RANGING THAT IT NO LONGER CONVEYS VERY MUCH.

DIONYSIAN

connected to Dionysus, the ancient Greek god of wine;

'drunken', 'orgiastic':

Barely a year into their existence, the Bravery are already steeped in a mythology of Dionysian proportions. They claim, for instance, to have slept with representatives from every major record company in the UK.

(Guardian)

Dionysus is the older Greek form of the deity known to the Romans as Bacchus, but where Bacchus is associated with drinking and having a good time, *Dionysian* can suggest a more extreme form of pleasure-seeking: something ecstatic, out of control. *Dionysian* is sometimes contrasted with *Apollonian* (see entry), since the sun-god Apollo represents restraint and rationality.

PRETENTIOUSNESS INDEX *!*

(see also *Bacchanalian*)

DISNEYESQUE

in the style of the films produced by Walt Disney (1901–66) or his studio;

'anthropomorphic', 'cute', 'sentimental':

> ...*we agreed on everything: mother love was not automatic, parenthood had become sealed in a smug and Disneyesque sentimentality, and children were capable of free will – and unspeakable evil.* (Observer)

Walt Disney and his brother Roy are supposed to have set off for Hollywood in the early 1920s with $40 between them. By the end of the decade Disney had created Mickey Mouse and started his cartoon factory. Walt's trick of giving cute human responses to animal characters, whether in cartoon films or in nature documentaries like *The Living Desert* (1953), and his willingness to exploit the pathos of a situation (for example, the death of Bambi's mother) have turned *Disneyesque* into a generally pejorative term. In the same way, *Disneyfication* describes the prettying-up of some place or event to make it more palatable or commercial. In fact, these definitions aren't altogether accurate or fair to Disney, since some of his films have a darkish or sinister aspect to them.

PRETENTIOUSNESS INDEX **Nil**

DISRAELIAN

characteristic of the style or politics of British Prime Minister Benjamin Disraeli (1804–81);

'imperialistic', 'reformist', 'believing in one-nation politics':

> *Here is a timely reminder of the Disraelian One Nation strand of conservative thought – which could become the Tories' credible passport back to power.* (Guardian)

Despite being regarded as an outsider and never entirely 'respectable', Disraeli was identified with the heyday of the British Empire and Queen Victoria's reign. His second period as Prime Minister (1874–80) oversaw various social reforms, and he is still regarded as a Conservative politician who looked to the interests of the whole nation rather than the advantage of a particular class.

PRETENTIOUSNESS INDEX *!*

DORIAN GRAY-LIKE

like the title character in Oscar Wilde's novel *The Picture of Dorian Gray* (1890);

'unnaturally youthful', 'eternally preserved':

> *For starters, he [Mick Jagger] could build that self-same rock'n'roll baaaand into one of the highest-grossing acts on the planet, amassing gazillions of greenbacks as he waggled his Dorian Gray-like derriere for the delectation of baby boomers from Berlin to Buenos Aires.* (Guardian)

In Wilde's story, Dorian Gray keeps his beauty and his youthful looks in spite of a dissolute way of life. The effects of ageing and decadence are reflected only in a changing portrait, which he keeps hidden away in the attic and which grows steadily more hideous. *Dorian Gray-like*, then, is not used about the genuinely young but about men who seem to be implausibly youthful. It's not really a compliment either since there's more than a hint of unnaturalness about the process.

PRETENTIOUSNESS INDEX *!*

DRACONIAN

connected to Draco, an Athenian legislator of the seventh century BC;

'very severe':

> *But in a final, pissed-off flurry, I appealed against getting such a draconian sentence for driving at 39mph on a dual carriageway in east London.*
> (Independent)

Draconian has recently become an oddly popular term, generally found in contexts where the user feels that some law or rule is a bit steep or 'out of order'. A *Draconian* punishment was genuinely harsh, however, since Draco set out to systematise Athenian laws and to impose public justice in place of private vengeance.

PRETENTIOUSNESS INDEX *!* THIS IS AN EXPRESSION THAT WOULD HAVE A BIT MORE FORCE IF IT WAS USED MORE SPARINGLY.

DYLANESQUE

in the style of singer-songwriter Bob Dylan (1941–);

'connected to political protest', 'unsentimental', 'bitter-sweet', 'surreal', 'poetic':

> *God will believe in your own ability to mend your ways. That is so*

effortlessly Dylanesque, yet so dripping in Biblical resonances, you have to
wonder whether he ad-libbed it or rehearsed it in his head beforehand.

(Observer)

Bob Dylan, born Robert Allen Zimmerman, defined the counter-culture of the 1960s with songs like 'Blowin' in the Wind' and 'The Times They Are A'Changin' '. Although Dylan came out of an American tradition of folk and blues and protest, he fused the various strands together to make something unique and instantly recognisable. Dylan's lyrics can be wryly realistic or hauntingly suggestive, while his playing and singing have never entirely lost a rough-hewn quality that only adds to his authenticity.

PRETENTIOUSNESS INDEX *!*

E

EDWARDIAN

characteristic of the reign of King Edward VII (1901–10);

'leisured', 'grand', 'imperial', 'innocent':

> *It even seemed that the further British power receded from its Edwardian heights, the more determined [Prime Minister Harold] Macmillan became to conceal the decline by presenting himself as a breezy Edwardian grandee.* (Dominic Sandbrook, *Never Had It So Good*)

Edwardian could describe the reign of any of the English kings of that name but, in popular use, it applies only to the period between the death of Queen Victoria and the outbreak of World War One. Since this coincided with the high point of British imperial confidence, the *Edwardian* years are sometimes seen as a golden age of peace, prosperity and power. For the upper classes it was certainly a leisured age, and the contrast with the horrors of the 1914–18 war has given to those few years – at least in the more rose-tinted interpretations – a kind of before-the-Fall innocence.

PRETENTIOUSNESS INDEX **Nil**

EEYOREISH

in the manner of Eeyore, an animal character in A.A. Milne's *Winnie-the-Pooh* (1926);

'gloomy', 'pessimistic':

> *While the trials of office might have been expected to temper his infamous optimism, he is in fact as Tiggerish as ever, jumping up and down with enthusiasm while the Eeyoreish Chancellor mopes next door.* (Daily Telegraph)

In *Winnie-the-Pooh* Eeyore is an old grey donkey, who thinks a lot and takes a gloomy view of things. Someone who is *Eeyoreish* could be said to make a profession out of being miserable.

(see also *Tiggerish*)

EINSTEINIAN

characteristic of the work, thinking or appearance of scientist Albert Einstein (1879–1955);

'brilliant but complex', 'difficult to understand', 'bringing about a revolution in human understanding':

> *How else can we explain why our underworked scientific research community is spending its man-hours thinking up cures for snoring, or promulgating algebraic solutions to the 'problem' of using chopsticks, which last week was illustrated in a flurry of difficult-looking Einsteinian formulae, courtesy of the graphics departments of all newspapers ...?* (Observer)

Einstein is seen not merely (merely!) as the greatest theoretical physicist of modern times but as the archetypal scientist, even the traditional mad scientist. His shaggy hair and generally disordered appearance – particularly in a famous photograph where he sticks out his tongue – contributed to this perception, so that Einstein in old age became a pop-culture icon. On a rather more important level, Einstein's work on the theory of relativity was revolutionary and led to the discoveries of quantum physics. Grasping what Einstein meant, however, lies outside most people's reach and thus the complexity of his theories becomes part of the legend of the brilliant thinker who operated on an intellectual plane denied to most of the rest of the world. So, if *Einsteinian* is not used in a specialist sense, it's likely to be synonymous with 'very difficult', as in the *Observer* quote above.

PRETENTIOUSNESS INDEX *!*

ELGARIAN

characteristic of the work of composer Edward Elgar (1857–1934);

'melancholy', 'romantic', 'quintessentially English', 'stirring':

> *After the sonorous opening chords, their [the double basses'] presence made the wistful first melody seem almost Elgarian, while whole swathes of the sumptuous and intense slow movement sounded uncannily close to Mahler's Fifth Symphony.* (Guardian)

Edward Elgar's best-known works, the *Enigma Variations* (1899) and the music to 'Land of Hope and Glory' (one of the *Pomp and Circumstance* marches of 1901), conveniently reflect two aspects of his composing personality. The *Variations* are a lyrical portrait in sound of several of Elgar's friends and their mood, whether elegiac, contemplative or lush, is a complement to the more triumphant tones of 'Hope and Glory'. Success came relatively late to Elgar and his period of greatest success was during the years leading up to World War One. Popular impressions of the composer and everything connoted by the term *Elgarian* are strengthened by his links with the Edwardian era. It's easy, perhaps too easy, to read into works like his First Symphony (1908) a nostalgia for the imperial heyday that preceded the slaughter of 1914–18. His music is frequently regarded as celebrating nature and the English landscape, in particular the area of Worcestershire around Malvern where Elgar grew up.

PRETENTIOUSNESS INDEX **Nil**

ELIOT-ISH

typical of the style or themes of poet, playwright and critic T(homas) S(tearns) Eliot (1888–1965);

'intellectual', 'dry', 'controlled', 'modernist':

> *Not that there's much about food in the Eliot canon. Had his mind set on higher things, I expect. Still, there is an almost Eliot-ish, New England restraint about the design of the New End and its menu.* (Guardian)

T.S. Eliot was born in Missouri but became a naturalised British citizen in 1927. By then he had already written what remains his most famous poem, *The Waste Land* (1922), which, with its disjointed narrative and sense of alienation, established him as a key figure in the modernist movement of the early 20th century. Eliot's public persona was somewhat aloof and restrained and he is identified with a high seriousness in his approach to culture. *Eliot-ish* may refer to his innovative impact on poetry or his sage-like role in literature, but it is as likely to describe his fastidious manner.

PRETENTIOUSNESS INDEX *!*

ELYSIAN

connected to Elysium, the place in ancient Greek mythology where those whom the gods rewarded lived a delightful after-life;

'paradise-like', 'delightful', 'heavenly':

> *… from the Elysian visions of William Morris, Stanley Spencer and The Wind in the Willows to the darker waters of the estuary and the glitzy*

brashness of Canary Wharf, here we have a river that seems, throughout its turbid course, to chart the social history of a nation. (Daily Telegraph)

Elysian still retains a bit more force than equivalents like 'heavenly', which often means no more than 'very nice'. Without any particular religious overtones, it can convey an experience or a vision that is other-worldly.

PRETENTIOUSNESS INDEX **!**

EMERSONIAN

reflecting the writings or philosophy of Ralph Waldo Emerson (1803–82);

'self-reliant', 'advocating the philosophy of transcendentalism':

Singularity – if one wanted a word to define Bellow's ambitions for the self it would be this. In many ways, he is an Emersonian individualist.

(Guardian)

Emerson, born in Boston and the son of a Unitarian clergyman, drifted away from the formal religion of which he was himself an ordained minister. He became one of a highly influential group of New England writers and thinkers in the first half of the 19th century who, in transcendentalism, evolved a half-mystical philosophy that revered nature and looked to their native land for inspiration. Emerson preached individuality, saying 'whoso would be a man, must be a nonconformist'.

PRETENTIOUSNESS INDEX **!**

(see also *Thoreauesque*)

EPICUREAN

following the doctrines of the Greek philosopher Epicurus (341–270 BC);

'seeking happiness', 'hedonistic':

The photographs in the diaries document this shift, as the cocktail-hour Tynan of his London regency morphs into the epicurean sage of his Hollywood exile, where, in one photo, he stares at the camera wearing sunglasses and sporting a white goatee, the very picture of the playboy philosopher. (Guardian)

Epicurus taught that if pleasure (or the absence of pain) is the only good, then the best pleasure is to be found in the harmony of body and mind, and the attempt to rise above the fear of death. This might be attained through living a simple, moral life. In other words, what the philosopher taught is almost the exact opposite of what the adjective *epicurean* has come to mean. The morality and simplicity aspects have gone and only the 'pleasure' part of the formula is remembered, so that an epicure is the same as a gourmet, while *epicurean* suggests 'pleasure-seeking'.

PRETENTIOUSNESS INDEX *!*

EROTIC

connected to Eros, the Greek god of love;

'sexy', 'suggestive':

Her account of the disappearance of erotic undressing before the onslaught of hardcore porn is a sad one; because, in its heyday, striptease was a lot of glamour and fun. (The Times)

In Greek and, later, Roman mythology (where he is known as Cupid) Eros is represented as a boy equipped with wings and a bow and arrow. As an adjective, *erotic* is found everywhere – one newspaper website alone lists over 3,000 uses. Standards have changed so that what would once have been regarded as pornographic is now seen as *erotic* and the adjective can be applied to anything that is sexual but not too explicit, hardcore or bizarre. *Erotic* just about manages to convey the idea of suggestion and subtlety but in the media the term seems to be used very casually, generally as a come-on.

PRETENTIOUSNESS INDEX **Nil**

F

FALSTAFFIAN

with the appearance or in the manner of Falstaff, a character in Shakespeare's *Henry IV* and *The Merry Wives of Windsor*;

'fat', 'boozy', 'jolly':

> *Nell's widowed mother, 'Madam' Gwyn, a Falstaffian figure fond of brandy, was reduced to running a bawdy house in Covent Garden.* (Spectator)

Sir John Falstaff – a corpulent and cowardly knight who deludes himself that he is acting as mentor to Hal, Prince of Wales and the future Henry V – is variously identified with fatness, drunkenness and a dissolute way of life. There is a less attractive side to his character but *Falstaffian* tends to accentuate the positive. The term is usually reserved for men and suggests a combination of good humour and fatness, but there seems no reason why it shouldn't be applied to a woman who liked her drink and ran a brothel (see quote), both typically *Falstaffian* interests.

PRETENTIOUSNESS INDEX *!*

FAUSTIAN

like Dr Faustus, a German magician and scholar of the early 16th century, who reputedly made a pact with the devil;

'seeking power and/or knowledge at any price, however destructive':

> *Likewise on television it is conventional wisdom that New Labour was born out of a Faustian pact whose signatories sold their socialist souls to the devil of electoral success.* (Prospect)

In legend, Faustus was presented by the devil Mephistopheles with a bargain whereby he would surrender his soul in exchange for knowledge and power in this world. (Among other versions, the story is dramatised in Christopher Marlowe's play *Dr Faustus*, in which the title character is granted 24 years of having Mephistopheles at his beck and call before being dragged down to hell.) *Faustian* has several meanings: when applied to a bargain or pact, it suggests a deal that brings a temporary benefit but lethal long-term consequences. When applied to an individual, *Faustian* might suggest someone who is desperate for knowledge or power, or a person who is spiritually in despair.

PRETENTIOUSNESS INDEX **Nil**

(see also *Mephistophelian*)

FELLINI-ESQUE

in the style of Italian film director Federico Fellini (1920–93);

'carnival-like', 'autobiographical', 'exuberant':

> *'Cannes is very Fellini-esque,' laughs Stephen Woolley. 'It's a complete zoo. Someone can be giving you a discourse on the French New Wave 1958–61, while someone's taking their clothes off on the table opposite you.'* (Observer)

After he became famous with *La Dolce Vita* – Anita Ekberg dancing in Rome's Trevi fountain – Federico Fellini made a series of films that seemed to alternate self-indulgently between autobiography and fantasy. With their elaborate set-pieces and parade of circus-like characters, they were essentially frames for the director's outsize personality.

PRETENTIOUSNESS INDEX *!*

FESTE-LIKE

in the style of the character of Feste in Shakespeare's *Twelfth Night*;

'humorous', 'sardonic', 'melancholy':

> *Yes, I was reassured in a kind letter, Clown was a curious, much misunderstood character, crucial to the message of the play, a strange, Feste-like figure, casting his ironic eye over all the events of this mighty catastrophe.* (Observer)

Although a professional jester, Feste is one of the more melancholy characters among Shakespeare's creations. Through his songs and witticisms, he pokes fun at his betters and organises practical jokes, but the role is usually played in a tears-of-the-clown fashion, as of someone laughing only to hide the sadness beneath. Feste doesn't take part in the general pairing-off at the end of *Twelfth Night* and the last song of the play belongs to him, with its characteristic refrain 'And the rain it raineth every day.'

PRETENTIOUSNESS INDEX *!*

FIRBANKIAN

in the style of the novelist Ronald Firbank (1886–1926);

'refined and artificial', 'high camp':

> *St Stephen's House when I was there was a Firbankian madhouse. The principal, a saintly man called Norah, made the fatal mistake of allowing the students to make their confessions to him.* (Daily Telegraph)

Aesthete and dandy, Ronald Firbank was wealthy enough to publish most of his own work himself. His very stylised novels, although an acquired taste, influenced later writers such as Evelyn Waugh. *Firbankian* suggests a hot-house atmosphere, with a dash of *fin-de-siècle* gayness.

PRETENTIOUSNESS INDEX *!!*

FITZGERALDIAN

typical of the life and writings of US novelist F. Scott Fitzgerald (1896–1940);

'precociously talented', 'self-destructive', 'glamorous but doomed':

> *Although critics have often castigated him for superficiality, I will still defend him [Jay McInerney] as a writer of popular serious fiction – best exemplified by his 1992 novel,* Brightness Falls, *an accomplished Fitzgeraldian study of the dimming of personal promise.* (The Times)

Fitzgerald had an instant success with his first novel, *This Side of Paradise* (1920), and together with his wife Zelda was seen as the embodiment of the fast-living, pleasure-loving world of the young and wealthy in the years between the two world wars. But Fitzgerald's sense of the doom that underlies fame and riches, exemplified in his most famous work, *The Great Gatsby* (1925), was borne out in his own life. Zelda descended into schizophrenia and Fitzgerald, a life-long alcoholic, died prematurely of a heart attack. For all his achievement he is sometimes seen as the archetype of failed promise, and *Fitzgeraldian* suggests a tragic glamour.

PRETENTIOUSNESS INDEX *!*

(see also *Gatsbyesque*)

FITZROVIAN

typical of the writers and artists who, in the middle decades of the 20th century, used London's Fitzroy Tavern as a base;

'bohemian', 'artistic', 'louche':

> *His achievements as a conductor have faded along with those who heard him; his skills as an arranger have been neglected; his hauntings of Fitzrovian bars and back streets have been trimmed to fit the familiar pattern of the period.* (Guardian)

The Fitzroy Tavern is in Charlotte Street, north of London's Oxford Street. For many years it was a drinking hole and meeting place for the likes of poet Dylan Thomas and painter Augustus John – as well as the more colourful Labour politicians of the day. *Fitzrovian*, deriving either from the pub itself or Fitzroy Street or Fitzroy Square, denotes a hard-drinking, cash-strapped, artistically inclined individual or group, but the reference is essentially a historical one.

PRETENTIOUSNESS INDEX *!!*

FLAUBERTIAN

characteristic of the style or themes of French novelist Gustave Flaubert (1821–80);

'dedicated to art', 'meticulous', 'non-judgemental':

> *[Cyril] Connolly's one novel, The Rock Pool, is sensual and funny, not an easy combination, but for someone who harboured a Flaubertian-masterpiece-or-nothing attitude to fiction-writing it was a light snack to set before the literary gods.* (Guardian)

Flaubert's best-known novel remains his first, *Madame Bovary* (1857), the story of the unhappy wife of a doctor in Normandy who commits suicide after an adulterous affair. The book provoked a scandal in its day, partly because Flaubert refused to adopt a judgemental attitude towards his characters – famously he said, '*Madame Bovary, c'est moi.*' Flaubert was known for his realism, his meticulousness (he was supposedly willing to spend days searching for the right word) and his conception of the writer's high obligation to literature. For these reasons he is often seen as the archetypal artist.

PRETENTIOUSNESS INDEX *!*

FORSTERIAN

typical of the themes or attitudes of writer E(dward) M(organ) Forster (1879–1970);

'liberal', 'humane', 'concerned with personal relationships':

For women, communication answers the Forsterian command to 'only connect'. (Observer)

E.M. Forster's novels, such as *Howards End* (1910) and *A Passage to India* (1924), were given a new lease of life by respectful film adaptations in the 1970s and 1980s. His humanism and his emphasis on the importance of personal relationships have sometimes seemed as dated as the Bloomsbury group with which he was connected, but the adjective *Forsterian* still conjures up a world in which sensitivity and personal loyalty take precedence. The 'only connect' comment in the *Observer* quote above comes from *Howards End* ('Only connect the prose and the passion, and both will be exalted, and human love will be seen at its height.')

PRETENTIOUSNESS INDEX *!*

(see also *Bloomsbury-ish*)

FRANKENSTEINIAN

connected to the scientist-creator in Mary Shelley's novel *Frankenstein* (1818);

'monstrous', 'unnatural', 'uncontrolled':

> *[The film]* Mimic *is about how a scientist genetically modifies cockroaches who further mutate into giant murderous beasties and take over the New York subway [...] It is a Frankensteinian tale, the moral of which is 'Be very careful where you stick that pipette.'* (Guardian)

Mary Shelley's novel, written when she was 19, has acquired the power of myth. And, like many myths, it can be read in several ways. In the original story, Victor Frankenstein takes on himself the god-like function of creating life by animating a body composed out of the parts of corpses. When the monster, who is never named, finds that the whole world shrinks from him in horror, he turns on his creator before disappearing into the arctic wastes to destroy himself. Among other interpretations, *Frankenstein* has been seen as a straightforward horror story; as an allegory of creation; as a disturbing parable of parenthood; and, most often, as a warning about the effects of uncontrolled 'tampering' with nature. It's not surprising that the expression should come to the fore again in the era of GM crops, cloning and designer babies. In fact the reference is so familiar that *frankenfoods* makes regular appearances in the headlines to describe genetically modified products.

PRETENTIOUSNESS INDEX **Nil**

connected to the life, teaching or writings of psychoanalyst Sigmund Freud (1856–1939);

'psychoanalytic', 'hidden', 'uncovering secrets', 'connected to guilt and repression', 'to do with the unconscious':

> *Sartre was coddled by his mother who dressed him like a girl. He was devastated when she remarried when he was 12 and he had to move to provincial La Rochelle. All in all, Sartre's early life provides a bundle of Freudian clues to his career – which probably explains why Sartre detested Freud and any suggestion that childhood determined character or the fate of the individual.* (Independent)

With the exception of Charles Darwin, no other scientific thinker and theorist has entered the public consciousness so completely as Sigmund Freud, even if his theories have become grotesquely simplified in the process. Freud, born in Moravia but practising psychoanalysis in Vienna for most of his life, evolved his theories while treating neurotic patients. The content of some his ideas was profoundly shocking at the time – for example, that children, far from being innocent creatures, experience sexual impulses early in life which have to be repressed to ensure normal development. However, concepts such as the Oedipus complex or penis envy or the symbolic value of dreams quite quickly established themselves as part of every thinking person's mental furniture. Freud has been strongly contested, however, with many arguing that what he produced was closer to myth or literature. *Freudian* is a very general term but it usually hints at something suppressed and probably sexual, something that if brought to light would provide an explanation for an individual's behaviour, outlook, etc.

PRETENTIOUSNESS INDEX **Nil**

G

GAITSKELLITE

describing the approach or outlook of politician Hugh Gaitskell (1906–63) or one of his followers;

(politically) 'social democratic', 'moderate', 'modernising':

He [Roy Jenkins] was the suave Gaitskellite who split the party and so made possible the triumph of Margaret Thatcher. (Guardian)

Hugh Gaitskell was leader of the Labour Party from 1955 until his sudden death in 1963. On the right wing of the party, he attempted to draw Labour away from its commitment to the nationalisation of key industries and he defended Britain's right to keep the nuclear deterrent. Subsequent Labour politicians, such as Roy Jenkins and (much later) Tony Blair, are sometimes described as being in the *Gaitskellite* mould.

PRETENTIOUSNESS INDEX **Nil**

(see also *Butskellite*)

GANDALF-LIKE

in the style of Gandalf, the white magician in J.R.R. Tolkien's *Lord of the Rings* trilogy;

'having magical powers', 'benevolent', 'wise', 'bearded':

Executive chairman Paul Reichmann is floating around before boarding his return flight to Canada, exuding a quiet, Gandalf-like wisdom in his long grey beard and black skullcap. (Daily Telegraph)

The global success of the *Lord of the Rings* films not only boosted the sales of Tolkien's original fantasy books but gave a new lease of life to at least two iconic figures: Gollum (see *Gollum-like*) and Gandalf. Half god and half father-figure, sage and mage, kindly but stern on occasion, Gandalf is the archetypal good wizard.

PRETENTIOUSNESS INDEX **Nil**

GANDHIAN

reflecting the style or beliefs of the leader of the movement for Indian independence, Mohandas (Mahatma) Gandhi (1869–1948);

'austere', 'preaching non-violence', 'campaigning for civil rights':

> On leaving the WMRE premises, Mr Dreyer was physically attacked by three of his irate fellow undergraduates. Unluckily for the assailants, he is not the Gandhian kind of pacifist but a champion boxer.   (Guardian)

Gandhi was the dominant figure in India's struggle to leave the British Empire and acquire self-rule. He led forms of protest that entailed civil disobedience but not violence, and which had a profound influence on later 20th-century struggles such as the civil rights movement in the US. *Gandhian* is most likely to refer to this doctrine of non-violence but it may also recall Gandhi's famously simple way of life in everything from his clothes to his vegetarianism.

PRETENTIOUSNESS INDEX *!*

GARBOESQUE

in the style of Greta Garbo (1905–90), Swedish-born Hollywood star;

'aloof', 'mysterious':

> Silence intensifies Beckham's Garboesque mystery.   (Observer)

Greta Garbo began in silent films but is remembered for talkies such as *Queen Christina* and *Grand Hotel*. It was in this latter film that her character uttered the line 'I want to be left alone', and this desire for withdrawal and privacy spilled over into her personal life. She retired from films in the 1940s and lived another 50 years; she never married and her own life seemed to be reflected in the doomed lovers whom she played on screen. And she was Swedish. It is not surprising that *Garboesque* has come to stand for an enigmatic and distant glamour.

PRETENTIOUSNESS INDEX *!*

GATSBYESQUE

in the style of Jay Gatsby, the title character in *The Great Gatsby* (1925), a novel by US writer F. Scott Fitzgerald (1896–1940);

'ostentatiously wealthy and mysterious':

His years spent honing his skills in the rag trade have turned him into one of Britain's richest men with a Monaco home, luxury yacht and fiftieth birthday party that was Gatsbyesque in its opulence. (Observer)

Scott Fitzgerald once wrote 'Let me tell you about the very rich. They are different from you and me.' (To which fellow-writer Ernest Hemingway's riposte was: 'Yes, they have more money.') The supreme example of the glamour of money is found in Fitzgerald's 1920s character Jay Gatsby, whose parties were as legendary as the sources of his wealth were shady. *Gatsbyesque* therefore stands for opulence, usually with a dash of romance and mystery.

PRETENTIOUSNESS INDEX *!*

(see also *Fitzgeraldian*)

GAZZA-LIKE

in the style of English footballer Paul Gascoigne (1967–);

'emotional', 'tearful':

But even the coach's permanent air of tranquillity can dissolve into Gazza-like surges of emotion, if his assistant Tord Grip is to be believed. (Guardian)

There are some sporting celebrities whose talents get buried in the wreck of their careers, so that they grow more famous for their drinking or their tantrums or their tears. Whatever Paul Gascoigne's skills as a footballer, he has become remembered for all three, particularly his tears on the field.

PRETENTIOUSNESS INDEX **Nil**

GETTYESQUE

connected either to multi-millionaire Jean Paul Getty (1892–1976) or to his son John Paul Getty (1932–2003), also a multi-millionaire;

'careful with money', 'philanthropic', 'reclusive':

England conceded 11 throws on their own ball, a charitable donation of Gettyesque proportions. (Daily Telegraph)

The sense of *Gettyesque* rather depends on whether the reference is to father or son. Getty senior, whose money and art collection helped to set up the Californian museum bearing his name, may have been a philanthropist but he had a reputation for meanness, based particularly on two stories: that he had a payphone installed in his Tudor mansion in Surrey, and that he at first refused to help pay a ransom when his grandson was kidnapped. The second Getty is more fondly remembered in Britain. He became a naturalised citizen in 1997, he was a passionate follower of cricket and he gave swathes of money to eminent institutions like the British Museum and Lord's cricket ground. John Paul Getty kept out of the limelight, so *Gettyesque* may also mean reclusive.

PRETENTIOUSNESS INDEX *!*

GILBERTIAN

typical of the style of lyrics produced by W(illiam) S(chwenck) Gilbert (1836–1911);

'light', 'witty', 'topsy-turvy':

> ... *the contortions necessary to conform to the recommendations of the Nolan report on standards in public life are positively Gilbertian in their ludicrousness.* (Daily Telegraph)

W.S. Gilbert, the writing half of the Gilbert and Sullivan partnership, was noted for plots and lyrics that could be both topical and fantastic. Any action by officials – particularly if they are in government and have elaborate titles – where they are seen to be behaving absurdly (and pompously) may be labelled *Gilbertian*.

PRETENTIOUSNESS INDEX *!*

GLADSTONIAN

connected to the Victorian politician William Ewart Gladstone (1809–98);

'liberal', 'principled':

> *But Mr Blair didn't go to war because he thought Britain was in danger of being attacked; he did it from a Gladstonian impulse to make things better in Iraq.* (Daily Telegraph)

Serving several times as Prime Minister, Gladstone was identified in foreign policy with a 'law of nations' approach, believing in the need for peace and diplomacy. The term *Gladstonian* could therefore, in an unsympathetic interpretation, come to mean 'do-gooding' and be contrasted with the more robust *Palmerstonian* (see entry) approach.

PRETENTIOUSNESS INDEX *!*

GODARDIAN

in the style of French film director Jean-Luc Godard (1930–) or one of his followers;

'experimental', 'intellectual', 'formal', 'cold':

Look at what happens to the possibly poisoned glass of milk Cary Grant brings to Joan Fontaine in Hitchcock's Suspicion when the Godardians go to work on it. 'The glass of milk is an "image" in two opposed yet interconnected ways,' opines Jacques Rancière. 'First, it is an agent of condensation. Second, it is an agent of dispersion.' (Guardian)

Jean-Luc Godard was at first a film critic and then a director at the beginning of the *Nouvelle Vague* movement in the early 1960s. Although, like other French intellectuals of the period, Godard paid enthusiastic tribute to American cinema and its hitherto unsung directors, his own films increasingly headed towards a cold formalism, with little in the way of conventional plot or character. (To Godard this would have been compliment and no criticism.) Godard's moment was the 1960s and 1970s when his combination of Marxism and experimental technique was in favour. His star has waned a bit since then. In any case, some people have always considered *Godardian* to be shorthand for 'pretentious' (see *Guardian* quote above).

PRETENTIOUSNESS INDEX *!!*

GOEBBELS-LIKE

in the style of Dr Joseph Goebbels (1897–1945), Hitler's minister for propaganda;

'shrill', 'lying':

Urbanski has been more forthright, referring to the film as 'almost a Goebbels-like piece of propaganda'. (Observer)

Goebbels was appointed propaganda minister in 1933 and used his control of the media to further Nazi interests and ideology. His principal propaganda technique was to repeat assertions or lies until people were conditioned to accept them as fact. Goebbels – who was Chancellor of Germany for the day and night between Hitler's suicide and his own (on 1st May 1945) – is so identified with the absolutely unscrupulous use of lies and misinformation that *Goebbels-like* remains something of a benchmark among insults.

PRETENTIOUSNESS INDEX **Nil**

GOLLUM-LIKE

in the style of Gollum, the ex-hobbit in J.R.R. Tolkien's *The Hobbit* and *The Lord of the Rings* trilogy;

'twisted and deformed', 'grotesque', 'conflicted', 'obsessed':

The BBC is still performing Gollum-like contortions over Gilligan.

(Observer)

Gollum is one of the more interesting characters in *The Lord of the Rings*, as shown by his prominence in the second and third of the blockbusting films. It has to be said that the interest springs from the fact that he's one of the few characters in both the books and films to show any complexity or internal conflict. Originally a hobbit named Sméagol, Gollum became solitary and repulsive through his obsessive pursuit of the ring. *Gollum-like* might refer to his 'twisted' shape or the gurgling voice that gives him his name, or to the moral contortions he goes through when he is arguing with himself.

PRETENTIOUSNESS INDEX **Nil**

GOONISH

in the style of the radio programme *The Goon Show*;

'zany', 'absurd', 'anarchic':

Like Nick Faldo, another great champion who could switch off his true personality in the workplace, [Steve] Davis is blessed with a goonish sense of humour.   (Daily Telegraph)

The Goon Show ran from 1951 to 1960 on the BBC Home Service (now Radio 4) and had an almost incalculable influence on the development of British comedy. The original Goons – Spike Milligan, Peter Sellers, Harry Secombe and Michael Bentine – operated in an area somewhere between the childish (silly voices) and the surreal (discussions about time), and gave their collective name to an authentic and new style of zany humour.

PRETENTIOUSNESS INDEX **Nil**

(see also *Pythonesque*)

GORDIAN (KNOT)

like the knot tied by Gordius, legendary king of ancient Phrygia;

'tangled', 'complex':

I untangle myself from the Gordian snarl of ticker tape relentlessly dribbling information from the stock markets of the world [...] and head on out. (Guardian)

In a delightful and rather comic legend, the Phrygians chose Gordius as their king because an oracle had told them that their troubles would be over if they picked the first man approaching the temple of Zeus in a wagon. It was their good or bad luck that the first person to turn up was a peasant. Gordius, duly chosen, dedicated his wagon to Zeus. The knot that secured the pole to the wagon's yoke was so complicated that it was supposed to be impossible to untie. *Gordian* may thus mean 'very tangled' with the implication that whatever is so described is in a mess. (Yet another legend said that whoever untied the knot would win the empire of Asia. In an early example of lateral thinking, Alexander the Great is supposed to have slashed the knot with his sword and applied the prophecy to himself.)

PRETENTIOUSNESS INDEX *!*

GOTHIC

in the style of architecture known as Gothic or connected to horror literature of the early 19th century or relating to gothic fashion in clothes and music;

'sinister', 'romantic', 'pleasurably frightening', 'dark and introspective', 'heavy metal':

The predominance of black and white, and the abundance of darkly romantic frills, are in keeping with the gothic mood which has also been in evidence on the catwalks of Christian Dior and Givenchy this week.

(Guardian)

Gothic (when spelled with a capital G) has a specific application to the style of architecture that evolved in the Middle Ages and was revived at the end of the 18th century. From there, however, the term starts to fan out in all directions. *Gothic* fiction, employing ruins, dark woods, and distressed maidens, enjoyed a great vogue during the time of Jane Austen, who sent up the whole genre in *Northanger Abbey* (published 1818). Jumping nearly 200 years, *gothic* (generally spelled with a lower-case *g*) characterises a distinctive dark style of dress, often accompanied with metal piercings and dead white make-up. But the versatility of the term is shown by the fact that it can also be used to describe romantic frills, as in the *Guardian* quote above. So, like a number of terms in this book, *gothic* has been diluted so as to mean pretty well whatever the user requires, as long as there's a tantalising hint of darkness.

<small>PRETENTIOUSNESS INDEX</small> **Nil**

GREENEIAN

in the style of British novelist Graham Greene (1904–91);

'bleak', 'spiritually anguished':

> *The [film] Consequences of Love offers a deadpan black comic insight into mafia violence, and a Greeneian meditation on the spiritual lives of those intelligent, middle-management types sucked into its web of fear.* (Guardian)

Graham Greene seemed to create his own world in novels like *The Heart of the Matter* (1948) or *The End of the Affair* (1951) as well as in the films he scripted, such as *The Third Man* (1948). The often exotic landscape of his fiction even prompted critics to coin the word *Greeneland* to describe the books' mixture of despair and danger. Greene's Catholic background was almost invariably a factor in his writing, but only to the extent that his characters could be sure of their own damnation. *Greeneian* therefore suggests a mixture of the spiritual and the squalid, but with a dash of exoticism.

<small>PRETENTIOUSNESS INDEX</small> *!*

H

HAMLET-LIKE

typical of the hero of Shakespeare's play *Hamlet*;

'broody and introspective', 'questioning', '(over-)intellectual', 'indecisive', 'noble':

> But, Hamlet-like, he may have agonised too long and too publicly to derive much benefit. (Daily Telegraph)

Hamlet-like could mean several things but, in practice, it tends to be used about a person who shilly-shallies and is unable to commit to any single course of action. (The 1948 Laurence Olivier film version of *Hamlet* was even advertised as the tragedy of a 'man who could not make up his mind'.) This is a reductive use of the term and not even an especially accurate one, since Hamlet is not so much indecisive as prevented from acting by various obstacles, internal and external. However, *Hamlet-like* will continue to be applied to any public ditherer when the person using the term wants to inject a bit of class into the discussion.

PRETENTIOUSNESS INDEX *!*

HAMMER-LIKE

typical of the style or themes of the films produced by Hammer studios;

'melodramatic', 'lurid', 'glossy':

> Parker's weird Faustian thriller opens noirishly then turns up the Technicolor to become a lurid Hammer-like horror. (Guardian)

The Hammer production company – based for many years at Bray studios near Windsor – was founded before World War Two but only gained recognition in the 1950s and, with its cycle of horror films, real prominence in the 1960s. Hammer's two best-known stars were Peter Cushing and Christopher Lee, with Lee tending to take the villainous roles (Dracula, Frankenstein's monster). It's hard to pinpoint exactly what made Hammer horror so *Hammer-like*. Partly it was the glossy look of the films, which belied their relatively cheap production costs. Partly it was the artful concentration on blood, gore and sex, more explicit than was usual in the cinema of the early 1960s. There was often a dream-like, enclosed quality to the films, probably because they were almost all shot in the grounds of Bray studios. It is doubtful if any English production company has come close to producing such a recognisable house style, certainly since the 1960s. Hammer eventually declined when mainstream cinema became either more explicit in its handling of sex and horror or more subtle, but the term *Hammer-like* has been used as a benchmark ever since.

PRETENTIOUSNESS INDEX **Nil**

HAMPSTEAD

connected to the north London district of Hampstead;
'intellectual', 'left-wing', 'out of touch':

> *Henceforth, business stories would be given air time without the tradition-al overtone of Hampstead-leftish disdain, and the insistence that such stories had to have wider social significance to merit being reported at all.* (Spectator)

The identification of Hampstead with high-minded socialism probably began in the 1950s when the then leader of the Labour Party, Hugh Gaitskell (1906–63), had a house there. A number of politicians and thinkers connected with Gaitskell also lived in the area. The fact that they were middle class, Oxbridge-educated and far removed from tradi-tional cloth-capped Labourism led to accusations of elitism. As if the political associations weren't bad enough, Hampstead and neighbour-ing Highgate have always had literary and artistic residents, while property prices in the area now make it a no-go area for all except the wealthy. It's easy, perhaps, to see why *Hampstead* became a term of abuse of the knee-jerk kind. However, the term is bit dated now and has been largely replaced in right-wing demonology by *Islingtonian* (see entry).

PRETENTIOUSNESS INDEX *!*

HARDYESQUE

typical of the works of English novelist and poet Thomas Hardy (1840–1928);
'pastoral', 'pessimistic':

As a result, I can't say I haven't entertained the odd daydream of a wed-
ding in the church up the hill, then being transported by horse and cart
back down to our house, friends and family following on foot, the perfect
picture of Hardyesque rural bliss. (Guardian)

For all the wealth of his writing, Thomas Hardy seems to represent two
things: the sometimes stark beauty of the English countryside and the
implacable workings of fate. The *Guardian* quote is representative of
Hardy's less gloomy side. There are wedding scenes in novels such as
Far from the Madding Crowd (1874) and *Tess of the D'Urbervilles* (1891)
but they are dogged by sinister consequences.

PRETENTIOUSNESS INDEX *!*

HEATHCLIFFIAN

**characteristic of the appearance or manner of the principal male
figure in Emily Brontë's *Wuthering Heights* (1847);**

'romantic', 'brooding', 'dangerous', 'untamed':

After all, if a man does a bit of shouting, demanding and stomping around,
he's admired for being fiery, passionate and Heathcliffian. (Observer)

From the moment of Heathcliff's introduction to the pages of
Wuthering Heights – 'a dirty, ragged, black-haired child' who has been
rescued from the streets of Liverpool – he becomes a dangerous, disruptive presence in the house of the Earnshaws. Violent and volatile,
he draws Catherine Earnshaw into an intense relationship which ends
with her premature death. Or does not end, since the implication of
the closing pages of the novel is that the pair are reunited beyond
death. Heathcliff is a genuinely wild creation, with similarities to
Rochester in Charlotte Brontë's *Jane Eyre* but without his civilising
attributes or that book's comparatively happy ending. *Heathcliffian*
suggests an extreme, Gothic model for the romantic hero.

PRETENTIOUSNESS INDEX *!*

HEATHITE

**describing the political approach or policies of Prime Minister
Edward Heath (1916–2005) or one of his followers;**

'managerial', 'interventionist', (politically) 'middle of the road':

After the election of Thatcher as party leader in February 1975 he
remained something of a Heathite or 'wet'. (The Times)

Edward Heath's premiership (1970–74) is generally regarded unfavourably. His one undisputed achievement was to negotiate Britain's entry into the European Union, or the Common Market as it was then known. Even this is looked on as an almost treasonous act by the devotees of Margaret Thatcher, who succeeded Heath as leader of the Conservative Party. *Heathite* is therefore defined partly by the Thatcherite era that followed, during which his government's moderate, Keynesian approach to economic affairs was regularly dismissed as 'wet'. In fact, 'wetness' was seen as characterising the entire one-nation approach of old-style Tories such as Heath. It is often forgotten that Heath began his government in a brisk, managerial style and that his attempts to treat Britain as an enterprise were regularly satirised in *Private Eye* magazine, which presented him as the director of a struggling company called Heathco forever issuing upbeat pronouncements and petty reprimands.

PRETENTIOUSNESS INDEX **Nil**

(see also *Keynesian* and *Thatcherite*)

HEATH ROBINSON-TYPE

typical of a character or device in a cartoon by William Heath Robinson (1872–1944);

'inventive but self-defeating', 'ridiculously complicated':

> *Jones's character spent years rigging up his own lair, an abandoned ship, into one marvellous Heath Robinson-type bomb. Happily, he got to see it blow up.* (Guardian)

Heath Robinson was a talented illustrator of children's stories but he is remembered for his almost surreal cartoons, with titles such as 'The professor's invention for peeling potatoes', in which some simple, everyday process is made absurdly complicated. Heath Robinson drew elaborate devices, rather medieval in appearance and involving wheels and pulleys and cords, attended by bustling functionaries. (*Heath Robinson* can also appear by itself as an adjectival phrase with the same meaning.)

PRETENTIOUSNESS INDEX **Nil**

HEEPISH

typical of Uriah Heep, a character in Charles Dickens's novel *David Copperfield* (1850);

'humble', 'obsequious and hypocritical':

Many [visitors' centres] are housed in fidgety new buildings that, trying to be polite and even Heepish – ever so 'umble – undermine the artistic integrity of the building or monument they are meant to serve.

(Guardian)

Uriah Heep is a lawyer's clerk in *David Copperfield*. A creepy figure, he is perpetually rubbing his clammy hands together and assuring people that he is 'a very umble person'. He crawls his way into his employer's confidence and then starts on a career of fraud. This is always a negative reference.

PRETENTIOUSNESS INDEX **Nil**

HEMINGWAYESQUE

in the style of the US writer Ernest Hemingway (1899–1961);

'terse', 'bragging', 'swaggering', 'macho':

But it is France none the less: I remember the anticipation of 1966 – I approached Europe then with Hemingwayesque intent. I would run with the bulls in Pamplona; lounge in the cafes of Paris and say things like, 'The wine, it is very good.' (Guardian)

Hemingwayesque denotes a style in two senses, a way of living and a way of writing. Ernest Hemingway's devotion to bull-fighting, big-game hunting and deep-sea fishing gave him an image that was the polar opposite of the sensitive writer shut up in his study. On paper he cultivated a style that was pared-down and hard-bitten. There's no doubt that Hemingway was a great writer, as he showed early on in *A Farewell to Arms* (1929), but his very public dedication to manly pursuits has sometimes raised a few eyebrows. Fellow US writer Gore Vidal – routinely described as waspish – said of Hemingway and their shared country, 'What other culture could have produced someone like Hemingway and not seen the joke?' So *Hemingwayesque* can cut two ways. As a comment on literary style it may be a compliment; as a description of behaviour it's probably a bit suspect.

PRETENTIOUSNESS INDEX *!*

HERCULEAN

in the manner of the Roman mythological figure of Hercules;

(of a person) 'very strong', 'giant-like'; (of a task) 'very difficult or effortful':

Every July my parents would embark on the Herculean task of transporting themselves, their five young sons and enough bottles of booze and packets of fags to keep drink-sodden uncles and cousins happy for the next year, by car and sea to County Galway. (Spectator)

Hercules (or Heracles to the ancient Greeks) was a legendary strong man who proved his prowess even as a baby by strangling two serpents in his cradle. *Herculean* can refer to an individual's size/strength but more usually alludes to an undertaking that requires great physical strength and stamina. This relates to the 12 labours of Hercules, a series of tasks imposed on him in penance for the crime of killing his wife in a fit of madness. The tasks included cleansing the Augean stables and bringing up from Hades the dog Cerberus, guardian of the entrance to the underworld.

PRETENTIOUSNESS INDEX **Nil**

(see also *Augean*)

HERMANN-ESQUE

in the style of US film composer Bernard Hermann (1911–75);

'tense', 'romantic':

An interview reveals that the echoes of Polanski and Hitchcock, including the Hermann-esque score, are deliberate. (Sunday Times)

Bernard Hermann enjoyed a long and distinguished career in film composing, from the score for Orson Welles's *Citizen Kane* (1941) to Martin Scorsese's *Taxi Driver* (1976). But he is best known for his association with director Alfred Hitchcock, and in particular for *Vertigo* (1958) and *Psycho* (1960). Everyone remembers the shrieking, stabbing strings from the shower-murder sequence in *Psycho*, and the way in which music contributes to the sense of unease and menace that hangs over the whole film. But Bernard Hermann also created the highly charged romantic accompaniment to *Vertigo*, with its echoes of Wagner, and laid down the mood of urban loneliness in *Taxi Driver* with a jazz-influenced score. He was one of the most versatile and important of the composers who escaped persecution by emigrating from Europe in the years before World War Two. Yet *Hermann-esque* is likely to refer only to that shower scene.

PRETENTIOUSNESS INDEX **!** THIS IS AN INSIDER'S REFERENCE PERHAPS, BUT IT DOES DESCRIBE A HIGHLY DISTINCTIVE STYLE OF FILM MUSIC.

(see also *Hitchcockian*)

HERODIAN

like Herod the Great (c.74–4 BC), king of the Roman province of Judaea around the time of Jesus's birth;

'tyrannical', 'anti-child':

When you have just been given a good hiding by an 11-year-old girl fresh from a primary school maths lesson, it does tend to make you lean slightly towards the Herodian view of children. (Daily Telegraph)

According to Matthew's gospel, it was King Herod who, suspicious of the predictions of a messiah and fearful of a rival, ordered the massacre of all male children under two in the attempt to kill Jesus. Warned in a dream by an angel, Joseph had already fled with Mary and the baby to Egypt. *Herodian*, rather than being used with absolute accuracy, tends to be applied, slightly flippantly, to someone who merely dislikes children (the *Telegraph* reference above is to a golfing prodigy).

PRETENTIOUSNESS INDEX *!*

HITCHCOCKIAN

typical of the style or themes associated with British-born film director Alfred Hitchcock (1899–1980);

'suspenseful', 'manipulative', 'threatening':

No one is dragging me anywhere near a field. I'm not going to be woken by the menacingly Hitchcockian noise of the dawn chorus.

(Daily Telegraph)

The reference is to Hitchcock's film *The Birds* (1963), in which birds turn against human beings, but the adjective derived from the director's name stands for a range of tension-inducing effects. Hitchcock specialised in the manipulation of the cinema audience, most famously in the finely cut shower scene in *Psycho* (1960). Frequently used, and often without justification, to describe any old thriller or whodunnit, the proper *Hitchcockian* experience is one that is carefully crafted, anxiety-provoking – and just a little cold in its view of human relations.

PRETENTIOUSNESS INDEX **Nil** BUT THIS IS ONE OF THOSE REFERENCES THAT ARE SO GENERAL OR VAGUELY APPLIED THAT THEY HAVE LOST PRECISION.

(see also *Hermann-esque*)

HITLERIAN

connected to the life, beliefs and actions of Adolf Hitler (1889–1945);

'dictatorial', 'totalitarian', 'Nazi', 'anti-Semitic', 'holding extreme racial beliefs', 'using dangerous rhetoric', 'warlike', 'having a little moustache':

> *But many opponents of GM food are wary of the Hitlerian concept of genetic super-species, even if this time round we are talking about broccoli.*
> (Guardian)

It's possible to attach almost anything negative to the name of Hitler, Nazi leader and German Chancellor from 1933 until his suicide in the Berlin bunker. Book-burning; crackpot theories about Aryan supremacy; pathological anti-Semitism; imperial hubris; aggressive nationalism; ranting oratory; warmongering: all this and more may be characterised as *Hitlerian*. The term may even extend to describing that little toothbrush moustache. As an expression, therefore, *Hitlerian* is something of a broad church.

PRETENTIOUSNESS INDEX **Nil**

HOBBESIAN

in the style of writer and philosopher Thomas Hobbes (1588–1679);

'bleakly realistic', 'harsh', 'merciless':

> *They depict an essentially Hobbesian nation in character. Every man must fend for himself. The rich, unimaginably comfortable by global standards, can take refuge in their affluence. The poor, most of them from ethnic minorities, looking like exiles from the Third World, are left to sink and die.* (The Times)

In person, Thomas Hobbes was apparently a mild or timorous individual – something he attributed to the fact that his mother was fearful of the Spanish Armada at the time she was pregnant with him – but he is remembered today for his uncomfortably objective assessment of the human condition. In his work of political theory, *Leviathan* (1651), Hobbes says that the natural state of man is 'a condition of war of everyone against everyone' and that therefore, without some powerful authority to keep people in check ('in awe' is how Hobbes puts it), the life of man is 'solitary, poor, nasty, brutish and short'. The adjective *Hobbesian* is an economical way of describing uncontrolled human nature, at least from a pessimistic viewpoint.

PRETENTIOUSNESS INDEX *!*

HOGARTHIAN

in the style of painter and engraver William Hogarth (1697–1764); 'squalid', 'satirical':

London is a place of endless fascination and scrapes; an immoral stew and a huge, heaving Hogarthian scrum. (The Times)

William Hogarth was best known for his series of paintings, later engravings, that charted the fortunes of a harlot or a rake or a newly married couple. The pictures are detailed and exuberant depictions of high and low life, with the emphasis on the latter. For example, the well-known *Gin Lane* shows a drunken woman whose unwatched baby is tumbling down a flight of steps while nearby a dead ballad singer still clutches his bottle, against a background of street crime and disorder.

PRETENTIOUSNESS INDEX *!*

HOLMESIAN

in the style of the world-famous detective Sherlock Holmes, created by Arthur Conan Doyle (1859–1930); 'brilliant', 'highly observant', 'eccentric':

By Friday, they were the Holmesian geniuses who, acting on behalf of the abovementioned banks, had swiftly located multi-million pound gaps in the books of Versailles, thus bringing in both the tontons macoutes and the receivers. (Guardian)

Sherlock Holmes has transcended even those other famous creations of 19th-century fiction, Frankenstein and Dracula, to establish himself in the world's consciousness as one of the oddest and most brilliant figures never to have existed. Conan Doyle started Holmes on his crime-solving career in *A Study in Scarlet* (1887) and concluded it nearly 40 years later in the short story 'The Retired Colourman' (1926). Doyle, who always rated his historical novels more highly than the rest of his fiction, famously attempted to kill Holmes off in 'The Final Problem' (1893) but public demand and a great deal of money prompted the author to bring him back to life. *Holmesian* can describe a variety of attributes, from the detective's hawk-eyed powers of observation to his deductive skills. It also touches on his cocaine habit as well as his stick-thin physique and his adeptness at disguise.

PRETENTIOUSNESS INDEX **Nil**

HOMERIC

reflecting the style or themes of the poems of the Greek writer Homer, the *Iliad* and the *Odyssey*;

'epic', 'mythical', 'heroic', 'on a large scale':

In 1910, a captain at last, he [Scott of the Antarctic] went south again in Terra Nova, and from that Homeric journey he never returned.

(Daily Telegraph)

Nothing certain is known about Homer or even whether there was a single writer who produced the two epic poems describing the fall of Troy and the subsequent wanderings of Odysseus. But *Homeric* can still used to describe a tale that is conceived on a grand scale and unfurls against a mythical backdrop or, as in the *Telegraph* quote above, to characterise a journey that is lengthy and dangerous, particularly if it has never been undertaken before.

PRETENTIOUSNESS INDEX **Nil**

HOPPER-ESQUE

typical of the style or subject matter of US painter Edward Hopper (1882–1967);

'urban', 'alienated', 'isolated', 'melancholy':

Imogen Cloet's two-tier set has the immensity of a cinema screen, black shutters sliding back and forth to reveal beautifully shadowy, Edward Hopper-esque interiors: here a smoky casino, there a neon-lit bar. (Daily Telegraph)

Hopper is identified with urban angst and isolation. His figures are posed alone in the frame or in isolation from each other, not quite connecting or staring at something out of range beyond the picture. He is known for his contrast of sun and shadow, and his urban interiors. Yet Hopper also painted images that suggested the almost infinite light and spaciousness of the American continent, and there is a sense of yearning in much of his work which may also define what is meant by *Hopper-esque*.

PRETENTIOUSNESS INDEX **!**

HOUDINI-LIKE

in the style of US magician and escapologist Harry Houdini (1874–1926);

'slippery', 'brilliantly elusive':

Are the public finances out of control, as some claim, or will Mr Brown emerge, Houdini-like, with his fiscal rules intact? (Guardian)

Although almost a century has passed since his death, Harry Houdini, the stage name of Hungarian-born Ehrich Weiss, remains the most famous escapologist of all time. He could get free from any number of handcuffs, ropes, chains, etc., delaying an escape until the last moment for maximum impact. *Houdini-like* (also *Houdinesque*) is almost always applied figuratively rather than to an actual illusionist. In particular, the expression tends to be used about politicians (as in the *Guardian* quote above) and has been applied to at least two US presidents, Franklin Roosevelt and Richard Nixon, reflecting their ability to wriggle out of trouble, at any rate for a time. It may also be that when used in this context *Houdini-like* reflects a faint distrust of politicians, if such a thing is conceivable, because of the connotations of trickery and illusion that go with the term.

PRETENTIOUSNESS INDEX **Nil**

HOWARD HUGHES-LIKE

in the style of film director, producer and millionaire Howard Hughes (1905–76);

'very wealthy', 'obsessed with flying', 'eccentric', 'reclusive':

Then he locked himself away in his Malibu estate for the rest of the decade in a state of Howard Hughes-like invisibility. (Guardian)

Hughes became an American legend long before his final protracted years, living out a strange existence in the Las Vegas hotels that he owned. Before that he had designed, built and test-flown planes, discovered and exploited stars such as Jean Harlow and Jane Russell, and run a Hollywood studio and an airline. The stories of Hughes's eccentricity are legion: that he was obsessed with hygiene and (less logically) the size of peas, that he wore empty Kleenex boxes in place of shoes, that he rarely had his hair cut or nails trimmed. His obsessive-compulsive behaviour has sometimes been interpreted as one of the symptoms of the syphilis he contracted when young. *Howard Hughes-like* might be a positive term in the sense of 'daring', 'innovative' and so on, recalling his extraordinary life as a designer, entrepreneur and movie mogul, but in practice it tends to focus on Hughes's peculiar last quarter of century and to be synonymous with 'hermit-like' if not 'mentally unbalanced'.

PRETENTIOUSNESS INDEX **!**

HUMBERT HUMBERTISH

in the manner of Humbert Humbert, the narrator of the novel *Lolita* (1955) by Vladimir Nabokov (1899–1977);

'obsessive', 'paedophilic':

In [the short story] 'Gators', for instance, a Humbert Humbertish tutor records his unsettling relationship with a teenage girl. (Guardian)

Humbert Humbert – a cultivated middle-aged man – is a more sympathetic character than the 'paedophilic' label suggests but his obsessive interest in the barely pubescent Lolita, which he considers love rather than lust, leads him to murder a rival. Unlike *Lolita-ish* (see entry), which is widely understood, *Humbert Humbertish* remains a fairly obscure literary reference.

PRETENTIOUSNESS INDEX *!*

(see also *Nabokovian*)

HYDRA-LIKE

similar to the Hydra, a mythical snake living in marshland in southern Greece;

'multi-headed', 'growing faster than it can be destroyed':

They didn't count on that hydra-like law of the blogosphere: take on one blogger, and dozens more will appear in his/her place. (Observer)

Disposing of the Hydra was one of the 12 labours of Hercules. As soon as one of its many heads was severed, others grew in its place. (Hercules solved this by searing each neck with fire as soon as the head had been cut off.) *Hydra-like* is a negative description, applied to problems such as regulating the traffic in drugs or combating terrorism. Not only is the 'hydra' intrinsically bad, but there is the implication that clumsy attempts to solve things may actually make the problem worse.

PRETENTIOUSNESS INDEX *!*

I , J

IAGO-LIKE

in the manner of Iago, the villain in Shakespeare's play *Othello*;

'cunning', 'deceiving while giving the appearance of honesty', 'devilish':

Deep down the wary Mr Brown is probably too canny to fall for Iago-like flattery. (Guardian)

In Shakespeare's tragedy, Iago is an officer serving under Othello, the commander of Venetian forces based on Cyprus. For a variety of apparent motives, but really acting from nothing more than simple malevolence, Iago decides to undermine and destroy his commander by insinuating that the latter's wife, Desdemona, has been unfaithful with another officer. Corrupted and goaded by Iago, Othello eventually kills Desdemona before committing suicide. Iago achieves his objectives by a show of bluff honesty, pretending that he is speaking out merely for the good of the listener. *Iago-like* therefore conveys the pretence of honesty, but also suggests destruction and malice.

PRETENTIOUSNESS INDEX *!*

(see also *Othello-like*)

ISLINGTONIAN

characteristic of Islington in north London and associated with the New Labour government first elected in 1997;

'characteristic of the Labour government under Tony Blair', 'liberal in appearance', 'innovative (but suspect)':

He was one of the earliest modernisers, but approached it from practicality and common sense rather than any Islingtonian desire for newness.

(Daily Telegraph)

The old charge against left-wing intellectuals was that they and their ideas were from Hampstead in north London. Fairly or not, the place was synonymous with out-of-touch pretentiousness and idealistic thinking. For the 21st century, however, Islington – a slightly less expensive district of London but still out of reach for most people – has more or less replaced Hampstead. Tony and Cherie Blair used to live in Islington, and the notorious deal (or non-deal) between Blair and Gordon Brown about the future leadership of the Labour Party was struck at the Granita restaurant in Upper Street, in the heart of Islington. The restaurant has gone and the Blairs have moved on, but *Islingtonian* remains a shorthand term of near-abuse for all those aspects of New Labour disliked by commentators on the political right (other similar terms include 'metropolitan', 'chattering classes', etc.).

PRETENTIOUSNESS INDEX !! THIS IS SOMETHING OF A SPECIALIST TERM, WHICHEVER SIDE OF THE POLITICAL FENCE YOU FIND YOURSELF.

(see also *Hampstead*)

JACOBEAN

characteristic of the reign of King James I (1603–25) and usually applied to the drama of that period;

'vengeful', 'bloody', 'scheming', 'filled with intrigue':

But the real power of this Jacobean morality tale is the warped price of newspaper ambition and survival. (The Times)

Drama before the days of James I could be violent and melodramatic too, but there was a particular taste in James's reign for plays filled with blood and intrigue, as in the works of John Webster (*The Duchess of Malfi*) or Thomas Middleton (*The Revenger's Tragedy*). Deaths are elaborate, often treated with black humour, and a whiff of decadence rises from the proceedings. Any or all of this may be suggested by *Jacobean*.

PRETENTIOUSNESS INDEX **Nil**

JAGGER-ESQUE

in the style of Mick Jagger (1943–), lead singer of the Rolling Stones;

'ageless', 'prancing', 'pouting':

In between bouts of Jagger-esque peacock posturing, the singer Pelle Almqvist promised to take us to the 'tenth level of soft rock detox'. (The Times)

Sir Michael Jagger's ascendancy over the world rock scene is remarkable. He qualified for membership of Saga some years ago and his band haven't had a true hit for even longer, but Jagger – and, to a lesser extent, the rest of the Stones – provides continual media fodder. *Jagger-esque* might refer to his singing style but other aspects about Jagger are more likely to be emphasised: his turbulent marriages and affairs, his crazy energy, his longevity, his lips, his bottom, his fossilised youth.

PRETENTIOUSNESS INDEX **Nil**

JAMESIAN

typical of the style or subject matter of US-born novelist Henry James (1843–1916);

'complex', 'refined', 'tortuous':

Messud's prose, with its erudite, Jamesian weave of clauses and sub-clauses, works like a tracker dog, forever chasing down a more exact compression of a feeling or thought. (Observer)

Henry James was born in New York but lived in England for most of his life, becoming naturalised just before his death. His novels, such as *The Portrait of a Lady* (1881) or *The Wings of the Dove* (1902), are notable for the extraordinary refinement of their style and dissection of feelings and circumstances. He said about himself that he was 'interminably supersubtle and analytic'. For such a civilised figure, James prompted some extreme responses, from near-worship to terminal impatience. Similarly *Jamesian* is a rather ambiguous expression, half praise, half blame.

PRETENTIOUSNESS INDEX **!**

JANUS-LIKE

like the Roman god Janus, guardian of doorways;

'facing two ways at once':

But SF [Sinn Fein]'s Janus-like stance on Bush and the US administration must surely cause them problems in the long run among the young radicals it is wooing in the Republic. (Observer)

Janus was originally more important in Roman mythology than his porter-like job of guarding doors suggests. He was the deity of beginnings (*January* derives from him) as well as entrances, and his two faces showed wisdom because he knew the past and could see into the future. *Janus-like* is now almost always used in a disparaging way to mean 'two-faced', 'hypocritical' – an interpretation that the Romans wouldn't have recognised but which is nevertheless an expressive description.

PRETENTIOUSNESS INDEX **Nil**

JEEVESIAN

in the style of the character created by P.G. Wodehouse (1881–1975);

'wise', 'ingenious', 'deferential':

The man behind the cash register was a model of Jeevesian emollience: 'Uh, these are the all-new dollar coins, sir. If you'll permit me to open the register I can also show you the new five-dollar bill. It's awful nice-looking.'
(Guardian)

Jeeves, the valet to Bertie Wooster, conforms to a master-servant pattern traditionally found in fiction in which the supposed inferior is actually smarter than the person he serves. While always tactful and aware of his subordinate position, Jeeves is Bertie Wooster's lifeline, a model of sense and dependability. *Jeevesian* therefore combines the idea of shrewdness with self-effacing service.

PRETENTIOUSNESS INDEX **Nil**

(see also *Woosterish* and *Wodehousian*)

JEFFERSONIAN

typical of the life, politics or philosophy of the third US President, Thomas Jefferson (1743–1826);

'committed to liberty', 'enlightened', 'elevated', 'brilliantly capable':

The general thrust seems to be a regretful acknowledgement that Title VII of the 1964 Civil Rights Act – with its noble, Jeffersonian, vision of a wholly equal and just American society – has still a long way to go. (Guardian)

Thomas Jefferson was one of the principal authors of the American Declaration of Independence and with him originates the stirring dedication to 'life, liberty and the pursuit of happiness'. Jefferson reflected the Enlightenment doctrines of his time, believing in the rights of man, the intrinsic goodness of humanity and the promise of the future, particularly for his native land. He was also a remarkably versatile individual – among other talents, he was a violinist, a lawyer and an architect (designing his own house at Monticello in Virginia) – but *Jeffersonian* is most likely to apply to his vision of the United States in that country's early years, a vision that seemed to combine rationalism and optimism in equal measure.

PRETENTIOUSNESS INDEX **Nil**

JEKYLL AND HYDE

connected to the principal character(s) in Robert Louis Stevenson's novel *The Strange Case of Dr Jekyll and Mr Hyde* (1886);

'two-faced', 'having violently conflicting personalities':

Diplomats, statesmen and psychologists alike all tried in vain to understand the inner workings of an often charming leader who combined a convivial Balkan bonhomie with a blind indifference to bloodshed. This Jekyll and Hyde personality helped Milosevic to maintain his standing on the international stage long past his sell-by date. (The Times)

Nineteenth-century novelists have given us three dominant figures of horror (the other two being Mary Shelley's Frankenstein and Bram Stoker's Dracula). The *Jekyll and Hyde* pairing is the only one to have a psychological basis, in that it corresponds to a belief that many – most? – people have the potential to show violently conflicting aspects of personality, good and bad. In Stevenson's original, Dr Jekyll experiments with a drug that gives him a separate identity. As Mr Hyde he is transformed into a gleeful murderer. The title figures of the story, which came to Stevenson in a dream and the first draft of which was written in three days, have served ever since to represent a dual personality. However, like the casual use of *schizophrenic* to describe someone who is undecided, *Jekyll and Hyde* is normally applied to a person with, say, a nasty temper rather than anything worse.

PRETENTIOUSNESS INDEX **Nil**

JOHNSONIAN

typical of the style, works or appearance of writer Samuel Johnson (1709–84);

'authoritative', 'scholarly', 'resonant', 'opinionated', 'influential in forming taste', 'eccentric in personal habits':

'In the United States, madam,' I said, in my richest Johnsonian tones, 'it may be seen as a privilege not to have to pay for a telephone call that one has not made. In the United Kingdom, we regard it as a right.' (Daily Telegraph)

Dr Johnson was one of the dominant figures in English life of the mid-18th century. A poet, critic and essayist, he also compiled the first

English dictionary of real substance and authority. Johnson's reputation grew after the publication of the dictionary in 1755 but his posthumous fame is largely the result of James Boswell's *Life* (1791), which devotedly recorded Johnson's table-talk and wide-ranging opinions. Johnson, a bear-like man with an awkward but imposing presence, delivered his views – quirky, maverick or commonsensical – with authority and conviction. *Johnsonian* is likely to refer to a rounded style of speech or writing, one that is assured of its own rightness. If applied to appearance, it suggests someone who is careless, even clumsy.

PRETENTIOUSNESS INDEX **Nil**

JORDANESQUE

in the style or with the appearance of celebrity model Jordan, real name Katie Price (1978–);

'exhibitionist', 'large-breasted', 'showing a genius for self-publicity':

> *Sprinters were arguably the inventors of the modern passion for self-exposure among male athletes, blessed as they are with an almost Jordanesque passion for displaying their expensively sculpted bosoms to the world.* (Guardian)

Jordan prefers being known as Katie Price these days and she has forged a highly successful new career as a best-selling author with books about herself. Her marriage to Pete Andre, whom she met during the 2004 run of *I'm a Celebrity, Get Me Out of Here!*, was the celebrity equivalent of a royal wedding. In fact, having started as a glamour model and page-3 stunner she is now an icon and well on her way to becoming – what else? – a national treasure.

PRETENTIOUSNESS INDEX **Nil**

JOYCEAN

connected to Irish-born writer James Joyce (1882–1941);

'in love with word-play', 'daring', 'experimental':

> *The tension was such that Le Tissier's initial gambit, a light smattering of oohs and aahs with a few non-sequiturs thrown in, quickly segued into incoherent Joycean streams of consciousness. 'Atmosphere ... yabber ... sunshine on the south coast ... blah ... 27 years ... yabber ... riverrun, past Rupert and Harry ...'* (Guardian)

After two relatively conventional works (*Dubliners* and *A Portrait of the Artist as a Young Man*), James Joyce went on to produce what was arguably the 20th century's most influential novel, *Ulysses* (1922), as well as its most famously unreadable one, *Finnegan's Wake* (1939). Joyce rejoiced in the difficulties he created, claiming that the reader 'should devote his whole life to reading my works'. *Joycean* may describe an obscure or demanding literary style, or it may refer to the frank content of his books – frequently regarded as obscene in their time. The most usual reference is to the 'stream of consciousness' technique which Joyce pioneered, a literary device whereby the reader is given the illusion of eavesdropping on the apparently random unfolding of someone's inner thoughts and feelings.

PRETENTIOUSNESS INDEX *!*

JUDAS-LIKE

acting like Judas, the disciple who betrayed Christ;

'traitorous':

> *So, after three long years, you discover that your dog has left you stinking, friendless and broke. You take walks only under cover of darkness and acquire a Judas-like capacity for disownership.*   (Guardian)

Judas betrayed Christ for 30 pieces of silver but a *Judas* may be a traitor without the spur of money. Although Judas's motives have been subsequently much debated, *Judas-like* remains a fairly insulting term.

PRETENTIOUSNESS INDEX **Nil**

JUNGIAN

connected to the life or teachings of Swiss-born psychiatrist Carl Jung (1875–1961);

'believing in the value of myth', 'archetypal', 'having opposed aspects of personality', 'seeking harmony':

> *Then it switches to psychological thriller territory as the body count and crack-ups increase before staggering to its conclusion as some kind of salutary fable about our Jungian dark sides.*   (The Times)

Carl Jung was for a brief period allied to Sigmund Freud but the two men diverged in the areas they regarded as significant in the fledgling science of psychoanalysis, and eventually came to occupy very distinct positions. Jung's doctrines may sometimes appear less rigorous than Freud's, with their emphasis on the value of myths and dreams, and ideas such as the 'collective unconscious' or the complementary psychic presences of anima and animus (respectively, the female component of men and the male component of women). *Jungian* philosophy has a mystical dimension that is absent from Freudian thinking, and it's no accident that Jung became one of the presiding figures of the spirit of the 1960s. If *Jungian* does not refer to specific psychoanalytic practices then it is likely to apply to a rather dream-like world of shadows, patterns and the quest for an over-arching unity.

PRETENTIOUSNESS INDEX **Nil**

JUNOESQUE

connected to Juno, the Roman goddess of women;

'large and attractive':

> *As Kathleen Turner's Junoesque Mrs R strips to her slip and then to the buff to entice Matthew Rhys's bewildered Ben, she announces, 'I'd like you to know I'm available to you.'* (Guardian)

Juno was the wife and the counterpart of the principal male god, Jupiter. In addition to her link with childbirth, her association with size, power and beauty seems to have been there from the beginning. When the word *Junoesque* is used now it tends to have a narrower focus, suggesting a mature attractiveness.

PRETENTIOUSNESS INDEX **Nil**

(see also *Rubenesque*)

K

KAFKAESQUE

reflecting the style or themes of Czech writer Franz Kafka (1883–1924);

'tortuously bureaucratic', 'enigmatic', 'nightmarish', 'impossible to escape from':

Instead the city is a trap, its grid of streets a net to capture the characters in external Kafkaesque nightmares … (The Times)

If Kafka hadn't existed it would have been necessary to invent him, so indispensable has the term *Kafkaesque* become, whether to those seeking to describe the modern human condition or to those who are simply fed up at being told to wait by an automatic answering service. The world of Kafka's narratives is a sinister, oppressive and enigmatic one. *The Trial* (published 1925) begins: 'Someone must have been telling lies about Joseph K., for without having done anything wrong he was arrested one fine morning.' Lack of control over one's life is the key – in Kafka's most famous short story, 'Metamorphosis', its central character wakes up one day to find himself turned into a giant insect. *Kafkaesque* can be used to describe a bleak and alienating city-scape just as easily as it can apply to an individual's struggles with bureaucracy, always 'faceless' of course. It is not surprising that the 20th century, with its dictatorships and persecutions and perpetual sense of threat, so took to Kafka. For all that, *Kafkaesque* is perhaps over-used, a reach-me-down term used whenever anyone gets impatient with officialdom rather than being applied to a genuine feeling of persecution.

PRETENTIOUSNESS INDEX *!*

KANE-LIKE

in the style of Charles Foster Kane, the title character in Orson Welles's film *Citizen Kane* (1941);

'ambitious and self-destructive':

Hollywood escapees Lucas and Coppola indulged in Xanadu-style empire-building in northern California, the former successfully while the latter fell victim to Kane-like hubris. (Guardian)

Kane was a fictitious newspaper magnate but closely based on the real-life figure of William Randolph Hearst, who tried to block the release of the film. Like Hearst, Kane was an aggressive and dynamic news proprietor with political ambitions. *Kane-like* may suggest either towering ambition or ultimate failure – or both.

Pretentiousness Index *!*

(see also *Wellesian*)

KEATONESQUE

typical of the style of silent-film comedian Buster Keaton (1895–1966);

'deadpan', 'unsmiling', 'involving slapstick':

By contrast, The Adventurer, in which Chaplin plays an escaped convict, is almost Keatonesque in its frenetic activity. (Guardian)

Along with Charlie Chaplin, Buster (born Joseph Francis) Keaton was one of the dominant figures of silent-film comedies. Whereas Chaplin managed a successful career after the coming of the talkies, Keaton fell victim to a combination of bad luck and alcoholism. *Keatonesque* suggests either the comedian's mournfully impassive face whatever disasters unfolded around him or the frantic movement typical of silent comedies.

Pretentiousness Index *!*

KEATSIAN

characteristic of the style, work or life of English poet John Keats (1795–1821);

'sweetly melancholy', 'passionate', 'short-lived':

Eighteen months ago, Haitink hadn't mined the edge of crazy excess in the score; this time round, alongside the gorgeous Keatsian melancholy and rapture, one heard all the urgency, all the fervour, all the madness that Wagner intended. (Daily Telegraph)

Of all the lives of the key poets of the Romantic period at the beginning of the 19th century, that of John Keats was the briefest and the most intense. His greatest writing was crammed into a two or three year period before he succumbed to tuberculosis in Rome at the age of 26. *Keatsian* may therefore describe any artistic life that is both brilliant and prematurely ended. If applied to poetry (or music, as above), the term generally suggests a lyrical combination of sadness and delight.

PRETENTIOUSNESS INDEX *!*

KENNEDYESQUE

typical of the life, style or policies of the 35th US President, John F. Kennedy (1917–63);

'charismatic', 'glamorous', 'youthful', 'optimistic', 'rhetorical and inspirational':

> *Bill [Clinton] does messianic Kennedyesque a million times better than poor old Tone, whose squirmy conference speech was just embarrassing.*
>
> (Daily Telegraph)

Jack Kennedy was the youngest man to be elected to the US presidency as well as the youngest to die. He came to the office with all the right credentials: heroic naval service in World War Two, good looks and a glamorous wife, and high political skills. Kennedy's term as President (1961–63) saw the most dramatic developments in the Cold War, from the building of the Berlin Wall to the Cuban missile crisis. The same years also witnessed the real emergence of the civil rights movement and the beginnings of America's manned space programme. For all these reasons, *Kennedyesque* might describe a time of hope and tense drama. But it is Kennedy's youth and his tragically early death that really give the term its resonance, so that *Kennedyesque* more often applies to style than to anything else, suggesting an individual with dash and charisma. Critics would claim that this is all too accurate since Kennedy's term in office didn't actually achieve much. The expression could also be used about JFK's less reputable side (his multiple sexual liaisons, the corruption rumours that hung about his election victory) but it's a measure of how nostalgically he is remembered that *Kennedyesque* is still found in a generally positive context.

PRETENTIOUSNESS INDEX **Nil**

KEYNESIAN

reflecting the beliefs and theories of economist John Maynard Keynes (1883–1946) or describing one of his followers;

'believing in state intervention in managing the markets and money supply':

> *Sir Edward [Heath] wanted to make the post-war settlement work better by the application of managerial methods. He was a Keynesian and what became known as monetarism was a fringe interest until at least 1972–73.*
>
> (The Times)

Keynes not only theorised about money and made himself rich by financial speculation but, through his writings and his advice to governments, had a profound effect on economic policy in the period following World War Two. Very broadly speaking, Keynes believed that markets weren't self-regulating but required government intervention to ensure high output and high employment. It was inevitable that his theories would dominate in the consensus-style British politics of the 1950s and 1960s, but the harsher monetarist climate of the 1980s – when the market was king if not god – saw the decline of Keynesianism.

PRETENTIOUSNESS INDEX **Nil**

KIPLINGESQUE

typical of the style or themes favoured by poet and novelist Rudyard Kipling (1865–1936);

'nostalgic for the days of the British Empire', 'imperial':

> *[Mark] Thatcher's lifestyle, founded in the days when JR Ewing was the face of corporate responsibility, remains preserved in a Kiplingesque time warp. His mock-Tudor mansion is run by 14 black servants ...* (Observer)

It is perhaps unfair that the term *Kiplingesque* should appear most often in a negative context, since Rudyard Kipling, author of *Kim* (1901) and *The Jungle Book* (1894), was an infinitely more subtle and ambivalent writer than the caricature imperialist or jingoist. However, *Kiplingesque* does inevitably recall the heyday of the British Empire and the Edwardian period before World War One.

PRETENTIOUSNESS INDEX *!*

KUBRICKIAN

in the style of US film director Stanley Kubrick (1928–99);

'cold', 'painstaking', 'obsessional':

> *Look at the clinical, Kubrickian tracking shots of the empty spaceship at the start – [director Ridley] Scott seems to prefer it that way, all neat and*

unmessed – or the shot of Jones the cat that punctuates Harry Dean Stanton's death: irises narrowing coolly, while the poor human fights for its life. (Tom Shone, *Blockbuster*)

Stanley Kubrick didn't make that many films (13 over nearly four decades) and his reputation rests not only on famous pictures like *2001* (1968) and *A Clockwork Orange* (1971), but on his reclusive lifestyle in a Buckinghamshire mansion and on his neurotic, even obsessional, approach to film-making. He spent literally years considering, preparing and often discarding projects, and the finished results were marked by a chilly perfectionism. Kubrick frequently seemed more interested in portentous themes and in set-design and camera lenses – in anything, really – rather than in people. (The most engaging and talkative character in *2001* is Hal the computer.) So *Kubrickian* suggests a somewhat detached approach to film, and to life, full of fine effects but a bit lacking in heart.

PRETENTIOUSNESS INDEX *!*

L

LADY MACBETH-LIKE

in the style of the character in Shakespeare's tragedy *Macbeth*;

'ruthless', 'highly ambitious', 'persuasive and manipulative':

> *Sometimes, according to the stories in Belgrade, [Mira Markovic's] irritation with his [Slobodan Milosevic's] reluctance to act reached Lady Macbeth-like proportions ('Thou art too full o' the milk of human kindness/To catch the nearest way').* (Daily Telegraph)

Commentators looking for an easy means of describing a powerful and unscrupulous woman, particularly when she uses a man to advance her cause, usually fasten on Lady Macbeth. The expression *Lady Macbeth-like* is more often found and more damning than the straightforward *Macbeth-like* (see entry), presumably because women just aren't expected to behave like that. In Shakespeare's play she teases and bullies her husband into committing the murder that will put him on the throne of Scotland. In fact, Shakespeare shows that Lady Macbeth is ambitious more for her husband than for herself and that she has a conscience which will eventually drive her to suicide. Not quite as bad as she's painted then…

PRETENTIOUSNESS INDEX **Nil**

LAINGIAN

connected to the writings and beliefs of Scottish psychiatrist R(onald) D(avid) Laing (1927–89);

'unorthodox', 'counter-cultural', 'questioning accepted notions of madness and sanity':

> *More seriously, the emptying of the old asylums – the process is euphemistically known as care in the community in Britain – has made romantic, Laingian notions of madness look horribly misguided.* (Observer)

R.D. Laing was one of the best-known figures of the counter-culture that emerged in the 1960s and whose effects rippled out through the next couple of decades. He developed an unorthodox view of mental illness, and particularly of schizophrenia, seeing it not solely as something that had to be treated but as a condition that had a validity and even a value of its own. Laing's ideas became distorted and simplified as they passed into general currency: for example, that the mad could possess a wisdom denied to the sane, that the family was often at the root of a schizophrenic's condition or that it was society which was truly 'mad'. Laing's writing and his soft-spoken persona – he came across as a kind of shaman – chimed with the 1960s. The *Observer* quote above indicates that Laing's influence has faded but he is still identified with the anti-authority, exuberant spirit of those times.

PRETENTIOUSNESS INDEX *!*

LARKINESQUE

reminiscent of the style or typical of the themes of poet Philip Larkin (1922–85);

'bleakly lyrical', 'wistful':

> *Even a song with the happy title I Love Life has a bleak, Larkinesque edge, starting: 'Here comes your bedtime story, Mum and Dad have sentenced you to Life.'* (Guardian)

Philip Larkin gave his name not just to a style of poetry but to a stoical way of looking at the world. His unillusioned later poems face death and decline, subjects that are pretty much at home in his early verse too. Larkin also 'celebrated' – not a word he would have had much time for – the everyday, and his work is full of local detail and commonplace references. He played up to his image as a dull, bespectacled bachelor librarian at Hull University so it comes as a relief (or perhaps a disappointment) when his biography shows that he had a rather more exciting private life than his verse suggested.

PRETENTIOUSNESS INDEX *!*

LAWRENTIAN

typical of the style and themes of writer D(avid) H(erbert) Lawrence (1885–1930);

'earthy', 'sexual', 'rhapsodic', 'intense':

It is all flesh and physicality, gender dysphoria and male emasculation, as the hapless Munrow, no doubt feeling the first tremblings of Lawrentian man, is torn between the powdered cleavage of a student nurse from Stockport and the handsome fortitude of a German widow. (Guardian)

Though D.H. Lawrence is secure in his position as a great writer, using the term *Lawrentian* about another writer's work is not necessarily a compliment (see above). There's a general feeling that Lawrence was often on the edge of self-parody: his intense approach to things, his sacramental attitude to sex, his deep seriousness, all seemed an affront to English evasion and moderation during his lifetime. For his own part, Lawrence found life in England intolerable and he and his wife Frieda lived in exile, in Mexico and Italy and elsewhere, for the last decade of his short life.

PRETENTIOUSNESS INDEX *!*

LAZARUS-LIKE

like the figure of Lazarus in the Bible;

'making an unexpected return', 'coming back from the dead':

A Lazarus-like return had put the horse back in a race which had seen more fall-out than a French bomb test in the Pacific. (Daily Telegraph)

The story of Lazarus, brother to Mary Magdalene, is told in John's gospel (11:43–4), where Jesus restores the man to life after four days shut up in a tomb. Any surprising restoration to form after a period of non-achievement or 'deadness' may be described as *Lazarus-like*, although the expression is a bit of a journalistic cliché.

PRETENTIOUSNESS INDEX **Nil**

LEAR-LIKE

connected to the character of King Lear in Shakespeare's play of the same name;

'marked by madness', 'raging furiously':

While pop's self-declared king descends into Lear-like hubris, madness and tragedy, young contenders for the crown merrily continue to state their musical case. (Daily Telegraph)

Lear-like is a convenient term to describe a person who once held a high position but who is starting to lose it, in both senses. In Shakespeare's tragedy, King Lear divides his kingdom between two daughters and banishes a third. The subsequent ingratitude of the first two drives him mad, but not before scenes of towering rage and self-pity.

PRETENTIOUSNESS INDEX !

(see also *Cordelia-like*)

LEAVISITE

in the style of English literary critic F(rank) R(aymond) Leavis (1895–1978) or describing one of his followers;

'high-minded', 'austere', 'rigorous':

> *The poets met regularly to have Leavisite 'close readings' of each other's work.* (The Times)

The most influential English literary and cultural critic of his generation, F.R. Leavis inspired devotion in his disciples and shaped an exacting and morally serious approach to literature. Cranky and difficult, he had a deep, almost mystical sense of the significance of English studies and the other humanities and was dismissive of much modern culture or ideas of 'progress'.

PRETENTIOUSNESS INDEX !

LECTERISH

in the style of Hannibal Lecter, hero-villain of the novels of Thomas Harris (1940–);

'insinuating and seductive', 'monstrous', 'ultra-malevolent':

> *He looks almost amused. His voice is really super-soft, almost Lecterish at this point. He might be reading me a bedtime story.* (Guardian)

Hannibal 'the Cannibal' Lecter, serial killer par excellence, has grown more baroque and improbable in each of his three fictional appearances to date. After a walk-on role in *Red Dragon* (1981), he took centre stage in *The Silence of the Lambs* (1988) and then gave his name to *Hannibal* (1999). Writer Thomas Harris knew a good thing when he created it. Lecter is a fairy-tale figure, with a bit of Dracula, a touch of Sherlock Holmes and a dash of the devil about him. Like all the best villains – Professor Moriarty, Ernst Stavro Blofeld – he seems to be immortal, and is as appealing as he is appalling. *Lecterish* might be connected to any of these attributes but the *Guardian* quote above specifically refers to his soft-spokenness – or rather to that feature of Anthony Hopkins's impersonation of him on screen.

PRETENTIOUSNESS INDEX !

LENNONESQUE

in the style of singer, songwriter and Beatles member John Lennon (1940–80);

'quirky', 'sharp', 'overtly working-class', 'anti-authority':

You can hear echoes of his style in every disaffected rock singer since, from the guttural whine of Kurt Cobain to the more obvious Lennonesque signature that Liam Gallagher stamps on every Oasis song. (Observer)

Lennon and McCartney were a match made in Liverpool if not heaven, with Lennon's brisk and often acerbic outlook complementing McCartney's sweeter, more conciliatory style. The often troubled relationship between the pair continued long after the Beatles split, with John complaining that songs by Paul such as 'Yesterday' were more often covered than his own. By then Lennon was established in the world's eyes as a 'Working Class Hero', in the words of one of his own titles, and bolshiness had become one of his defining characteristics.

PRETENTIOUSNESS INDEX **Nil**

LEWINSKY-LIKE

relating to Monica Lewinsky, an intern in Bill Clinton's White House;

'sexually scandalous', 'curvaceous':

In America, the contrast is even greater. Back in 1950, the average US woman was a curvy 36B–26–37. Today, she is a Lewinsky-like 37D–30–40.

(Guardian)

For most people, the Lewinsky affair is likely to be the dominant memory of Bill Clinton's presidency. Clinton denied having 'sexual relations with that woman', either lying or convincing himself that fellatio didn't really count as sex. No one emerged with much credit from this scandal, neither the President nor his friends nor his persecutors. As for Monica Lewinsky herself, she was regarded in some quarters as having exploited the fame or notoriety that dogged her afterwards even if, at 21, she was the youngest of all the participants. Although it could be argued that the Lewinsky episode was America's equivalent of the Profumo affair (see *Profumo-esque*), there was a farcical and toe-curling aspect to the scandal that was missing in the British version. As well as being a shorthand reference to a sex-and-politics scandal, *Lewinsky-like* might also allude to Monica's fairly generous size (as in the *Guardian* quote).

PRETENTIOUSNESS INDEX **Nil**

(see also *Clintonian*)

LILLIPUTIAN

connected to the imaginary land of Lilliput in Jonathan Swift's satirical novel *Gulliver's Travels* (1726);

'tiny', 'insignificant':

> *No doubt Admiral Horatio Nelson is an authentic hero of British history, of a sort that makes our leaders today seem Lilliputian.* (The Times)

Lilliput is the first place that Lemuel Gulliver visits in his fanciful travels. In a country where the inhabitants are only six inches tall, he is treated as a freak. For his part, Gulliver finds the concerns and the politics of the Lilliputians ridiculous although they consider themselves very important. (Swift intended the country and its inhabitants to be a satire on contemporary English politics.) *Lilliputian* generally refers less to physical smallness than to moral insignificance or pettiness.

PRETENTIOUSNESS INDEX **Nil**

(see also *Brobdingnagian* and *Swiftian*)

LOACHIAN

in the style or typical of the themes of films made by British director Ken Loach (1936–);

'naturalistic', 'politically committed', 'radical':

> *Disconcertingly, [the film] looks not at all like a gritty Loachian realist drama, but is shot in the rigorous style of a high art film […] and is accompanied by serene music by Elgar, Harvey and Purcell.* (Independent)

Ken Loach began his career in television with filmed dramas such as the highly influential *Cathy Come Home* (1966). Loach's cinema films, the best known of which remains *Kes* (1969), are famous for their concentration on social areas and problems overlooked by mainstream cinema, especially of the Hollywood variety. The experience of ordinary working life, the reality of hardship and the exploration of political activism are dealt with in documentary style and using a cast as far removed from traditional stardom as possible. All of this may be suggested by *Loachian*.

PRETENTIOUSNESS INDEX *!*

LOLITA-ISH

like Lolita, the title character of a novel by Vladimir Nabokov (1899–1977);

'pubescent and sexy':

But before Shakira could incorporate rock'n'roll into her Lolita-ish pop act, news arrived that an executive from Sony's Latin division was staying at a posh hotel in town. (Observer)

Even in its day, *Lolita* (first published 1955) was a notorious book – and, arguably, had it been written in the last few years it would never have seen the light of day at all. The story of an older man's obsession with a 12-year-old girl, *Lolita* attracted little interest at first. But when it was attacked by a *Sunday Express* columnist as pornography, the novel excited the attention of the authorities and the instincts of publishers worldwide so that, not for the first or last time, outrage became a handy marketing tool. The fastidious writer Vladimir Nabokov – Russian-born but living in the United States – found fame. It is an irony that in the current climate of extreme nervousness on the subject of paedophilia, it seems unlikely that many artists and writers would welcome *Lolita* as they did in the less liberal atmosphere of the 1950s. Nevertheless, the adjective *Lolita-ish* survives to suggest a self-aware, pre-pubescent sexuality that toys with innocence.

PRETENTIOUSNESS INDEX **Nil**

(see also *Humbert Humbertish* and *Nabokovian*)

LOWRYESQUE

typical of the style or subject matter of painter L(aurence) S(tephen) Lowry (1887–1976);

(of figures) 'stick-like', 'child-like'; (of landscape) 'industrial', 'bleak':

After all that volcanic ballet aggression, Linehan's five little people in street clothes seem almost Lowryesque, suffused in anxiety … (Daily Telegraph)

Lowry forged an approach and style of painting that is instantly recognisable. His city-scapes with their figures scurrying and preoccupied below grey skies or against a backdrop of chimneys recall the great conurbations of northern England in the early part of the 20th century. Such scenes might seem quaint now, a matter of historical curiosity, but there is a bleakness and steadiness of gaze in Lowry's vision that keeps him contemporary.

PRETENTIOUSNESS INDEX *!*

LUCAN-LIKE

connected to the disappearance of Lord Lucan;

'mysteriously disappearing', 'frequently sighted':

Ten years on, Richey's disappearance remains imbued with a Lucan-like mythology by those who love a good mystery. (Observer)

Whenever someone well-known disappears in dodgy circumstances, the chances are that there will be a Lucan reference. Richard Bingham, seventh Earl of Lucan, unsuccessful gambler and not much else, vanished after the murder of his children's nanny in 1974. He has never given himself up or been found, and in 1999 the High Court declared him dead on an application made by his family. Lucan has supposedly been sighted from time to time around the world but seems as elusive as the Loch Ness monster, if less interesting. (The other reference in the *Observer* quote above is to Richey Edwards, guitarist and lyricist for The Manic Street Preachers, who vanished in 1995. His car was later discovered near the Severn Bridge, indicating that he might have committed suicide.)

PRETENTIOUSNESS INDEX *!*

LUCULLAN

in the manner of Lucius Licinius Lucullus (c.114–57 BC), Roman general and pleasure-lover;

'luxurious', 'extravagant':

Which is not to say that scenes of Lucullan excess were entirely lacking. It was calculated on Sunday morning that, during the 18-hour binging session that the rest of the world knew as Saturday, several stags consumed at least 14 pints of lager each. (Guardian)

After a military career in Asia Minor, Lucullus returned to Rome and flaunted his wealth and extravagant tastes. He built no fewer than three villas for himself in the Bay of Naples and had tunnels driven through mountains to supply salt water to his fish-ponds. *Lucullan* behaviour is therefore synonymous with luxury and excess in eating and drinking.

PRETENTIOUSNESS INDEX *!!*

LUDDITE

connected to the Luddites, an anti-industrial movement at the beginning of the 19th century;

'hostile to progress', 'disruptive', 'backward-looking':

None of this would have happened had the Net Book Agreement still been in place, which forced books to be sold at a fixed price. Yet we should not be Luddite either. The book industry has not collapsed since the NBA was abolished.   (The Times)

In the early stages of the Industrial Revolution, some textile workers in the north of England who feared unemployment because of the introduction of new plant began a campaign of organised machine-breaking. Their name was supposedly derived from one Ned Ludd or 'King' Ludd, who was said to have his base in Sherwood Forest. The Luddite movement was itself smashed by the execution of 17 of their number in York in 1813. Oddly, no great romance or idealism has ever seemed to attach to the word *Luddite* and the expression generally indicates a head-in-the-sand attitude to change.

PRETENTIOUSNESS INDEX **Nil**

M

MACBETH-LIKE

connected to the tragic hero of Shakespeare's play of the same name;

'ruthless', 'murderous', 'trapped', 'easily manipulated':

A colleague, expert in the Macbeth-like world of Scottish Labour, explained to me later that, on the death of the former Labour leader John Smith, Mr McFall was one of the first Scottish MPs to declare for Mr Blair instead of Mr Brown. (Daily Telegraph)

Macbeth is less straightforward to pin down than his wife (see *Lady Macbeth-like*). Sometimes he is a byword for the man who is easily manipulated into doing wrong by women, in his case the witches and his wife. *Macbeth-like* may also be used to describe someone's ruthlessly ambitious behaviour in the quest for power, as well as suggesting a sense of despair and entrapment when that power has been obtained. And, finally, *Macbeth-like* obviously has a special application in the world of Scottish politics which, if the *Telegraph* reference above is to be taken literally, is full of double-dealing and back-stabbing.

PRETENTIOUSNESS INDEX **Nil**

MACHIAVELLIAN

in the style or following the doctrines of the Italian politician and writer Niccolò Machiavelli (1469–1527);

'devious', 'ruthless', 'expedient':

Of the 14 starters, in fact, Tim had seemed the least sparky or Machiavellian. The least likely, in other words, to force himself to the top in the ruthlessly driven culture of Sugarland. (The Times)

Niccolò Machiavelli, born in Florence, held various posts in the government of that city-state before writing *The Prince* (1513), a treatise on statecraft. He recommended that rulers should, if necessary, use deceit or unethical methods to hold on to power. Known for assertions such as 'To be feared gives more security than to be loved', Machiavelli rapidly came to be seen as an exponent of amoral politics and unscrupulous power-seeking, someone to be condemned even when his policies were being followed on the quiet. Before the end of the 16th century his name had become synonymous with cunning and treachery, and as the *Times* example indicates, *Machiavellian* is still widely used to characterise devious self-seeking.

PRETENTIOUSNESS INDEX **Nil** A 600-YEAR-OLD REFERENCE TO A FLORENTINE MAY SEEM OBSCURE BUT THE TERM IS SO USEFUL, AND NOT JUST IN POLITICS, THAT WE WOULD BE THE POORER WITHOUT IT.

MAGRITTE-LIKE

typical of the style or subject matter of Belgian-born painter René Magritte (1898–1967);

'surreal', 'humorously incongruous':

> *[The picture] is a consciously surreal image, with an incongruous Magritte-like juxtaposition of abruptly separate objects.* (Independent)

Magritte began his working life designing posters, and something of the clear-cut, immediate style associated with advertising can be glimpsed in his paintings. Magritte uses familiar objects in an unfamiliar or contradictory fashion: a steam train emerging from a fireplace, a picture of a pipe with a legend underneath that reads in French 'This is not a pipe'. Magritte is one of the more accessible of the surrealists and although there are disquieting elements in his work – for example, the hooded couple titled *Lovers* – *Magritte-like* tends to suggest a whimsical or witty playing with reality.

PRETENTIOUSNESS INDEX **!**

MAJORISH

characterising the personal style of Conservative politician John Major (1943–) or the style of government and political programme he initiated as Prime Minister (1990–97);

'middle of the road', 'provincial':

> *These were classic English murder mysteries, the sun (and the sun is nearly always shining in a Morse yarn) illuminating the mellow Cotswold stone of a timeless Oxford, in a John Majorish landscape of warm beer and female undergraduates on bicycles.* (Independent)

It's hard to believe that the expression *Majorism*, probably more often found than *Majorish*, would ever have been created without the precedent of *Thatcherism* or *Thatcherite* (see entry), but it was obviously considered that every British Prime Minister should be distinctive enough to leave his or her stamp on country and government. *Majorism* isn't remembered very fondly these days and it is difficult to say exactly what political policies it embodied, but at least the man's style – understated, non-messianic – came as a relief after Mrs Thatcher's. The allusion in the *Independent* quote is to a speech by Major in which he invoked a rather implausible-sounding English landscape. (*Majorism* is sometimes used to describe a tortuous or artificial-sounding piece of speech, supposedly characteristic of the then Prime Minister.)

PRETENTIOUSNESS INDEX **Nil**

MALTHUSIAN

connected to the theories of economist Robert Malthus (1766–1834);

'entailing overpopulation and starvation':

Apparently the surviving monuments had been central to high cities where millions of people were jammed into vertical compounds, victims of a Malthusian nightmare of overpopulation in a land of limited resources.

(Gore Vidal, *The Golden Age*)

Robert Malthus was both clergyman and economist. In his *Essay on the Principle of Population* (1798) he theorised that human populations are always likely to rise at a rate that is faster than the growth in food supplies. He was against birth control but thought that population could be regulated by 'prudence', the alternative being forcible control through famine or some other disaster. Malthus, who could be 'civil to every lady' as long as she wasn't pregnant, has therefore come to be identified with a rigorous or pessimistic view of human development, and the adjective *Malthusian* has overtones of this. Charles Darwin was influenced by Malthus's ideas and, like *Malthusian*, *Darwinian* (see entry) equates with a scientific, unsentimental way of regarding the world.

PRETENTIOUSNESS INDEX **Nil**

MALVOLIO-LIKE

in the style of the character Malvolio in Shakespeare's *Twelfth Night*;

'pompous and priggish', 'unintentionally comic', 'self-deluding':

[Kelsey] Grammer might not be a natural Lear or Shylock, but as the Malvolio-like Dr Frasier Crane he has turned in some of the finest, smartest, most bittersweet sitcom acting America has produced. (The Times)

In *Twelfth Night* Malvolio is the steward of the household of the wealthy and beautiful Olivia. Tricked into believing that she loves him, he dresses up in bright yellow stockings and behaves so absurdly that she has him shut up for a madman. Malvolio is to be laughed at for his priggishness and his grand airs, but there is also pathos to his character – he tries to cling to his dignity but it is stripped away, while no one will love him except himself. *Malvolio-like* generally refers to the pompous, self-deceiving side of someone's character.

PRETENTIOUSNESS INDEX *!*

MANDARIN

connected to the ruling class of mandarins during the Chinese Empire;

'elitist', 'elevated', 'remote from ordinary people':

One of the liberations of contemporary art has been to free us from the mandarin view of 'everlasting monuments to the human spirit'. (The Times)

Mandarin is used as a noun or adjective, and almost always in a disparaging sense, to describe a remote caste of officials who lay down the law or set the rules of taste. The word comes from the Portuguese version of a Malayan term for 'counsellor'. Arguably, use of the word is itself something of a *mandarin* reaction since it's unlikely to be widely understood.

PRETENTIOUSNESS INDEX *!*

MANDELA-LIKE

characteristic of Nelson Mandela (1918–), one-time political prisoner and President of South Africa between 1994 and 1999;

'charismatic', 'revered', 'forgiving', 'conciliatory':

The fresh, virtuous-looking Kim Dae-jung is a poignant contrast to Kim Jong-il; his entire life has been a strenuous, even dangerous fight for democracy and public service, tortured and arrested by previous military regimes, a Mandela-like figure in Korean politics. (Guardian)

Nelson Mandela is probably the closest thing to a secular saint that the world currently possesses. Sentenced for life in 1964 for his anti-apartheid activities under the banner of the African National Congress (ANC), Mandela's imprisonment on Robben Island turned him into the most famous political prisoner on earth. Following his release in 1990, he was elected the first black president of South Africa after a landslide victory for the ANC. Mandela was widely admired for advocating reconciliation and harmony between the races, and it was generally accepted that the country would not have made its peaceful transition to democracy and majority rule without him. *Mandela-like* is sometimes almost synonymous with 'saintly', but the usual application of the term suggests a leader with charisma, one who possesses the ability to transcend barriers of race and colour, and the power to bind wounds.

PRETENTIOUSNESS INDEX **Nil**

MANDELSONIAN

connected to Peter Mandelson (1953–), Labour politician and European Commissioner for Trade;

'highly skilled at public relations/spin-doctoring', 'concerned with style rather than substance', 'ruthlessly effective':

> *Progressive is one of the quintessential New Labour words; a word that, if one was trying to sow discord, one would even describe as Mandelsonian.*
>
> (Guardian)

It is difficult to come up with a complimentary definition for *Mandelsonian*, though even Peter Mandelson's many critics and enemies would give him at least some of the credit for restoring the fortunes of the Labour Party, culminating in the 1997 election victory after almost 20 years out of power. Crucially, Mandelson backed Tony Blair rather than Gordon Brown for leader after the death of John Smith, and Blair rewarded him by giving him a key role in the election campaign and then a Cabinet post. Mandelson has twice resigned from office, first because of an undeclared loan received from a fellow minister and the second time because of allegations that he acted improperly in trying to secure British citizenship for an Indian businessman (he was cleared in a subsequent enquiry). He has a talent for attracting flak and vitriolic criticism, mostly from his own side, and many traditional Labour supporters see him as representing all that is most typical of New Labour (concern with image, obsession with winning at all costs, etc.). So *Mandelsonian* is not a term of praise, as shown by the quote above, though there may be grudging admiration if it is applied to spin-doctoring skills.

PRETENTIOUSNESS INDEX *!* THIS IS SOMETHING OF A SPECIALIST TERM THOUGH QUITE WIDELY UNDERSTOOD.

MANICHAEAN

connected to the beliefs of Mani (or Manichaeus);

'dualistic', 'absolute', 'black-and-white':

> *None has boasted more proudly that the subtle greys of real life do not fit in with their Manichaean view of the universe. For them, it's either black or white, good or evil, with us or against us.* (Independent)

Not many names of religions or heresies having their origins in the early centuries after the birth of Christ have survived to be quite widely used terms in the 21st century, but *Manichaean* (or *Manichean*) is an exception. Mani – a title of respect rather than a name – was born in western Persia around 210 AD and formulated the belief that the two principles that governed the universe were light and dark, or good and evil, and that they were engaged in perpetual struggle. Mani declared himself a follower of Christ but was condemned as a heretic. Despite that, his doctrines were influential and didn't die out until the Middle Ages. It is easy to see how, in the current world climate of stark beliefs and opinions (whether religious or cultural), the term *Manichaean* has come back into favour, usually as a way of branding the extremism of one's opponents.

PRETENTIOUSNESS INDEX *!*

MANSONESQUE

connected to Charles Manson (1934–), cult leader in 1960s Los Angeles;

'murderous', 'dangerously cultish':

> *Thanks to his straggly beard and piercing eyes, Liman looks like the shaman of a Mansonesque cult.* (The Times)

Manson was a failed rock musician who exerted a hypnotic influence over members of his 'family', a collection of deluded and deranged individuals who provided the nightmare underbelly to the hippy dream of the 1960s. The climax of the Manson family exploits was the murder of five people in the Los Angeles house of film director Roman Polanski in 1969, the victims including Polanski's pregnant wife Sharon Tate. Like other late 20th-century cult leaders who led their followers to disaster – Jim Jones of the People's Temple, David Koresh of the Branch Davidians – Manson was attributed with messianic or satanic looks and powers. Serving his sentence in a Californian prison, he is reportedly eligible for parole in 2007.

PRETENTIOUSNESS INDEX *!*

MAOIST

reflecting the life or political doctrines of Chinese Communist leader Mao Tse-tung (1893–1976) or describing one of his followers;

'revolutionary', 'authoritarian', 'dictatorial', 'centralising', 'encouraging a cult of personality':

> *The Government's somewhat Maoist exhortations to the public to 'Back the Bid' may also stick in the craw of those who simply like to watch sports.*
>
> (Daily Telegraph)

Regardless of the degree to which Mao's life and achievements were distorted or fabricated for propaganda purposes, his brand of Communism became a model for extreme revolutionary movements and cells around the world. *Maoist* may describe one of these, much diminished since the collapse of Communism. More likely, the term will be used to mean 'authoritarian' or 'tyrannical', particularly to evoke a *1984*-style world in which everyone is officially devoted to the state/party/leader and parrots the same empty slogans. In such contexts *Maoist* is always a pejorative expression, as in the *Telegraph* quote above.

PRETENTIOUSNESS INDEX **Nil**

MARLOVIAN

characteristic of the style, themes or approach of Elizabethan poet and playwright Christopher Marlowe (1564–93);

'rebellious', 'strident':

> *Farr turns the Marlovian antihero, who is as dangerously hubristic as Faustus, into an individual driven and divided by demons, whose nature is coruscatingly exposed in the spellbinding performance of Greg Hicks.*
>
> (The Times)

Marlowe's life, from the fragments that are known of it, was as noisy and controversial as Shakespeare's was the opposite. Reputedly a spy, he was to die in a tavern brawl that conspiracy theorists have pored over ever since. Marlowe arguably created the dramatic anti-hero, the dynamic figure who revels in his own evil daring, in plays such as *The Jew of Malta* and *Dr Faustus*. Unless used in a literary context to refer to Marlowe's development of blank verse, *Marlovian* generally describes an aggressive, anti-authority stance.

PRETENTIOUSNESS INDEX *!*

MASOCHISTIC

connected to the life and writings of Leopold von Sacher-Masoch (1836–95);

'having a taste for suffering', 'enjoying humiliation and discomfort':

If, like my colleagues on this newspaper, I worked next door to a super-market I would have to develop an unusually masochistic streak not to shop at it after work, and to dedicate my precious weekend to trawling around my local shops instead. (The Sunday Times)

Sacher-Masoch's novel *Venus in Furs* (first published 1870) tells us of a man who desires to be treated as a slave by his female lover and degraded for his own pleasure. The book was apparently a reflection of Masoch's own sexual preferences. He has gone down in history not as the originator of this particular bent, which must be as old as the hills, but as the one to give his name to it. Significantly this labelling comes from that period of the late 19th century when sexual behaviour was beginning to be studied and categorised. Like *sadistic* (see entry), *masochistic* has wandered quite a long way from its sexual roots, so that it is now employed routinely to describe any action or attitude that causes the doer a self-inflicted inconvenience or pain, even a mild one. At a guess, four out of five uses have no sexual component at all.

PRETENTIOUSNESS INDEX **Nil**

MAUGHAMESQUE

typical of the style or themes favoured by novelist and playwright W(illiam) Somerset Maugham (1874–1965);

'exotic', 'worldly', 'gripping':

Whatever else may be said of Paul Theroux's fiction, he has never run short of good ideas, and Blinding Light *positively thrums with Maughamesque narrative bounce.* (Spectator)

Somerset Maugham enjoyed a remarkably sustained and successful career from the period in his early 30s when he had four plays running simultaneously in London until near the end of his long life. Though he fell out of fashion and accepted that he would never be seen as a ground-breaking artist, Maugham has generally been admired for the economy of his prose, his evocation of foreign locales (especially in what in his time was known as the Orient) and the drive of his narratives. *Maughamesque* might refer to any of these.

PRETENTIOUSNESS INDEX *!*

MAXWELLIAN

characteristic of publisher and newspaper proprietor Robert Maxwell (1923–91);

'on a large scale', 'crooked', 'combative', 'controversial':

By then, the scandal that would ultimately wrest control of the Telegraph Group from him and catapult him into Maxwellian disgrace was gathering pace. (Guardian)

Robert Maxwell was an MP, a publisher of academic books and the owner of the *Daily Mirror* among other newspapers. His life was dogged by controversy and scandal, and his death was as sensational and mysterious as the rest of the story. He fell overboard from his yacht while it was cruising off the Canary Islands, whether by accident or as a suicide (although there were later theories that he had been murdered). After his death it was revealed that he had been taking money from the *Mirror* pension fund in order to paper over the cracks in his crumbling business empire. There is something *Kane-like* (see entry) about Maxwell's fall – although, in fact, he fell more than once during his business career, always clambering back to new wealth and status. *Maxwellian* might refer to a number of things: his posthumous disgrace, his tendency to resort to litigation if there was any hint of criticism, his larger-than-life appearance, style and appetites.

PRETENTIOUSNESS INDEX **!**

McCARTHYITE

connected to the anti-Communist campaign waged in the US by Senator Joseph McCarthy (1909–57);

'vehemently anti-Communist', 'hysterical', 'witch-hunting':

In the US, the hysterical reaction to child abuse by priests is beginning to take on a McCarthyite aspect – which is not to deny that paedophile priests exist, just as there really were Communist subversives. (Daily Telegraph)

Joseph McCarthy, a lawyer by training and elected to the Senate in 1946, leapt to fame – or notoriety – when he claimed that the State Department, in charge of US foreign policy, was employing Communist sympathisers. The charges, though generally baseless, reflected legitimate public fears in the early 1950s, a period when the Cold War was well entrenched and the Soviet Union had recently developed the atom bomb. Senator McCarthy became so popular that his opponents were wary of openly criticising him. Undeterred by lack of evidence and supported by press and public opinion, McCarthy eventually went too far when he tried to establish the presence of reds in the US Army. He died, an alcoholic, in 1957 but bequeathed his name to any frenetic attempt to suppress civil liberties through persecution and to the hysterical whipping-up of public anger against a supposed enemy. *McCarthyite* is a loaded term, the use of which seems to preclude argument, and its thoughtless application to the policies of one's opponents could be seen as something of a *McCarthyite* trick in itself.

PRETENTIOUSNESS INDEX **Nil**

McCARTNEY-ESQUE

typical of the style of singer, songwriter and Beatles member Paul McCartney (1942–);

'nostalgic', 'melodious', 'upbeat', 'campaigning':

Riding to Vanity Fair is notable not only for a glorious chorus that rises from the song's murky strings and minor chords in a way that is so inimitably, ridiculously McCartney-esque, you can virtually feel your thumbs involuntarily twitching aloft, but also because it offers a previously unheard noise: Paul McCartney sounding bitter. (Guardian)

Early in their songwriting careers Lennon and McCartney agreed to take joint credit for the songs they produced, regardless of the exact contribution of each. For all that, it was generally easy to distinguish between their work: Lennon was identified with the more surreal or harder-edged numbers, while McCartney was perceived as the 'cosier' of the pair. This neat pigeon-holing may have been unfair to McCartney, who lacked Lennon's well-advertised rawness and authenticity. Yet songs like 'Yesterday' and 'Eleanor Rigby' have a wistfulness and sympathy that seemed out of Lennon's range. *McCartney-esque* may suggest the hummable quality of his work with the Beatles and later with Wings. It may point to a kind of sweetness and optimism. Or it may refer to the various causes that McCartney campaigned for with his first and second wives, Linda and Heather: for vegetarianism, against seal-culling, etc.

PRETENTIOUSNESS INDEX **Nil**

McLUHANITE

connected to the ideas of Marshall McLuhan (1911–80) or describing one of his followers;

'believing in the global village', 'about the mass media':

Will Self writes about Big Brother in the review section. The show is 'a synec-
doche of the British polity' and an 'enactment of McLuhanite prophecies'.
Quite. (Guardian)

The Canadian academic Marshall McLuhan was once hailed as the most important thinker since Darwin or Freud. It was he who, in the 1960s, pinpointed a change in the means of communication from the old and so-called 'hot' culture of movable type to a new 'cool' world of mass communication. He also developed the idea that the means of communication is more important than whatever is being communicated ('the medium is the message'), and the notion of the Global Village. McLuhan was briefly ultra-cool himself, but his profile dimmed and it's doubtful if many people under, say, 40 recall him now.

PRETENTIOUSNESS INDEX *!!*

MEPHISTOPHELIAN

in the manner of Mephistopheles, the devil who tempted Faust to sell his soul;

'seductive but dangerous', 'subtly wicked':

Anakin is gradually being lured to the Dark Side by Chancellor Palpatine.
There are few young actors who could invest this kind of Mephistophelian
pact-in-a-packet (boil in three minutes) with any conviction, and Hayden
Christensen sadly isn't one of them. (Independent)

In legend, Mephistopheles presented Faustus (a German magician and scholar) with a bargain whereby he would surrender his soul in exchange for knowledge and power in this world. Among other versions, the story is dramatised in Christopher Marlowe's play *Dr Faustus*, in which the title character is granted 24 years of having Mephistopheles at his beck and call before being dragged down to hell. Mephistopheles is generally presented as a rather smooth, urbane character – bad but interesting.

PRETENTIOUSNESS INDEX *!*

(see also *Faustian*)

METHUSELAN

like the figure of Methuselah in the Bible;

'unimaginably old', 'long-lived':

Should I be lucky enough to survive into the Methuselan zone with some miracle of modern medicine, I may even be reserving my seat on the bus to Winnipeg. (Guardian)

Methuselah's name appears early in the book of Genesis, part of a list of Adam's immediate male descendants, the patriarchs. He is distinguished only by the fact that he was the longest-lived of them all, dying when he reached 969 and fathering the first of his children at the comparatively tender age of 187. *Methuselan* (or *Methuselah-like*) is synonymous with 'very old', although it's a rather dated reference now, in every sense.

PRETENTIOUSNESS INDEX *!!*

MICAWBERISH

typical of Mr Micawber, a character in Charles Dickens's novel *David Copperfield* (1850);

'debt-ridden but cheerful', 'financially naive':

Clearly, Gordon Brown is now fast running out of road, with the claim that something will turn up before the end of the year looking more and more Micawberish as each month goes by. (Guardian)

In Dickens's *David Copperfield*, Wilkins Micawber and his large family live in chronic debt. A volatile character, Mr Micawber is always either plunged in gloom or planning confidently for better times 'in case anything turned up', his favourite and faintly forlorn expression. *Micawberish* suggests a rather naive faith that some lucky chance is going to rescue you from financial difficulties.

PRETENTIOUSNESS INDEX *!*

MICKEY MOUSE

connected to the famous cartoon mouse created by Walt Disney at the end of the 1920s;

'unimportant', 'not to be taken seriously', 'derisory':

He saw cathedrals with their standards in music, art, and erudition as rescuing us from Mickey Mouse religion, not playing safe but prepared to take risks in prophecy and preaching. (Guardian)

Since the famous mouse was often seen as symbolising American cheerfulness, it may seem odd that *Mickey Mouse* is now used to describe something that is somewhere between a joke and an object of contempt.

Supposedly, it derives from wristwatches introduced in the 1940s that featured images of Mickey, his arms serving as the hands telling the time. Anyone wearing such a watch could hardly expect to be taken seriously.

PRETENTIOUSNESS INDEX **Nil**

MIDAS-LIKE

like the legendary Midas, king of Phrygia (in what is now central Turkey);

'wealthy', 'having a magic touch, particularly when it comes to making money':

> *The final touch evaded him, but his Midas-like Irish fly-half, Burke, was there to turn the opportunity into seven points.* (Daily Telegraph)

Midas wasn't the name of a specific individual but the title of all the kings of Phrygia, as with the pharaohs of Egypt. In one of the myths associated with him, Midas was granted a wish by the god Dionysus and asked that everything he touched be transformed into gold. He changed his mind when food turned to gold in his mouth and was relieved of his gift by bathing in a river. *Midas-like* refers not so much to these unfortunate consequences but to an unstoppable gift for making money – a kind of financial green fingers. However, the term has a wider application and in the *Telegraph* quote above suggests a consistent ability to turn something to advantage.

PRETENTIOUSNESS INDEX **Nil**

(see also *Croesus-like*)

MILLS & BOONISH

in the style of the novels produced by the publishing house of Mills & Boon;

'conventional', 'sentimentally romantic', 'escapist':

> *But his romance with Sian, or what passes for it, is very Mills & Boonish in tone – full of italicised I want, I wants and sentences such as 'his eyes twinkled with mischief'.* (Daily Telegraph)

Founded nearly a century ago by Gerald Mills and Charles Boon, the publishing house that still bears their names has long been synonymous with mass-produced romantic fiction. Their paperbacks reputedly have a regular annual readership of 3 million in the United Kingdom. The imprint and the style of the covers are better known to outsiders than any of their authors (many of them pseudonymous). In the conventional view, a Mills & Boon romance must feature a manly hero and a quivering heroine for whom, until not so long ago, virginity would have been a vital qualification. In the end, true love will conquer all the difficulties that strew their path ('strew' is somehow a *Mills & Boonish* word). Jane Austen was doing this kind of thing two centuries ago, so Mills & Boon have an honourable pedigree. But the expression *Mills & Boonish* still suggests a rather soft-centred and escapist view of love and romance, written in a formulaic way.

PRETENTIOUSNESS INDEX **Nil**

MILTONIC

connected to the style, themes or subject matter of English pamphleteer and poet John Milton (1608–74);

'epic', 'grand', 'involving the struggle between good and evil':

> In Cardiff['s production of opera Billy Budd], Christopher Maltman and Phillip Ens played Billy and Claggart, their encounters forming a series of homoerotic duels between a damaged cherub and a glamorous Miltonic Satan. (Guardian)

Milton was deeply involved in the political life of his time and a strenuous supporter of republicanism (he was briefly put under arrest when Charles II was restored to the throne). But his legacy and influence lie in his poetry, in particular the 12-book *Paradise Lost* (1667), an epic narrative of the expulsion of Adam and Eve from the Garden of Eden. To trace out the origins of the human Fall, Milton went back to the earlier fall of Satan from Heaven, and much of *Paradise Lost* is set in Hell, visualised as a place of horrific grandeur. Arguably, the dominant figure of the poem is not God or even Adam but Satan, with whose defiance and desperate predicament some have felt that Milton was secretly in sympathy. *Miltonic* might refer to any work conceived on a grand scale, particularly if it involves a good–evil conflict, or may be applied to a glamorous but demonic figure. The term is also used of the poetic style that Milton created for his English epic, a sonorous, musical verse that depends heavily on Latinate words and constructions.

PRETENTIOUSNESS INDEX **Nil**

MIRANDA-LIKE

like the character of Miranda in Shakespeare's *The Tempest*;

'innocent', 'naive', 'full of wonder':

128

He retained what was described by a friend last week as 'a Miranda-like ability for wonder about the world'. (Observer)

In Shakespeare's final play, Miranda is the daughter of Prospero, the exiled Duke of Milan (see *Prospero-like*). Brought up by her father on an empty island, her first encounter with the real world is when a group of people is shipwrecked there. Seeing the assorted group, which contains plotters and fools as well as the odd good man, she says, 'How beauteous mankind is! O brave new world,/That has such people in't!' (Her father's comment – kindly or pitying – is ' 'Tis new to thee'.) *Miranda-like* therefore suggests an innocence and capacity for wonder that will be hard to preserve in the light of experience.

PRETENTIOUSNESS INDEX *!*

MISS HAVISHAM-STYLE

similar to Miss Havisham, a character in Charles Dickens's *Great Expectations* (published 1861);

'abandoned', 'eccentric', 'reclusive':

Guests reported that she battered the groom over the head with the wedding bouquet before hiding away, Miss Havisham-style, in her own bridal gown. (Guardian)

Miss Havisham was jilted on her wedding day and, in shock and grief, locked herself away in her house, surrounded by all the paraphernalia of the wedding, including the decaying food. She still wears her bridal dress. But *Miss Havisham-style* may be applied casually to any oldish woman who leads an eccentric and reclusive life, without any necessary reference to failed marriages, etc.

PRETENTIOUSNESS INDEX *!*

MONROE-ESQUE

in the style of film star Marilyn Monroe (1926–62);

'beautiful and alluring', 'ultra-feminine':

A few months earlier, these same fashion journalists had been crowing over Sophie's 'curvaceous beauty', her 38DD chest and her Monroe-esque femininity. (Daily Telegraph)

Marilyn Monroe's fame seems to grow with the years. Her troubled personal history, her marriages to baseball star Joe DiMaggio and then to playwright Arthur Miller, her involvement with Jack and Bobby

Kennedy, her increasing inability to meet the demands that shooting a film imposed on her – all these things, and her sexual presence on screen, have combined to feed the Monroe legend. *Monroe-esque* might be applied to her neurotic decline, culminating in suicide, to her iconic status in American culture or, simply, to her beauty and femininity.

PRETENTIOUSNESS INDEX **Nil**

MOSLEYITE

connected to British politician Oswald Mosley (1896–1980);

'narrowly nationalist', 'fascistic':

> … *many pens and voices [...] have been trying to rouse the spirit of English nationalism – while shedding crocodile tears at the prospect of a Mosleyite rebirth* …   (Guardian)

Born into a wealthy family, Oswald Mosley had a volatile political career following service in the Royal Flying Corps in World War One. He began as a Conservative MP in 1918 before crossing the floor eight years later to be elected for Labour. Then in 1932, 'inspired' by the successes of Hitler and Mussolini, he founded the British Union of Fascists. He was interned during World War Two and continued a political life of sorts in the years afterwards. Mosley was a glamorous and charismatic figure and a powerful orator. *Mosleyite* is usually shorthand for a particularly British form of fascism, with overtones of nationalism and anti-Semitism.

PRETENTIOUSNESS INDEX **Nil**

MOZARTIAN

reflecting the life, music or style of composer Wolfgang Amadeus Mozart (1756–91);

'lucid', 'delicate', 'balanced', 'showing prodigious and early talent', 'dying tragically early':

> *Simultaneously suggesting happiness, regret, and a keen awareness of the hurt that lies at the heart of love, Dench achieves a Mozartian richness of feeling.*   (Daily Telegraph)

It was Josef Haydn – 24 years Mozart's senior – who told Mozart's father that his son was 'the greatest composer that ever will be known'. Certainly, Mozart has attracted the kind of reverence that attaches itself to a saint and his music is sometimes claimed to be divinely inspired, heavenly, etc. The picture of Mozart as someone producing other-worldly music is at odds with the sometimes difficult circumstances of his life and the poignant legends surrounding his death. Like other terms associated with artistic geniuses, such as *Shakespearean* and *Dickensian, Mozartian* has many applications but, in general, the term is used to suggest work that has a steely delicacy to it.

PRETENTIOUSNESS INDEX **Nil**

MURDOCHIAN

characteristic of Australian-born media tycoon Rupert Murdoch (1931–);

'having worldwide influence', 'market-driven':

Howells admits to lying awake at night musing on jargon about flextech and licensing, and on the fight to protect British TV from being overrun by Murdochian values. (Guardian)

Murdochian is not a neutral adjective. As the head of the worldwide conglomerate News Corporation – an empire that covers a range of media outlets from 20th Century Fox to *The Times* – Rupert Murdoch inspires fear, suspicion and admiration in about equal proportions, and the term *Murdochian* may reflect any or all of those responses. Generally speaking, Murdoch is identified with devotion to market forces, whose priorities are likely to be different from public-interest values.

PRETENTIOUSNESS INDEX *!*

MUSSOLINI-LIKE

reminiscent of the character, tastes or ruling style of the Italian dictator Benito Mussolini (1883–1945);

'tyrannical', 'grandiose', 'bombastic':

As editor at the time, I was asked by Maxwell to 'pop up' to his Mussolini-like office, where the following conversation took place: 'Your mate is taking the piss out of me,' boomed Maxwell, before I was through the door.
(Guardian)

It is interesting that of the three principal dictators involved in World War Two – Stalin, Hitler and Mussolini – it is only the latter who gets off relatively lightly when his name is invoked as a term of abuse. While *Hitlerian* and *Stalinist* (see entries) evoke images of totalitarian rule and genocide, *Mussolini-like* is more a matter of style than substance. The expression may recall the large, grandiose buildings of the fascist period in Italy or the bombastic, ranting style of the leader known as 'il Duce', and there's generally a suggestion of hollowness about it. The *Guardian* reference above is to newspaper proprietor Robert Maxwell, a *Mussolini-like* figure in size at least and in his imposing, flashy style.

PRETENTIOUSNESS INDEX **Nil**

N

NABOKOVIAN

typical of the style or themes favoured by Russian-born novelist Vladimir Nabokov (1899–1977);

'stylised', 'elegant', 'cold':

> *There is a Nabokovian cruelty in the way Sandrine seduces a decent middle-ranking executive but once she and Nathalie fall for a corporate de Sade, the film becomes an absurd baroque whirl ...* (The Times)

Vladimir Nabokov left Russia with his family after the Revolution and lived in Europe before moving to America in 1940. He became famous, or notorious, with the success of his novel *Lolita* (1955), which enabled him to retire from university teaching in the US and devote himself more fully to writing. In fact he had produced a considerable body of work before then. Nabokov's prose style is glittering, intricate and playful. There can also be a certain detachment, even cruelty, in his approach to character – for example, in *Laughter in the Dark* (1932), a pair of lovers take advantage of the husband's blindness to conduct their affair under his nose. It's this aspect of Nabokov that is referred to in the quote above from a film review.

PRETENTIOUSNESS INDEX *!*

(see also *Humbert Humbertish* and *Lolita-ish*)

NAPOLEONIC

relating to the life and achievements of the French emperor Napoleon Bonaparte (1769–1821);

'toweringly ambitious', 'over-reaching', 'heroic', 'supremely skilled as a military commander and strategist':

> *For a club with such strong Gallic connections it is perhaps ironic that Arsenal's hubris may have taken on Napoleonic proportions. After all, like the French emperor's, their conquest has been undone by a Russian.* (Guardian)

It is probably fair to say that what Winston Churchill represents to the British finds its equivalence in Napoleon's status among the French: that is, a figure who was a dominating and supremely charismatic leader in times of crisis and one who, in ways that are almost beyond definition, seemed to embody quintessential qualities of his nation. Both men have a near-mythical reputation and Napoleon's life is a source of as much fascination – though of a more benign kind – as Hitler's is. Bonaparte, born in Corsica, became commander-in-chief of the French army at the age of 27 and emperor in 1804. He was the dominant figure in Europe, much of which he ruled, until he met his Waterloo in the battle of 1815. Napoleon's programme of modernisation and centralism is still very evident in France, while his legacy is continually celebrated in French culture. Yet at the same time, *Napoleonic* may be applied to arrogant, hubristic actions that ultimately lead to tragedy and downfall.

PRETENTIOUSNESS INDEX **Nil**

NARCISSISTIC

like the Greek mythological figure of Narcissus;

'self-loving', 'vain':

> *Finally, with the news that Daniel Craig is odds-on favourite to inherit the 007 mantle, it makes complete and satisfying sense to know that one of the most attractive and narcissistic male icons in cinema might be transformed into something ugly – no, something sexy-ugly.* (The Times)

In the myth, Narcissus was a young man whose great beauty made the nymph Echo fall for him. He wasn't interested in her and, in punishment, the goddess Aphrodite caused Narcissus to fall in love with his own image, which he glimpsed in a pool of water. He died either by tumbling into the water or in grief that he could not embrace his own reflected self (and was transformed into the flower that bears his name). In its extreme form, narcissism can be a pathological condition, but the adjective *narcissistic* tends to mean no more than 'vain' and 'self-absorbed', although it also implies a lack of interest in others.

PRETENTIOUSNESS INDEX **Nil**

NELSONIAN

in the style of English naval commander Horatio Nelson (1758–1805);

'heroic', 'gallant', 'charismatic as a leader':

Wayne Rooney has a message for the French that is almost Nelsonian in its brevity and understated impact. Today, in the biggest game of his career, he is going to do his best. (Observer)

Nelson reigns supreme in the gallery of British heroes, but the term *Nelsonian* usually refers to one of three particular anecdotes. He put a telescope to his blind eye at the battle of Copenhagen (1801) so as not to see a signal demanding withdrawal. Before the battle of Trafalgar (1805), he signalled the fleet, 'England expects that every man will do his duty' (this is the reference in the *Observer* quote above). The third story, of course, is his dying request to his flag-captain, 'Kiss me, Hardy'.

PRETENTIOUSNESS INDEX **Nil**

NERO-ESQUE

in the style of the Roman emperor Nero (37–68 AD);

'cruel', 'tyrannical', 'enjoying destruction':

Thus the German director Roland Emmerich destroyed half of New York in Independence Day *(1996), much to the approbation of audiences [...] and Nero-esque critics who described the obliteration of Manhattan as 'exhilarating and gleeful'.* (The Times)

Apart from *Augustan* (see entry), the terms associated with the Roman emperors tend to point to their madness or their badness or both. *Nero-esque* (or *Neronian*) is no exception. Nero, who ruled between 54 and 68 AD, persecuted the Christians, had his mother murdered and, most famously, is supposed to have played and sung while he watched Rome burn. This is the reference in the *Times* quote above.

PRETENTIOUSNESS INDEX **!**

NIETZSCHEAN

connected with the writings and doctrines of German philosopher Friedrich Nietzsche (1844–1900);

'believing in the power of will', 'identified with the concept of the superman', 'Darwinian':

Whether he [Arnold Schwarzenegger] was cast as a Nietzschean barbarian warrior, a ruthless special-forces soldier, or an indestructible super-robot parachuted in from the future, what you saw on screen was, more or less, what you got. (Daily Telegraph)

Nietzsche's complex philosophical ideas have filtered into modern consciousness in very simplified form, and he is best known for his statement 'God is dead', and for the way in which the Nazis appropriated some of his ideas, particularly those to do with the necessary dominance of the weak by the strong and the concept of the superman (the *Übermensch* in German). Although his teaching was distorted by the Nazis, the term *Nietzschean* is loosely used to describe a state of society in which power goes inevitably to those who have no qualms about using it, and suggests a world in which 'soft' qualities like pity and mercy have little place. In this respect the expression is not unlike *Darwinian* (see entry).

PRETENTIOUSNESS INDEX *!*

NIXONIAN

connected to the life, behaviour and doctrines of the 37th US President, Richard Milhous Nixon (1913–94);

'devious', 'scandal-haunted', 'supporting policy of détente':

> *They are developing Nixonian desires to bug without warrants from judges and to pity themselves, but not others.* (Observer)

Richard Nixon served as President of the United States from 1969 to 1974 and was the only one to resign while in office, as a consequence of the Watergate scandal. Partly because of his Republican Party base, Nixon was less hamstrung in foreign affairs than Democratic predecessors like John F. Kennedy or Lyndon Johnson. He established a policy of détente with the Soviet Union and China, and he was more liberal in home affairs than several of his successors. Nixon's life was one of triumph, defeat and comebacks and he was haunted by the 'tricky Dicky' label attached to him early in his political career. Finally driven from office by his involvement in the attempts to cover up the Watergate scandal, he regained a statesmanlike reputation in the last two decades of his life. The adjective *Nixonian*, however, is most likely to refer to his frequently paranoid outbursts, his unscrupulous and often illegal attempts to do down his opponents, and his overwhelming sense of being misjudged. History has already been kinder to him than his contemporaries were.

PRETENTIOUSNESS INDEX **Nil**

O

OATES-LIKE

in the manner of Captain Lawrence Oates (1880–1912), a member of Scott's Antarctic expedition;

'disappearing mysteriously', 'heroic', 'self-sacrificing':

Alarm bells should have rung the night before, when his 'nip out' for ice turned into a worryingly long Captain Oates-like absence. He returned 90 minutes later clutching two bags of water. (Observer)

Returning from the South Pole, Captain Oates deliberately sacrificed himself, fearing that his severe frost-bite would endanger the survival of the rest of the expedition. In the event, the whole party perished. Oates is often seen as a model of understated courage, as shown by Scott's journal: 'There was a blizzard blowing in the morning when Oates said "I am just going outside and may be some time" and he stumbled out of the tent. We knew that poor Oates was walking to his death, but though we tried to dissuade him, we knew it was the act of a brave man and an English gentleman.'

PRETENTIOUSNESS INDEX **Nil** BUT THE COMPARISON SOMETIMES APPEARS IN A SLIGHTLY TACTLESS AND HUMOROUS CONTEXT, AS IN THE *OBSERVER* QUOTE.

(see also *Scott-like*)

ODYSSEAN

connected to the mythical Greek figure of Odysseus (known as Ulysses to the Romans);

'cunning', 'much-travelled', 'homesick':

I am still waiting for the book to describe the experience of so many British families who search for la bonne vie in France: only to find hostility, boredom, isolation, illegal Sky TV transmitters and an Odyssean longing for home. (Daily Telegraph)

Odysseus, the hero of Homer's poem the *Odyssey*, wandered the seas for ten years after the fall of Troy before the gods permitted him to return to the island of Ithaca, of which he was king. During the siege of Troy, Odysseus was noted for his cunning (the ruse of the Trojan horse was his idea). Later he turns into the archetypal wanderer and also a symbol of endurance and survival as he faces one danger after another. Finally, in his longing for his kingdom and his wife Penelope, Odysseus becomes the image of the homesick man. *Odyssean* might suggest any of these attributes, although its most usual application is to the idea of the wanderer.

PRETENTIOUSNESS INDEX *!*

OEDIPAL

connected to Oedipus, the king of Thebes in Greek mythology who killed his father and married his mother;

'suppressed', 'incestuous':

Throwing in repeated contributions by the devastatingly sexy Angelina Jolie, who, as Alexander's evil mother, fosters Oedipal turmoil in the young hero, does not lend the film any subtlety. (Daily Telegraph)

It was Sigmund Freud who used the myth of Oedipus to explore what he saw as a psychological truth, namely that in very early life males are in a state of unconscious rivalry with their fathers for the attention of their mothers. *Oedipal* therefore hints at a sexual closeness and tension, usually unacknowledged. More generally, *Oedipal* could be used to describe any kind of uneasy or anti-parent behaviour, suggesting fraught relations with mother and/or father.

PRETENTIOUSNESS INDEX **Nil**

(see also *Freudian*)

OLYMPIAN

from Mount Olympus in north-east Greece, in traditional mythology the home of the gods;

'god-like', 'lofty':

Nobody has since emerged to match Young's combination of soaring ideals, substantial argument and Olympian grandeur. (Spectator)

At almost 3000 metres, Olympus is the highest mountain in Greece and so the appropriate home for gods such as Zeus. The idea of loftiness leads quickly to a sense of superiority, and the term *Olympian* generally carries overtones of 'arrogant'.

PRETENTIOUSNESS INDEX **!**

(see also *Parnassian*)

OPHELIA-LIKE

connected to the life and death of Ophelia in Shakespeare's *Hamlet*;

'driven mad', 'drowned':

> *The latest is poor Patsy Kensit, languishing in a private clinic, trembling on the brink of Ophelia-like misery and madness, beaten to an emotional pulp by her attachment to Liam Gallagher.* (Guardian)

The two things everyone knows about Ophelia are that she is in love with Hamlet, although rejected by him, and that she dies by drowning, possibly a suicide. In fact, she is driven to distraction by the murder of her father Polonius (for which Hamlet is responsible). Nevertheless, her death is sometimes seen as archetypally romantic, the result of a broken heart but a gentle result, since she glides downstream half-asleep. The famous pre-Raphaelite picture by Millais contributes to this rosy view of Ophelia's death. So, even though it's slightly misleading, *Ophelia-like* suggests lovelorn suffering and plenty of pathos.

PRETENTIOUSNESS INDEX **!**

OPRAH-ESQUE

reflecting the style or life of US television host Oprah Winfrey (1954–);

'achieving great success after early adversity', 'very influential in culture and the media', 'doing high-profile charity work', 'having the common touch':

> *Happiness might be a trivial quality when compared with wisdom or knowledge, but the older I get the happier I am when around my family and friends. I know, it sounds Oprah-esque, but there you have it.* (Spectator)

Oprah Winfrey is the most powerful celebrity on American television and, arguably, across the US media culture. Just one strand of her activities – the Oprah Book Club – has had a profound effect on reading habits, since the selection of a title guarantees enormous sales. Unlike some chat-show hosts, Oprah has not focused only on the rich and famous but on 'ordinary' people, dealing with heavyweight topics such as child abuse. Coming from an impoverished Mississippi background and with first-hand experience of sexual abuse and racism, Winfrey is the exemplar of the American dream in her achievement of billionaire status and an influence that she has tirelessly and shrewdly extended across her own country and beyond.

PRETENTIOUSNESS INDEX **Nil**

ORPHIC

connected to the legendary lyre-player Orpheus;

'ravishing', 'beautiful and melodious':

> *In the lobby of the Metropolitan Opera House in New York, murals by Marc Chagall, also derived from designs for The Magic Flute, dangle from the ceiling and do their best to persuade the raucous city to pause and listen to the Orphic harmony of the spheres.* (Observer)

Orpheus's playing was so seductive that not only animals but stones and trees were drawn to listen to him. In the best-known part of the legend he goes to the underworld in search of his dead lover Eurydice and wins her back from its ruler Pluto by the beauty of his music (only to lose her once more when, disobeying instructions, he turns round to look at her as they ascend from underground). *Orphic* (also *Orphean*) is a fairly specialised term, suggesting not just supreme skill in music but an almost other-worldly power.

PRETENTIOUSNESS INDEX *!*

ORTONESQUE

in the style or typical of the themes of playwright Joe Orton (1933–67);

'macabre', 'blackly humorous', 'outrageous':

> *There is some lightweight fun to be had here, but the play hasn't told you much more by the end than you can deduce in the opening minutes, and it cries out for some really black Ortonesque dialogue to expose the rot in a world where you can put a price on anything – even a wife.* (Guardian)

Joe Orton's life was short – he was murdered by his gay lover – and his dramatic output small, but the word *Ortonesque* had already entered the language by the time of his death. In only three full-length plays, *Entertaining Mr Sloane* (1964), *Loot* (1965) and *What the Butler Saw* (1967), Orton fashioned a style that combined high camp and deadpan humour against a backdrop of outrageous events on stage, all of them to do with sex, death and money. Time has dulled the shock of some of it but *Ortonesque* is still a useful and evocative term for theatre writing that is calculated to offend while employing genteel language or gestures.

PRETENTIOUSNESS INDEX *!*

ORWELLIAN

in the style of or connected to the themes and subjects favoured by writer George Orwell (1903–50);

(relating to writing style) 'clear', 'classic'; (relating to subject matter) 'nightmarish', 'totalitarian':

After all this, there is a growing sense that Burma's rulers – who go under the Orwellian title of the State Peace and Development Council (SPDC) – now realise they are dealing with an opponent they cannot beat. (Observer)

The essayist, journalist and novelist George Orwell produced an astonishingly varied body of work in his relatively brief life. His influence on our culture is far-reaching, even at a basic level. (The television titles *Big Brother* and *Room 101* both derive from his final novel, although largely purged of their most sinister associations.) Like the similar expression *Kafkaesque* (see entry), *Orwellian* is a popular piece of shorthand for a range of attributes and attitudes. The principal use of the term relates to his last two books, *Animal Farm* (1945) and *1984* (1949). Both are satires, the first on the Russian Revolution and second on the creation of a totalitarian state in Britain. *Orwellian* may describe the way that language is twisted and corrupted in the service of power. In *1984*, words point in the opposite direction to the truth – political dissidents are tortured in the Ministry of Love, war is waged by the Ministry of Peace. Current military/political euphemisms, such as 'collateral damage' to describe the unintended victims of an air attack, are frequently described as *Orwellian*. (This distortion of language is the reference in the *Observer* quote above.) Equally, the term may describe the nightmare world of repression and state violence that characterised Hitler's Germany and Stalin's Russia or any other totalitarian regime. *Orwellian* therefore has largely negative connotations. But if the term is used to apply to a writer's style, it is complimentary, since Orwell was noted for his lucid and persuasive prose.

PRETENTIOUSNESS INDEX **Nil**

(see also *Big Brotherish* and *Stalinist*)

OTHELLO-LIKE

in the manner of Othello, the tragic hero of Shakespeare's play of the same name;

'easily deceived', 'insanely jealous':

Anger is, late in the game, exacerbated by sexual paranoia (the alcoholic's impotence translates into jealousy of Othello-like intensity). (Guardian)

In Shakespeare's tragedy, Othello is the commander of Venetian forces based on Cyprus. For a variety of apparent motives, but really acting from nothing more than basic malevolence, his trusted lieutenant Iago decides to undermine and destroy his commander by insinuating that the latter's wife, Desdemona, has been unfaithful with another officer. Corrupted and goaded by Iago, Othello eventually kills Desdemona before committing suicide. *Othello-like* chiefly relates to a person's furious jealousy but it may also refer to the ease with which someone can be taken in over sexual matters.

PRETENTIOUSNESS INDEX *!*

(see also *Iago-like*)

OXBRIDGE

connected to Oxford and Cambridge universities and the social/ class attitudes and influences that supposedly emanate from them;

'elitist', 'privileged':

His [Andrew Neil's] vision of an Old Britain, consisting of an Oxbridge ruling class versus a meritocratic New Britain, crystallised in his libel case against Sir Peregrine Worsthorne and has indirectly provoked some of his best journalism. (Independent on Sunday)

Oxbridge can be a neutral term but it is most often found in a critical context hinting at privilege. As the oldest universities, and the ones most associated with power and wealth, Oxford and Cambridge are traditionally seen as the home – or the cradle – of Britain's rulers, movers and shakers. Between a half and a third of recent government and shadow cabinets have been made up of *Oxbridge* graduates.

PRETENTIOUSNESS INDEX **Nil**

OXONIAN

connected to Oxford and its university;

'distinctive', 'superior':

There are flashes of the Oxonian drawl, which seems to have been taught to all doctors of his generation. (Guardian)

Oxonian has a neutral, dictionary meaning to define a person who went to Oxford University, but it carries quite a freight of associations, most of them tending towards the negative. Just as *Etonian* nails down a class, style, voice, etc., so to a lesser extent does *Oxonian* carry overtones of elitism, despite being (or perhaps because it is) a rather dated term now.

PRETENTIOUSNESS INDEX *!*

OZYMANDIAN

reminiscent of the figure of Ozymandias in a poem of the same name by Percy Bysshe Shelley (1792–1822):

'proud', 'imperious', 'desolate':

Ozymandian despair in New Orleans wasteland (headline in The Times)

'Ozymandias' is a brief poem giving a traveller's description of discovering the remnants of a great statue in a desert. What remains of the face shows a proud sneer while the inscription on the pedestal boasts 'My name is Ozymandias, king of kings:/Look on my works, ye mighty, and despair!' Nothing is left around the shattered image but the endless sands. Shelley's poem is a comment on the arrogance of power, ultimately undone by time, and the name Ozymandias is thought to refer to the Egyptian pharaoh Rameses the Great. *Ozymandian* might mean 'proud' but it could also suggest the desolation that follows the fall from greatness, as in the *Times* quote above.

PRETENTIOUSNESS INDEX *!*

(see also *Shelleyan*)

P

PALMERSTONIAN

related to politician and Prime Minister Henry Temple, third Viscount Palmerston (1784–1865);

'assertively patriotic', 'imperial-minded':

> *Current American certitude of the rightness of its cause is as unshakeable as that of any Victorian missionary society or Palmerstonian gunboat skipper.*
>
> (Guardian)

Palmerston served 58 years in the House of Commons and was twice Prime Minister. Famous for his assertive defence of British interests, as Foreign Secretary he ordered the British fleet to Athens in 1850 when an English subject's property was destroyed in that city. The term *Palmerstonian* almost always comes coupled with 'gunboat (diplomacy)', reflecting an era of over-arching imperial confidence.

PRETENTIOUSNESS INDEX *!*

PANDARUS-LIKE

in the style of Pandarus, a character in Shakespeare's play *Troilus and Cressida*;

'making sexual arrangements for others', 'pimping':

> *First a Pandarus-like sergeant from the Kinema Corps tries to get him into bed with the centre's German secretary.* (Guardian)

In Shakespeare's version of the doomed love story of Troilus and Cressida with its background of the Trojan war, Pandarus is uncle to Cressida. For no very clear reason, except a sort of voyeurism, he encourages their affair and sees them into bed. The character, also found in versions of the story other than Shakespeare's, gives us the word *pander* with the general sense of 'indulge', but *Pandarus-like* tends to refer only to the sexual manipulation of others.

PRETENTIOUSNESS INDEX *!*

PANDORA'S (BOX)

like the box carried by Pandora in Greek mythology and which, when opened, releases everything harmful;

'containing unknown problems and dangers':

> *What a lot about human nature she [Jane Austen] knew, this witty spinster, scarcely 40 when she died, and how deftly, almost imperceptibly, she allows us to peer into her Pandora's box of the world's follies.* (Spectator)

Pandora, the first woman according to the myth, was created by the gods so that they could have vengeance on Prometheus. She carried a box or jar that she was forbidden to open. She did so, and all the evils that have dogged the world ever since flew out, leaving only Hope at the bottom of the box. *Pandora's box* is occasionally (and wrongly) used as to describe a selection of items, some good, some bad, but it (correctly) applies only to unseen dangers. The implication is always that the box is better left tight shut.

PRETENTIOUSNESS INDEX **Nil**

(see also *Promethean*)

PANGLOSSIAN

like the character of Dr Pangloss in Voltaire's novel *Candide* (1759);

'mindlessly optimistic':

> *There is a Panglossian tendency to overstate oil reserves by oil-producing countries and oil companies alike, as we have learned from Shell.*
>
> (Observer)

Dr Pangloss is Candide's tutor in Voltaire's satire. Whatever disaster happens, he interprets it as being for the best (since we live in the best of all possible worlds). *Panglossian* characterises a rose-tinted way of looking at the world, whether out of a wilful ignoring of the facts or out of stupidity.

PRETENTIOUSNESS INDEX *!*

(see also *Candide-like*)

PARNASSIAN

connected to Mount Parnassus in central Greece;

'inspiring', 'poetic':

Like Arnold, Woodhead has a lofty, Parnassian concept of the teacher's role – handing on 'the best that has been known and said in the world'.

(Daily Telegraph)

In Greek mythology, Mount Parnassus was the home to Apollo and the Muses. Not often used now, *Parnassian* is generally connected to poetry and suggests the elevated, 'god-given' nature of a high art form. Like *Olympian* (see entry), *Parnassian* may also suggest a certain detachment from the world if not an active superiority to it.

PRETENTIOUSNESS INDEX *!!*

PARTHIAN (SHOT)

like the arrows shot by the Parthian horsemen of ancient Persia;

'parting (blow)', 'retaliating in defeat':

Their Parthian shot is becoming an electoral liability for the Democrats. It is time for them to draw a line under the Clinton era.   (Daily Telegraph)

The Parthians fired arrows at their pursuers when they were retreating or running away. The survival of this metaphor from ancient military tactics may have to do with the similarity of sound between *parting* and *Parthian*, but the urge to administer a final kick in defeat is as old as humanity.

PRETENTIOUSNESS INDEX **Nil**

PAVLOVIAN

connected to the work of Russian physiologist Ivan Petrovich Pavlov (1849–1936);

'conditioned', 'reflexive', 'unthinking':

The word 'culture' produces Pavlovian sympathy among many Western politicians, intellectuals and artists.   (Spectator)

Pavlov worked at Saint Petersburg University, studying conditioned reflexes. Believing that an automatic reflex could be 'learned', he experimented with dogs by associating their feeding with the ringing of a bell. After a time, the dogs would salivate at the sound of the bell alone, without any food being provided. Pavlov was awarded a Nobel Prize in 1904 for his work on the physiology of digestion. Although *Pavlovian* comes from the neutral world of scientific experimentation, applications of the word tend to be negative when it comes to human beings, suggesting an unconsidered, even foolish, response to something.

PRETENTIOUSNESS INDEX **Nil**

PAXMANESQUE

in the style of TV interviewer Jeremy Paxman (1950–);

'abrasive', 'inquisitorial':

> *The questions were hardly Paxmanesque. Why are the press so horrible to you? was the gist of the gentle lob Mrs Booth Blair used as a vehicle to bat away the claims she was piggybacking on her husband's visit.* (Guardian)

Jeremy Paxman has been fronting BBC2's *Newsnight* for the best part of two decades, although he has branched out into other types of programme, notably the revival of *University Challenge* in 1994. Paxman has become famous for his robust – some would say aggressive, others would even say offensive – style of questioning politicians and others. His 'Paxo' nickname may be half-affectionate but, of course, it also refers to the well-known brand of poultry stuffing.

PRETENTIOUSNESS INDEX **Nil**

PECKSNIFFIAN

like the character of Mr Pecksniff in Charles Dickens's novel *Martin Chuzzlewit* (published 1843);

'hypocritical':

> *As recently as 1994, the title [of Lord Haw-Haw] was deemed unparliamentary language by the Speaker of the House, so joining a list of banned terms including 'ruffian', 'Pharisee', 'cad', 'jackass' and 'Pecksniffian cant'.*
> (Spectator)

In *Martin Chuzzlewit*, Pecksniff claims to be an architect, although he has never actually designed anything. Similarly he claims to be moral but is in fact a mean and bullying figure. *Pecksniffian* is a fairly rarefied piece of abuse, so it is good to know that it is on a list of expressions that are banned in the House of Commons.

PRETENTIOUSNESS INDEX *!!*

PEPYSIAN

relating to Samuel Pepys (1633–1703) or his diary;

'curious', 'vivid', 'detailed and inclusive':

> *But luckily, readers, I jotted down everything I saw that day as I walked up and down: […] confetti; dancers soaked where a fire-hydrant springs the lost River Walbrook high into the air; three topless women with 'Drop the*

Debt' written on their breasts. (I feel these notebooks offer a Pepysian historical record.)   (Guardian)

Samuel Pepys started his diary on New Year's Day in 1660 and closed it nearly ten years later when he feared that his eyesight was failing (it wasn't). He wrote vivid first-hand accounts of such historic events as the Fire of London as well as detailing his domestic life, including quarrels with Mrs Pepys over his pursuit of other women. *Pepysian* might stand for 'immediate' and 'observant' – as well as 'frank' or 'curious' in relation to sexual matters. But Pepys was frank in a private way: his diaries, deposited in his Cambridge college, were written in a cipher that wasn't cracked until the beginning of the 19th century.

PRETENTIOUSNESS INDEX *!*

PERICLEAN

connected to or in the style of Pericles (c.500–429 BC), the dominant figure in Athens;

'marking a golden period in culture', 'persuasive in speech':

The main speaker was one Edward Everett, former governor of Massachusetts, who was deemed so important that the event was postponed because he needed longer to prepare his speech. Everett spoke for two hours, in the Periclean manner.   (Guardian)

Pericles was the leading Athenian politician of the fifth century BC. Because of the ascendancy of Athens over the rest of Greece during his life, and because of his association with writers and philosophers, *Periclean* sometimes signifies a golden age. More often it describes a lofty, persuasive style of oratory – although in the *Guardian* quote above its use seems partly ironic.

PRETENTIOUSNESS INDEX *!!*

PHILIPPIC

in the style of the speeches delivered by the Greek orator Demosthenes in the third century BC;

'severe or condemnatory (speech)':

By convention, panning shots are banned [in the US Senate], for the simple reason that these important gentlemen would be seen delivering their Philippics to rows of empty benches.   (Independent)

Demosthenes attempted to stir up his fellow Athenians to take action against the aggressive policies of King Philip of Macedonia, which were threatening Athenian territories. A *Philippic* might describe any extended oratorical attack. It's interesting to note that, like other expressions drawn from Greece and Rome and to do with public speaking, such as *Ciceronian* or *Periclean*, the term feels more at home in the context of US than British politics.

PRETENTIOUSNESS INDEX *!*

PHILISTINE

belonging to the Philistines, enemies of the Israelites in the Old Testament;

'hostile to art and culture':

> *Starring Jennifer and Felicity Kendal [...] the film told the affectionate story of a travelling Shakespeare troupe in an increasingly philistine post-colonial India.* (The Times)

Just as the ancient Greeks put foreigners in their place by terming them barbarians, so the Philistines were regarded as stupid and ignorant by their long-term enemies, the Israelites. The term has come down through the centuries and, usually spelled with a lower-case *p*, denotes anyone who is not so much indifferent as actively hostile to the arts and other refinements in life. A few people might rejoice in being called *philistine* but it's generally a dismissive expression.

PRETENTIOUSNESS INDEX **Nil**

PICKWICKIAN

in the style or with the appearance of Samuel Pickwick, the title character in Charles Dickens's *Pickwick Papers* (1837);

'plump and cheerful':

> *In life, he cut a Pickwickian figure, pleasingly plump and full of benevolence.* (Guardian)

Pickwickian neatly combines size and good nature, and the adjective rarely refers to one quality without implying the other. This is one of the more mainstream literary references and Pickwick is, along with Scrooge, the most instantly familiar of the Dickensian characters.

PRETENTIOUSNESS INDEX **Nil**

PILATE-LIKE

in the manner of Pontius Pilate, the Roman administrator of Judea when Jesus was crucified;

'indifferent', 'evasive', 'denying responsibility':

What should concern us is the implication that somehow, in the midst of a very dirty war [...] we British can somehow walk through the middle of the inferno in white suits, untouched and unsullied. There is a dangerous Pontius Pilate-like washing of our hands.   (Guardian)

Pontius Pilate is famous for one action only: literally washing his hands of responsibility for the death of Jesus. When the Jewish high priest and elders demanded his execution (which could only be carried out under Roman law), Pilate examined Jesus but could find no reason to put him to death. However, the elders persisted and when 'Pilate saw that he could prevail nothing, but that rather a tumult was made, he took water and washed his hands before the multitude, saying, I am innocent of the blood of this just person; see ye to it' (Matthew 27:24). Ironically, this gesture of buck-passing has caused Pilate to be remembered down the ages and made his name synonymous with evasiveness and guilt. He is the most infamous hand-washer in fact as opposed to fiction (there the title would go to Lady Macbeth).

PRETENTIOUSNESS INDEX **Nil**

PINTERESQUE

in the style of the playwright and screenwriter Harold Pinter (1930–);

'enigmatic', 'menacing', 'marked by pauses':

Still, I ask brightly, how many hamsters could I buy today? There is yet another pause. My afternoon is becoming distinctly Pinteresque. 'How many do you want?' Mr Overalls replies.   (Guardian)

Harold Pinter's plays mark out a distinctive landscape of humour and oblique threat. *Pinteresque* is a very versatile term and covers not only the mood of his drama but predominant themes such as betrayal and jealousy. But the most usual application of *Pinteresque* is to describe a pause in conversation – whether pregnant, puzzling or sinister – since Pinter has raised the hesitations and silences of everyday speech into a stylised aspect of his art.

PRETENTIOUSNESS INDEX *!*

PIRANDELLIAN

connected to the style or works of Italian dramatist Luigi Pirandello (1867–1936);

'blurring the boundary between reality and illusion', 'questioning identity', 'tricksy':

> *It has been like living in that classic childhood fantasy [...] that what seems like reality is actually a giant play everyone else is performing for your benefit. Only this play has a Pirandellian twist: while they are putting on a performance for you, you are putting on a performance for them. Or are they? (And are you?)* (Guardian)

In Pirandello's best-known drama, *Six Characters in Search of an Author* (1921), six mysterious figures burst in on a play rehearsal and demand that the producer stage their life story instead. In another drama, *Henry IV* (1922), a man strikes his head by falling off a horse and, waking up, believes himself to be a king. Pirandello's plays are about identity, illusion and reality. *Pirandellian* is a convenient, shorthand term to describe a kind of game-playing with reality and illusion.

PRETENTIOUSNESS INDEX **!**

PIRANESIAN

in the style of pictures by Italian artist Giovanni Piranesi (1720–78);

'cavernous', 'threatening', 'surreal':

> *Alien, too, is a beautiful film, most obviously when it alights on the alien planet, with its Piranesian vistas.* (Tom Shone, *Blockbuster*)

Piranesi was influenced by the remains of ancient Rome and produced images of that city. But he is best known now for his many etchings of great, empty structures full of stairs, vaults and great machines. These 'imaginary prisons' (*carceri di invenzione*) are without the human presence, indeed they seem to be on a superhuman scale, reflecting a paranoid, nightmarish world.

PRETENTIOUSNESS INDEX **!**

PLATONIC

connected to the ideas of Athenian philosopher Plato (c.427–348 BC);

'philosophical', 'non-sexual', 'archetypal', 'idealised':

> *But, of course, Gillian was right, the village was like a Platonic idea of a village – a packhorse bridge, a beck, skirted with yellow flag irises, that*

threaded its way amongst the grey stone houses, the old red telephone box, the little postbox on the wall, the village green with its fat white sheep grazing unfettered. (Kate Atkinson, *Case Histories*)

Plato produced his philosophical work in the form of dialogues, some involving his friend and mentor Socrates. The term *Platonic* is in very widespread use to describe a relationship that is non-sexual – the up-market equivalent of 'just good friends'. This sense of *Platonic* is related to the rather more serious application of the term to mean 'in an ideal form'. In his writing Plato developed a belief that things in the world are copies or shadows of perfect and archetypal forms that exist in a realm beyond the senses. All English villages, to take the example from the quotation above, are therefore imitations of some ideal English village that exists in a sphere above our knowledge.

PRETENTIOUSNESS INDEX **Nil**

(see also *Socratic*)

POIROT-ESQUE

in the style of the detective Hercule Poirot, created by mystery-writer Agatha Christie (1890–1976);

'eccentric', 'logical', 'soft-spoken', 'dandified':

The White House [in Dover] retains some art deco features, including its Poirot-esque staircase and original aluminium and frosted glass bathroom door. (Daily Telegraph)

Together with Agatha Christie's other fictional detective, Miss Marple, Hercule Poirot became one of the most famous sleuths of the 20th century. Christie took care to give her Belgian hero some odd or endearing speech mannerisms, as well as a trim moustache and an excusable vanity. *Poirot-esque* might refer to any of these features or to his logical brilliance in unmasking murderers, but the books and TV adaptations are so redolent of their period that the expression can be used as shorthand even for a style of architecture or interior design, as in the *Telegraph* quote.

PRETENTIOUSNESS INDEX **Nil**

(see also *Christie-like*)

POLLYANNA-ISH

in the manner of Pollyanna, the title character of children's stories by US author Eleanor Hodgman Porter (1868–1920);

'naively optimistic':

All this Pollyanna-ish positivity could be off-putting, were it not earthed by Janie's sense of integrity. (Daily Telegraph)

Pollyanna was a child heroine who looked for the best in every situation. This became the 'just being glad' game – played, for example, by telling a sick woman that she should be glad the rest of the world was well. Rather than childhood innocence, *Pollyanna-ish* suggests an almost wilful naivety and optimism in the face of the facts. The context generally makes the meaning clear but it's not a widely used reference.

<small>PRETENTIOUSNESS INDEX</small> *!*

POLONIUS-LIKE

connected to Polonius, a character in Shakespeare's play *Hamlet*;

'opinionated', 'wordy':

The nearest [presidential candidate Howard Dean] comes to voicing an inflexible article of faith is his Polonius-like insistence that budgets can and must be balanced. (Guardian)

In Shakespeare's tragedy, Polonius is a talkative courtier and advisor to Claudius, the king of Denmark (who murdered his brother, the previous king and Hamlet's father). Usually characterised as an old windbag, convinced of the rightness of his own opinions, Polonius is killed while eavesdropping on a scene between Hamlet and his mother. The *Guardian* reference above is to one item in a lengthy speech of advice Polonius gives to his son, Laertes, as he departs for the fleshpots of Paris: 'Neither a borrower nor a lender be.' It's not exactly about balancing budgets, perhaps, but more to the point may be the tacit hint that the would-be US President Howard Dean was, like Polonius, a bit of a bore.

<small>PRETENTIOUSNESS INDEX</small> *!*

POOTERISH

like the fictional character Charles Pooter in *The Diary of a Nobody* (1892) by the brothers George and Weedon Grossmith;

'conventional', 'trivial':

On and on they come, their Pooterish authors bizarrely convinced that what is really only a perfectly nice magazine feature – why I love frocks; my peculiar grandmother; how baking bread saved my life – deserves to be preserved between two hard covers for all eternity. (Observer)

The Diary of a Nobody began as a series of articles in the comic magazine *Punch*. Its popularity swiftly ensured publication in book form and it has never been out of print since. Charles Pooter is an office clerk living in Holloway in London who details his suburban life with unconscious humour. Originally a satire on self-important diaries by public figures, *The Diary of a Nobody* showed some affection for Pooter. But the term *Pooterish* is pretty dismissive.

PRETENTIOUSNESS INDEX **Nil**

POTEMKIN-STYLE

in the style of the fake villages supposedly constructed by Russian minister Grigori Aleksandrovich Potemkin (1739–91);

'fake', 'designed for show or to impress':

> *And if you want to know the difference, you should try visiting one of those Potemkin-style Maasai villages in Kenya whose only purpose is to extract money from tourists. At least when you visit the Himba ones, you know they really couldn't care whether you turn up.* (Daily Telegraph)

When Catherine the Great, Empress of Russia, went on a tour of the newly annexed territory of Crimea in 1787, the story goes that Potemkin – an immensely ambitious and industrious minister – ordered the construction of sham villages that could be viewed during the royal progress along the river Dnieper. This was to impress Catherine, a former lover of Potemkin, with his success in transforming a backward region. Although any royal or presidential tour is going to bring out the paintbrush and the broom there is a difference between tidying-up and constructing the 18th-century equivalent of a film set. However, it seems likely that the 'Potemkin village' tale was either an early example of an urban legend or a story deliberately spread by his enemies. Either way, *Potemkin-style* has come to connote something sham.

PRETENTIOUSNESS INDEX *!*

POTTERISH

connected to the world-famous character created by J.K. Rowling and first appearing in *Harry Potter and the Philosopher's Stone* (1997);

'magical', 'bespectacled', 'traditional':

> *Few at the Universities UK annual conference in the Harry Potterish*

surroundings of Keble College, Oxford, believe that undergraduate fees of up to £3,000 a year from 2006 are the magic wand to solve their problems. (Guardian)

Potterish – or *Potteresque* – looks like an adjective in search of something or someone to attach itself to. It is quite often used to describe boyish-looking men (glasses, neat hair, vaguely intellectual), particularly if they are in politics. But *Potterish* may also apply to a type of school or a style of architecture (Gothic, ivy-clad). At the moment the adjective looks like rather lazy shorthand but maybe it will come into its own.

PRETENTIOUSNESS INDEX **Nil**

POUJADIST

in the style of French politician Pierre Poujade (1920–2003);

'anti-tax and pro-small business', 'hostile to big government':

This is a fight against the forces of conservatism – a popular front of Poujadist small businessmen, farmers, cab drivers and truckers. (Guardian)

Pierre Poujade was a briefly popular and influential politician in the France of the early 1950s. The owner of a stationery shop, he founded a union and then a political party to defend the 'little man' against the encroachments of the authorities. *Poujadist* can sometimes be equated with 'petit-bourgeois', particularly when used in a hostile context (as in the *Guardian* quote).

PRETENTIOUSNESS INDEX *!!*

POWELLITE

in the style or with the outlook of British MP Enoch Powell (1912–98);

'anti-immigrant', 'anti-European', 'patriotic':

But the Powellite fear that old England's in her winding-sheet remains a powerful element in the Tory appeal to stability. (Guardian)

The politician Enoch Powell is best remembered today for his anti-immigration stance in the 1960s and for a single notorious speech (the 'rivers of blood' one), which got him kicked out of the Shadow Cabinet. Powell was also fiercely opposed to British entry into the European Union (or the Common Market as it was then known) and stood four-square for the preservation of British sovereignty. A brilliant but maverick figure, and ultimately an isolated one, Powell held a romantic view of national identity. The adjective *Powellite* might refer to this but is just as likely to describe his attitude towards immigration.

PRETENTIOUSNESS INDEX *!*

(*Powellite* may also refer to the policies backed by or the supporters of Colin Powell, US Secretary of State between 2001 and 2004.)

PRESCOTTIAN

in the style of British politician and deputy Prime Minister John Prescott (1938–);

'bluff', 'inclined to get tangled up in speech':

> *But we have high hopes for this Prescottian observation made recently at the National Institute for Clinical Excellence: 'As you know yourself, the proof of the pudding is in the eating here and there is a lot of eating being done by others of the pudding being produced.'* (Observer)

To have an adjective derived from one's name marks some kind of success, almost irrespective of the actual meaning of the word. In the media John Prescott – old Labour rather than New Labour, surely? – is often derided for his convoluted sentences and his blundering vocabulary as well as his general truculence. There's a metropolitan snootiness, not to say snottiness, at work here, and parliamentary sketch writers no doubt see Prescott as an easy laugh. Now the habit seems to have spread to the rest of the country as well.

PRETENTIOUSNESS INDEX **Nil**

PRIAPIC

connected with Priapus, ancient Roman god of gardens and fertility;

'lustful', 'sex-obsessed':

> *His friendships confuse people. He plotted with the late Alan Clark, priapic diarist of the Thatcher years, and is on good terms with that very different Clarke, Ken.* (Observer)

As a deity, Priapus came to the Romans from Asia Minor. Often depicted as a dwarfish figure with a great phallus, Priapus is the embodiment of male desire. *Priapic* suggests someone in a state of perpetual arousal, or close to it. On balance, it is probably closer to an insult than a compliment, although an insult of a rather literary and rarefied kind.

PRETENTIOUSNESS INDEX *!!*

PROCRUSTEAN

connected to the mythical figure of Procrustes;

'forcing into conformity':

> *Rather than trying to squeeze the 25 European states into this single Procrustean polity, we should build a bigger, better, brighter, looser union.*
> (Guardian)

In the Greek legend Procrustes was a robber who set on travellers and compelled them to lie on an iron bed. If the unfortunate traveller's legs overhung the end of the bed, Procrustes chopped them off. If the traveller was too short, Procrustes stretched him until he fitted the bed. *Procrustean* has therefore come to stand for the attempt to make people or things conform to a single standard, against protests as well as common sense. Only occurring in negative contexts, *Procrustean* may also imply threat or the use of force.

PRETENTIOUSNESS INDEX *!*

PROFUMO-LIKE

connected to the career and scandal surrounding John Profumo (1915–2006), a government minister in the early 1960s;

'sexually scandalous':

> *Demonised by the press, he does a Stonehouse-style disappearing act, then reappears as a Profumo-like figure, seeking redemption through charitable works, in his case doling out soup and sympathy to the homeless.*
> (Daily Telegraph)

In 1963 John Profumo was Minister for War, as it was then called, in the Conservative government of Harold Macmillan. He had an affair with Christine Keeler, a 19-year old showgirl, as they were then called. When the relationship came to light, it supposedly raised issues of national security, since Keeler was also involved with a naval attaché at the Russian embassy in London. An ideal scandal, the Profumo affair combined sex and spies, the upper classes and various low-life figures. John Profumo resigned and was greatly admired for the way in which he sank from the public eye and dedicated himself to charity work – in his case, washing up and cleaning at an East End centre for the homeless and the addicted. *Profumo-like* is sometimes used as a benchmark adjective for post-resignation behaviour by government ministers who've lost their jobs.

PRETENTIOUSNESS INDEX *!*

(The 'Stonehouse-style' mentioned in the *Telegraph* quote above is a reference to John Stonehouse, a minister in Harold Wilson's Labour government of the mid-1970s. Facing financial disaster, Stonehouse staged his own 'death by drowning' off a Miami beach in 1974. He eventually turned up in Australia.)

PROMETHEAN

like the Greek mythological figure of Prometheus;

'heroic', 'rebellious', 'daring':

> *Boyle presents a heroic but inevitably flawed figure, almost Promethean in his determination to confront the conservatives of his time.*
>
> (Independent on Sunday)

In the most famous story about Prometheus he steals fire from the gods for the benefit of humanity. For this he is chained by Zeus to a rock, where an eagle feeds each day on his liver, which regrows overnight so that the torment can be renewed the next day. Hercules eventually kills the eagle and releases Prometheus. *Promethean* has therefore come to signify any heroic figure who stands up in a noble cause and against overwhelming odds – and probably suffers in consequence.

PRETENTIOUSNESS INDEX *!*

PROSPERO-LIKE

like the character of Prospero in Shakespeare's play *The Tempest*;

'controlling', 'detached', 'having magical powers', 'sage-like':

> *Despite Godard's reputation as an aloof, Prospero-like figure, he is a surprisingly gracious interviewee.* (Guardian)

In Shakespeare's final complete play, Prospero is the exiled Duke of Milan. Banished with his young daughter to a deserted island, he masters the forces of magic and causes the shipwreck of his old enemies on the island. After that he must decide whether to avenge himself or to forgive them. An almost god-like figure because of his supernatural powers and his oversight of the little world of the island, Prospero is sometimes seen as a self-portrait by Shakespeare. *Prospero-like* suggests someone who is fundamentally wise and benevolent but capable of being severe.

PRETENTIOUSNESS INDEX *!*

PROTEAN

like Proteus, originally a sea-god in Greek mythology;

'multi-faceted', 'changeable':

> *Overwhelming guilt, at least where it is not in proportion to terrible wrong-doing, is one of the protean forms of self-importance.* (Spectator)

Proteus had the gift of prophecy but, to escape questioning, would adopt different shapes ranging from animals to natural objects such as trees. *Protean* tends to be used in a complimentary sense to describe people who have a mixture of talents – for example, the actor who is very versatile and can play in different styles. The negative context of the word in the *Spectator* quotation above is less usual.

PRETENTIOUSNESS INDEX *!*

PROTESTANT

connected to the Protestant churches and characterising an outlook supposedly associated with them;

'serious', 'suspicious of enjoyment', 'believing in hard work':

> *Middle-class Americans, like myself and my fellow seekers, have been raised with the old-time Protestant expectation that hard work will be rewarded with material comfort and security.* (Guardian)

The original *Protestants* were the groups who protested against official denunciations of the Reformation in the early 16th century; in other words, those denominations that sought to break away from Catholic hegemony. The term *Protestant* is quite often used outside religious contexts to suggest a rather dour attitude to life, one that looks sceptically at pleasure and believes in the virtues of hard work (and, by implication, the financial rewards that follow), as suggested by the expression *Protestant work ethic*.

PRETENTIOUSNESS INDEX **Nil**

PROUSTIAN

reminiscent of the style or subject matter of French writer Marcel Proust (1871–1922);

'evoking intense early memories', 'nostalgic':

> *The family had holidayed there and the visit unleashed some Proustian moments of childhood gastronomic excitement.* (The Times)

Proust's monumental, multi-volume work, generally known in English as *Remembrance of Things Past*, deals in part with the recovery through memory of the past. *Proustian* therefore generally indicates a moment of intense nostalgia, triggered by some taste or smell. The standard reference – it occurs early in the first volume of the work – is to the experience of eating a madeleine cake soaked in tea, which brings back to the narrator an overwhelmingly intense childhood memory that he can't quite pin down. Given the difficulty of reading Proust's work, it's interesting to note how far the notion of a *Proustian* moment has entered popular culture. Although use of the term is, arguably, a touch pretentious, it does describe an almost universal experience.

PRETENTIOUSNESS INDEX *!*

PRUFROCKIAN

typical of the style and manner of the narrator of T.S. Eliot's poem 'The Love Song of J. Alfred Prufrock' (published 1915);

'self-analysing', 'timorous', 'uncertain':

> *This leads to a self-examination of Prufrockian proportions, and the narrative is packed tight with philosophical platitudes, which are about as useful as having books for sandbags.*   (Guardian)

'Prufrock' was Eliot's first substantial work, introducing a distinctively modern tone and character to poetry. The narrator is divided between banal concerns, such as whether he is going bald, and dream-like visualisations of mermaids or the evening fog. Above all, Prufrock is conscious that he is not cut out for heroism or any kind of distinction.

PRETENTIOUSNESS INDEX *!!*

(see also *Eliot-ish*)

PUCKISH

in the style of Puck or Robin Goodfellow, an imp or goblin in Shakespeare's *A Midsummer Night's Dream*;

'impish', 'mischievous':

> *He is surprisingly softly spoken, his severe grey eyes lightened by a puckish smile.*   (Daily Telegraph)

A *puck* is an old and generic term for a malignant imp, but Shakespeare gave him a capital *P* and turned him into a figure of mischief rather than malice – in the epilogue to the play, the character calls himself 'an honest Puck'. So *puckish* is without any negative connotations and can even convey a touch of benevolence along with the mischief.

Pretentiousness Index **Nil**

PYRRHIC (VICTORY)

relating to the victory won by Pyrrhus, the king of Epirus (318–272 BC);

(of success) 'won at too great a cost', 'self-defeating':

It seems only yesterday that the nation was rejoicing at news of the victory, albeit pyrrhic in his case, of Lord Nelson at the Battle of Trafalgar, and now here we are celebrating its bicentenary year. (The Times)

Pyrrhus was a skilled military commander and king of Epirus in northern Greece. He campaigned against Rome and won the battle of Asculum in southern Italy in 280 BC. However, Pyrrhus lost the best part of his army during the battle and is reputed to have said afterwards, 'Another such victory and we are ruined.' The expression *Pyrrhic victory* is less often applied to military campaigns than it is to ambivalent success in other areas of life.

Pretentiousness Index *!*

PYTHONESQUE

in the style of the television series *Monty Python's Flying Circus*;

'surreal', 'wacky':

Watch the film, revel in the battle scenes, laugh at the bad acting and the blond mullet and the Pythonesque plot delivery. (Daily Telegraph)

Monty Python's Flying Circus ran between 1969 and 1974 for a total of 45 episodes over four series, and spawned several films and recently a stage musical based on the film *Monty Python and the Holy Grail* (1974). It seems hardly necessary to describe the humour of the 'Pythons' (Graham Chapman, John Cleese, Terry Gilliam, Eric Idle, Terry Jones and Michael Palin) but for the record the TV shows consisted of a sequence of sketches, sometimes incomplete or lacking a punch-line, which were bizarre or plain bonkers. Some of the items – the dead parrot sketch, John Cleese's turn as a civil servant from the Ministry of Silly Walks – have become classics of eccentric humour which is sometimes seen as peculiarly English. Very influential, *Monty*

Python's Flying Circus was to those growing up in the 1960s and 1970s the equivalent of what *The Goon Show* had been to the previous generation. On a personal and perhaps rather plaintive note, am I the only person who never found the Pythons particularly funny?

PRETENTIOUSNESS INDEX **Nil**

(see also *Goonish*)

Q, R

QUIXOTIC

like Don Quixote, the chivalrous knight in the novel *Don Quixote of La Mancha* (1605) by Miguel de Cervantes;

'idealistic', 'naive', 'deluded', 'selfless':

He's also a brilliant mimic who can slip in or out of character, and while never betraying his principles is equally capable of acts of wilful cruelty and quixotic deeds of kindness. (Spectator)

In Cervantes' famous story, Don Quixote is a kindly gentleman whose brain has been addled by reading too many tales of chivalry. Accompanied by his squire Sancho Panza and dressed in rusty armour, he sets off on a broken-down horse in search of adventures. In his confused mind, a village girl becomes a noble lady and windmills are transformed into giants who must be attacked. *Quixotic* is an odd adjective, since it seems to convey both approval and disapproval, affection and impatience. On the one hand, Quixote believes he is doing the selfless, chivalrous thing; on the other, he is deluded to the point of insanity. Use of the expression generally suggests a sporadic, inexplicable act of kindness/gallantry, as in the quote above. *Quixotic* may also refer to someone who has the fictional knight's appearance: tall and gaunt.

PRETENTIOUSNESS INDEX **Nil**

RABELAISIAN

typical of the style or subject matter of French satirical writer Francois Rabelais (c.1494–1553);

'bawdy', 'good-humoured', 'insatiable':

It stretched also from the more Rabelaisian days of Fleet Street being Fleet Street, staffed by characters who could have walked off the pages of Evelyn Waugh's Scoop [...] to the more clinical world of dispersed offices and cold screens that lacked the camaraderie with his competitors that he relished.
(Guardian)

Rabelaisian, like *Proustian* (see entry), is an interesting example of a French-derived word that is fairly widely known and understood even though few people will be familiar with the original works that gave rise to the term. Broadly speaking, *Rabelaisian* is identified with a tolerant, good-humoured approach to life, bordering on the gross or the grotesque. It's not exactly a compliment but nor is it an insult. There may be a trace of approval in its application, as in the *Guardian* quote above.

PRETENTIOUSNESS INDEX *!*

RACHMANITE

like the crooked landlord Peter Rachman (1919–62);

'violent', 'racketeering':

He made his mark in Parliament in particular by his concern for transport and health issues and by his opposition to the Rachmanite practices encouraged by the Rent Act 1957. (Daily Telegraph)

Peter Rachman, a Polish refugee in London in the period after World War Two, became notorious for his racketeering practices as a slum landlord. Taking advantage of the 1957 Rent Act (which enabled landlords to evict long-serving tenants from unfurnished property provided that it was replaced by furnished accommodation), Rachman 'persuaded' his reluctant tenants to leave their rent-controlled flats with the aid of gangs of wrestlers and boxers. The empty flats or rooms were then let at grotesquely inflated prices to immigrant families, who frequently had difficulty finding accommodation elsewhere. Even many years after the man's death, *Rachmanite* still represents a benchmark in property exploitation and racketeering.

PRETENTIOUSNESS INDEX *!*

RAMBOESQUE

connected to the fictional character of John J. Rambo;

'violently patriotic and ruthless':

McNab, who was leading the mission, claimed in his book that they killed or wounded 250 Iraqis before they were overwhelmed. Asher says this is nonsense, a Ramboesque account that might shift books but has no basis in fact. (Guardian)

Rambo, played by Sylvester Stallone, appeared in the film *First Blood* (1982) based on a novel by thriller-writer David Morrell. The Stallone character was an unstable Vietnam veteran who took his revenge on an entire backwoods town after being arrested by the local sheriff. But Rambo's ask-no-questions, take-no-prisoners stance chimed with the newly assertive America of the Ronald Reagan era, and the enormous box-office success of *First Blood* spawned two sequels. President Reagan, whose government had just negotiated the release of hostages in Lebanon, joked after watching one of them: 'Boy, I saw *Rambo* last night. Now I know what to do the next time this happens.'

PRETENTIOUSNESS INDEX **Nil**

REAGANITE

typical of the style, attitude or politics of the 40th US President, Ronald Reagan (1911–2004), or describing one of his followers;

'right-wing', 'anti-communist', 'folksy', 'easy-going':

Financed by the Media Research Centre, a privately funded organisation founded by Reaganites in the late Eighties, it is dedicated to 'exposing and combating liberal media bias', according to its masthead. (Observer)

Ronald Reagan gave back to Americans the optimism and sense of ease that they had lost in the troubled post-Vietnam years under presidents such as Richard Nixon and Jimmy Carter. Reagan became not merely a standard-bearer for the religiously inclined right but a kind of secular saint to them, and he regularly figures at or near the top of any list of the greatest presidents. Admirers also credit Reagan with ending the Cold War, bringing about America's economic recovery after the doldrums of the 1970s, and restoring the country's self-respect and standing in the world. His detractors acknowledge – but are also annoyed by – his folksy charm, and are baffled how a one-time film actor who was apparently indifferent to political details could have achieved such a hold on the nation's affections. They suggest that other leaders like the USSR's Mikhail Gorbachev had a good deal to do with the end of hostilities between east and west, and they point out that the national debt rose to unprecedented levels during Reagan's two terms (1981–89). In other words, *Reaganite* and the softer-sounding *Reaganesque* can be terms of either high praise or condemnation, depending on which side of the political fence the user is standing.

PRETENTIOUSNESS INDEX **Nil**

REBECCA-LIKE

in the style of the title character of Daphne du Maurier's novel *Rebecca* (published 1938);

'ghostly', 'haunting':

> For all Royal Ballet dancers, the company's Prima Ballerina Assoluta *[Margot Fonteyn] is both an inspiration and a burden. Her memory lingers, Rebecca-like – to haunt her successors.* (Daily Telegraph)

The unnamed heroine of *Rebecca* marries the suave Max de Winter who sweeps her off to his Cornish estate. The housekeeper, Mrs Danvers, is devoted to the memory of de Winter's first wife, Rebecca, and taunts the anonymous new wife with her inferiority. Deriving from a modern classic with echoes of the great 19th-century Gothic romances, such as *Jane Eyre*, *Rebecca-like* almost invariably suggests a haunting and sinister atmosphere or memory.

PRETENTIOUSNESS INDEX *!*

REITHIAN

in the style or with the approach of John Reith (1889–1971), an early Director-General of the BBC;

'dour', 'edifying':

> Something you, as a strike-breaking BBC management geek, could never *normally justify even if it fell squarely within the terms of your noble Reithian mission to edify.* (The Times)

John (later Lord) Reith was the first general manager of the BBC and then Director-General (1927–38). The creation of the BBC as a reliable and independent national institution is usually credited to him. In particular, Reith believed that the BBC's role was as much to educate as it was to entertain, and his stated creed was: 'Give the public slightly better than it thinks it likes.' (Reith's paternalistic style had its female counterpart in the 'Auntie' nickname, half affectionate, half mocking, given to the BBC in the 1950s.) The adjective *Reithian* is sometimes used to evoke those high-minded days before and after World War Two and more often as a stick with which to beat the present-day BBC if it seems to be straying too far down-market in search of ratings.

PRETENTIOUSNESS INDEX *!*

REMBRANDTESQUE

typical of the style of Dutch painter Rembrandt van Rijn (1606–69);

'dark', 'using shadow', 'self-examining':

> *The latter film followed Hurt's acclaimed stage performance of the role, which inspired one critic to froth that he has the right face for Krapp, 'full of wrecked, Rembrandtesque fascination, suggesting acres of pained and mysterious hinterland'.* (Observer)

One of the greatest painters of all time, Rembrandt is famous for his portraits, and particularly self-portraits, as well as his employment of light and dark on canvas. *Rembrandtesque* may refer to this use of shadow but it can also characterise a depiction of oneself or others that is marked by real insight and yet tinged with mystery.

PRETENTIOUSNESS INDEX *!*

RENOIRESQUE

typical of the style or subject matter of French painter Pierre Auguste Renoir (1841–1919);

'lush', 'sensuous', 'warm':

> *To start with they took to her because of her Renoiresque beauty and her ebullient vitality, but some of the most distinguished minds of the 20th century remained her friends because of her intelligence, sensibility, wonderful generosity ...* (Daily Telegraph)

One of the best-known of the impressionist painters, Renoir produced landscapes and portraits that are characterised by their frequently lush colours and spontaneous feel. In particular, his female figures are noted for their fullness and vibrancy. *Renoiresque* is likely to refer either to this or to an unabashed use of colour.

PRETENTIOUSNESS INDEX *!*

RIMBAUDIAN

characteristic of the life or work of French poet Arthur Rimbaud (1854–91);

'modernist', 'anarchic', 'self-destructive', 'wandering':

> *Equating death with glory, the song firmly pins its creator's colours to the mast of Rimbaudian excess at a time when his [Pete Doherty's] only remaining friends seem happy to join him for this final chaotic ride.* (The Times)

Rimbaud is not much read now, although his poetry was regarded as avant-garde in its day. But, like Byron (see *Byronic*), he remains famous for living the life of the archetypal bohemian artist. Together with his lover, the poet Paul Verlaine, Rimbaud embarked on a spree of drug and alcohol excess that scandalised his contemporaries and culminated in Verlaine's shooting him (though the resulting wound was minor). Rimbaud later abandoned poetry and spent years wandering in Europe and the Middle East, including a stretch as a gun-runner in north Africa. His life was the equivalent of a rock star's flashy descent, hence the comparison with Pete Doherty above.

PRETENTIOUSNESS INDEX *!*

ROONEYESQUE

in the style or with the success of footballer Wayne Rooney (1985–);

'achieving sudden and startling success', 'uncontrolled':

In March 2000 Gaucci burst on to the scene in a positively Rooneyesque manner by threatening to lock his squad in their training complex until the end of the season if they failed to beat Venezia. (Guardian)

Brought up on a Liverpool housing estate, Wayne Rooney briefly held the title of the youngest player to score a Premiership goal, when playing for Everton against Arsenal. He continues to hold the record for the highest transfer fee paid for a teenage player, when he moved to Manchester United in a deal that is likely to end up costing around £25 million. Rooney also breaks records on the literary front, having secured a publishing contract in 2006 worth £5 million, the highest sports book deal to date. *Rooneyesque* could therefore apply to any football wunderkind who is both successful and young, but the term is as likely to be used about his outbursts of temper (usually blamed on his youth) or the sexual exploits that earned him some tabloid attention. Every football generation – that is, every period of five or six years – seems to need a figure to hold up for admiration, fascination and derision in about equal proportions, and the mantle has passed from David Beckham to Wayne Rooney.

PRETENTIOUSNESS INDEX **Nil**

ROUSSEAUESQUE

following the style or doctrines of the Swiss writer and philosopher Jean-Jacques Rousseau (1712–78);

'free', 'simple', 'natural':

The rams have to be put on the islands in November, and taken off, exhausted, in January, but apart from that the [sheep] lead the most wonderfully free, Rousseauesque existence, being themselves in a way that their Home Counties cousins [...] could only sadly yearn after. (Daily Telegraph)

Rousseau believed that living in a structured society had taken human beings away from their proper condition in a 'state of nature'. Human nature was intrinsically good but was corrupted by the requirements of living in society. He originated the concept of the 'noble savage', proclaiming the superiority of those who had never been tainted by contact with civilisation. *Rousseauesque* tends to be equated with the simple life or with a kind of naive optimism about human nature in its untouched state.

PRETENTIOUSNESS INDEX *!*

RUBENESQUE

in the style of the paintings of Peter Paul Rubens (1577–1640), particularly his pictures of women;

'exuberant', 'fleshy', 'voluptuous':

Nineteenth-century women struggled to preserve a deathly pallor and plump themselves up like Rubenesque cushions. (Daily Telegraph)

Rubens painted religious pictures as well as scenes of mythology but it is the rounded female figures of the latter to which he has given his name. *Rubenesque* has been equated with an attractive fleshiness for at least a couple of centuries now and the term is a roundabout compliment.

PRETENTIOUSNESS INDEX *!*

RUMSFELDIAN

characterising words or attitudes seen as typical of US politician and defence secretary Donald Rumsfeld (1932–);

'tough and aggressive', 'verbally tortuous':

His latest, Rumsfeldian line on tough sentencing begs the obvious question: what has happened to Lord Woolf? (Guardian)

Donald Rumsfeld has in fact served two US presidents as defence secretary. Appointed by Gerald Ford in the mid-1970s, he was the youngest man to fill the post. By the time he took up the job again under George W. Bush in 2001 he was the second oldest. Rumsfeld enjoyed a high profile during the Iraq war in 2003, thanks to his combative performance at press briefings. *Rumsfeldian* therefore suggests a no-nonsense, hard-line stance. However, the defence secretary also became something of a cult figure for his elaborate verbal musings ('There are known knowns. These are things we know that we know. There are known unknowns …'), and the word may also characterise these.

PRETENTIOUSNESS INDEX *!*

RUNYONESQUE

in the style of US writer and newspaperman Damon Runyon (1884–1946);

'criminal but colourful', 'slangy':

> *But the prospect of the Runyonesque colour of the on-course bookies fading to the monochrome grey of the laptop screen seems far more depressing than the odd bent trainer engaging in a little light robbery.* (Daily Telegraph)

Damon Runyon was born in Kansas and grew up in Colorado but is forever identified with New York, and in particular the Prohibition years. He wrote for the papers on baseball and boxing, while his stories centre on the world of gamblers, bootleggers and small-time crooks. Runyon gave them distinctive nicknames (Nathan Detroit, Harry the Horse) and developed a knowing, big-city style using slang and strung-out sentences. Any humorous 'larger than life' treatment of the underworld, especially when it focuses on the little men, is likely to be called *Runyonesque* – or would have been once, since people now prefer the in-yer-face mockney gangster-style of Michael Ritchie's films.

PRETENTIOUSNESS INDEX **Nil**

RURITANIAN

connected to Ruritania, the imaginary mid-European country created by Anthony Hope (Hawkins) in the novel *The Prisoner of Zenda* (1894);

'romantic', 'colourful and intriguing':

> *The sparkly carriages of '81, bringing in all that foreign royalty in their Ruritanian uniforms, were replaced by a couple of buses filled with what looked like extras from Four Weddings and a Funeral.* (Daily Telegraph)

A fine late-Victorian tale of romance and adventure, with a dash of politics, *The Prisoner of Zenda* is the best-known work of Anthony

Hope (1863–1933). Hope, a barrister, dropped his surname Hawkins to provide himself with an elementary pseudonym and was later knighted for his role in the British propaganda campaign of World War One. Often filmed, *Zenda* is a story of royal impersonation, midnight assignations in palace summer-houses and skulduggery in hunting-lodges. Accordingly, *Ruritanian* has come to mean 'exotic and intriguing', but the adjective may also refer to the political scheming that characterised the imaginary German-style statelet as well as the flamboyant costumes and ceremonies that were a feature of life there.

PRETENTIOUSNESS INDEX *!*

(see also *Balkan*)

S

SADISTIC

relating to the practices or writings of the Marquis (Donatien Alphonse) de Sade (1740–1814);

'enjoying the pain and humiliation of others, particularly in a sexual context':

> A real-life former drill sergeant, R. Lee Ermey, steals the show as the sadistic camp commander who relishes torturing his new recruits, with Matthew Modine and Vincent D'Onofrio leading the young cast.   (The Times)

De Sade wrote much of his work in prison. The extreme nature of his writings, with their celebration of perverse and pathological sexuality, means that they have only recently become available for general publication although they have long been circulated in privately printed or expurgated editions. The term is so widely used that it frequently wanders free of its sexual context.

PRETENTIOUSNESS INDEX **Nil**

SAMSONESQUE

connected to the biblical figure of Samson;

'strong but vulnerable', 'destructive', 'long-haired':

> And for another, he is reluctant to leave his reputation in the hands of a mischievous journalist who might want to cast him as a Samsonesque figure, ready to bring the ancient home of the golfing establishment down on the heads of the grey-haired, blazer-wearing members supping soup in the dining room below.   (Guardian)

Samson or *Samsonesque* stands for a number of things, some of them contradictory. In the Old Testament book of Judges, Samson belongs to the Nazarite sect, one of whose vows is not to cut their hair. He is represented as a fighter of superhuman strength but one betrayed by his lover, Delilah, when she discovers that the secret of his prowess lies in his long hair. She has it cut while he is sleeping so that he is captured, blinded and imprisoned by the Philistines, who mock him inside a temple devoted to their pagan god. Samson's strength has, however, been restored as his hair has grown again and, guided by the lad who escorts him during his blindness, he pulls on the pillars that support the temple, destroying himself but also killing many thousands of Philistines in the process. In the traditional view, Samson stands for the man whose muscles are no match for feminine wiles. *Samsonesque* could also be used either in connection with his long hair and its association with virility, or with his period of blind captivity. Finally, Samson's behaviour was (self-)destructive, as in the *Guardian* reference above.

PRETENTIOUSNESS INDEX *!*

SAPPHIC

connected to the Greek poet Sappho, born in the seventh century BC on the island of Lesbos in the eastern Aegean;

'lesbian':

> *Take a walk on the Sapphic side of the street in art as opposed to reality and from* The Well of Loneliness *to* Mulholland Drive, *it's a right old sob-a-thon.* (The Times)

Sappho is said to have gathered round her a group of women for the teaching of music and verse or for worship of the goddess Aphrodite. Only fragments of her love poetry survive. *Sapphic* is occasionally used as an up-market or knowing alternative to *lesbian*, and in more repressed times would have been a mildly coded way of referring to female homosexuality.

PRETENTIOUSNESS INDEX *!!* THIS IS A FAIRLY RESTRICTED TERM AND IS ARGUABLY A RATHER COY USAGE THESE DAYS.

SARTREAN

connected to the writings and theories of French philosopher and novelist Jean-Paul Sartre (1905–80);

'intellectual', 'existentialist', 'acting in good faith':

> *Hooligans come in different types. There is the baffled simpleton who destroys out of simian rage, and there is the brute who is violent because that is his nature. His is, in Sartrean terms, a consistent and indeed existential statement.* (Daily Telegraph)

Jean-Paul Sartre – chain-smoking, café-haunting, attractive to women despite his ugliness – conforms to the popular notion of the Gallic thinker. He was the best-known proponent of the philosophical doctrine known as existentialism, which emphasises both the isolation of the individual and the necessity for each person to create his or her own system of values and decide on the standards by which to act. An action proceeding from these grounds is 'authentic'. *Sartrean* may also suggest the kind of refined intellectualism that Sartre seemed to embody as well as referring to the Marxist and even Maoist positions he adopted during his long involvement with French political life.

PRETENTIOUSNESS INDEX *!*

SCOTT-LIKE

in the manner of Captain Robert Scott (1868–1912);

'stoical', 'heroic':

> *Increasingly we are allowed to witness that final wait: to experience not Scott-like heroism but the banality, pathos or sheer terror of the moment. Technological change has given us unprecedented access to the process of dying.* (Guardian)

On 17th January 1912, Scott arrived at the South Pole on his second expedition to the Antarctic. However, an expedition led by the Norwegian Roald Amundsen had reached the Pole a month earlier. Scott and his men are remembered not so much for this 'failure' as for their heroic endurance in terrible conditions and their deaths on the return trip.

PRETENTIOUSNESS INDEX **Nil**

(see also *Oates-like*)

SCROOGE-LIKE

like the character of Ebenezer Scrooge in Charles Dickens's moral fable *A Christmas Carol* (1843);

'grouchy', 'miserly':

> *In justifying a move likely to underline its Scrooge-like image, Europe's largest discount airline said it did not believe using a mobile phone charger at work was acceptable.* (Guardian)

On the night of Christmas Eve, Scrooge is visited by the ghost of his dead business partner and three spirits, the ghosts of Christmas Past,

Present and Yet to Come, who show him the error of his miserly ways. He ends the story a genial, twinkling figure, bestowing blessings and presents on all. *Scrooge-like* refers only to his skinflint, tight-fisted existence. Oddly, the expression does not seem to be as insulting as 'miserly' although that is what it means.

PRETENTIOUSNESS INDEX **Nil**

SHAKESPEAREAN

characteristic of the style, work or life of William Shakespeare (1564–1616);

1) (of his plays) 'universal', 'wide-ranging', 'profound', 'large-scale', 'comic', 'tragic', etc.:

His [Seve Ballesteros's] long fall from the ramparts of golfing domination is positively Shakespearean in its nature. (Daily Telegraph)

2) (of his style) 'flowing', 'innovative', 'unique', 'bawdy', 'elevated', etc.:

The highest judges in the land are mandated to deliver justice, not Shakespearean rhetoric. (Observer)

It is impossible to characterise Shakespeare without deploying a substantial number of epithets, many more than the ones I've listed above. Virtually any description of his plays or poetry can be contradicted or qualified by a different or opposing term. For the English-speaking world, and for large areas outside it, William Shakespeare remains the universal writer and artist, even for those who scarcely know his work or are unaware that when they say 'a sorry sight' or 'dead as a doornail' they are quoting from him. Above all, there is the idea of range: while other dramatists are known for their excellence in a particular field, Shakespeare produced surpassing work in comedy, history, tragedy, romance and hybrid versions of all of these genres. And the range is accompanied by insight and profundity, with the result that many people consider him to possess an almost unmatched grasp of human motivation. Similarly, Shakespeare's style encompasses everything from the crudest (and most feeble) jokes to poignant love lyrics to stirring rhetoric. He has always served as a benchmark for artists, and has inspired countless other works across the world in music, painting, literature, opera, ballet, film and drama, to say nothing of whole libraries of critical commentary and explication. Nearly four centuries after his death Shakespeare remains the foundation of English drama and much else. If the term *Shakespearean* is applied to his or someone else's life, then again there is a wealth of possible meanings from 'enigmatic' or 'elusive' (since much of his personal life is unknown or unexplained) through to more mundane descriptions like 'unprivileged', 'emerging from a provincial background', etc.

PRETENTIOUSNESS INDEX **Nil**

SHANDYESQUE

in the style of the novel *Tristram Shandy* by Laurence Sterne (1713–68);

'self-referential', 'rambling', 'eccentric', 'experimental':

Laurence Sterne (about whom he writes well) is one of his heroes, and he allows some whimsical Shandyesque digressions. (Spectator)

One of the oddest books in English, *Tristram Shandy* is a sort of autobiography but one that begins at the moment of the narrator's conception, before shooting off in random directions. Sterne is sometimes seen as a forefather of the 20th-century 'stream of consciousness' novel and other forms of experimental fiction. The book doesn't so much finish as stop (with the words 'cock and bull' in the last sentence), while on the way Sterne employs devices such as a blacked-out page to signal a character's death. Among other targets, he sends up the whole process of writing novels.

PRETENTIOUSNESS INDEX *!*

SHANGRI-LA-LIKE

similar to the imaginary land depicted in James Hilton's novel *Lost Horizon* (published 1933);

'paradise-like', 'utopian':

Last year there were hundreds of backpackers visible on the streets of Leh, Ladakh's colourful Shangri-La-like capital. (Guardian)

The fictional Shangri-la was a remote pass in the Himalayas, a benign Buddhist retreat from the world. The expression might once have been the height of romance and graced a thousand retirement bungalows, even if it seems slightly naff now. It is interesting that the American presidential retreat in Maryland was originally called Shangri-la by President Roosevelt in 1942 before it was renamed Camp David by President Eisenhower (after his grandson).

PRETENTIOUSNESS INDEX *!*

SHAVIAN

typical of the style or themes favoured by writer and dramatist George Bernard Shaw (1856–1950);

'unorthodox', 'witty', 'thought-provoking':

Indeed, you go on to marvel at the benign figure who bumbles around the stage, apologetically dispensing Shavian good sense and deferentially ensuring that family crisis never becomes family disaster. (The Times)

Shaw produced not only more than 50 plays but also volumes of music criticism and varieties of political writing. He enjoyed setting the cat among the pigeons, being controversial and sometimes perverse in his views whether they were directly expressed in the interminable prefaces to his plays or through the mouths of his characters. The controversy has pretty well disappeared by now but Shaw is still highly regarded for his well-constructed dramas as well as his wit and robust outlook.

PRETENTIOUSNESS INDEX **Nil**

SHELLEYAN

connected to the life, writings or beliefs of poet Percy Bysshe Shelley (1792–1822);

'rebellious', 'anti-authority', 'free-spirited':

Claire, who dragged the Shelley household halfway across Europe in her pursuit of Lord Byron, displayed a readiness to embrace the Shelleyan ideal of free love and nude bathing that was held as a perpetual rebuke to her half-sister's prudery. (Guardian)

Shelley is sometimes regarded as the archetypal romantic poet, the embodiment of the desire for self-fulfilment and of dedication to art. His life, with its unhappy affairs and wanderings, fits our image of the driven artist while his premature death – in a boat lost at sea during a storm off the Italian coast – only adds to his lustre. He's not much read now apart from a handful of poems like 'Ozymandias' but *Shelleyan* still stands for ideas of freedom from convention, particularly for those who see him as a kind of proto-hippy.

PRETENTIOUSNESS INDEX *!*

SIBYLLINE

in the style of a sibyl, a prophetess in ancient Greece or Rome;

'mysterious', 'prophetic':

His model might be Henry Kissinger, who cuts a dashing social figure in town while running a consultancy business and maintaining his image by emitting sibylline rumbles about world affairs. (Daily Telegraph)

Sibyl was the title given to a woman who could predict the future and issue warnings. The sibyls were legendary figures – the earliest of them uttered prophecies connected to the Trojan war – and books of their prophecies circulated in the Near East or, in Rome, were held secure in the Capitol temple. Like most oracles the sibyls seemed to have used mystery as a marketing tool, so *sibylline* carries the sense of 'obscurely prophetic'.

PRETENTIOUSNESS INDEX *!*

(see also *Delphic*)

SISYPHEAN

relating to the task performed by Sisyphus, mythical king of Corinth, in the underworld;

'endless and futile':

With mud and sunscreen running down my forehead and into my eyes, I hacked away at the earth for what seemed like a Sisyphean eternity.

(The Times)

In one of those imaginative punishments imposed for crimes committed on earth and beloved by Greek myth, Sisyphus was condemned to roll a large stone to the top of a hill. When he reached the top it rolled down so that the whole process had to be started again. Hence, anything *Sisyphean* is both pointless and unending as well as requiring effort.

PRETENTIOUSNESS INDEX *!*

SITWELLIAN

typical of the style or appearance of poet and writer Edith Sitwell (1887–1964), or of her brothers Osbert (1892–1969) and Sacheverell (1897–1988);

'eccentric', 'flamboyant', 'refined':

No wardrobe mistress could have fetched her up in such a magnificent display of Sitwellian grandeur – the jewelled hands with their long, pearly fingernails, the gold hoop earrings, the aureole of burnished curls rising like fine wire from her domed forehead. (Daily Telegraph)

The Sitwells grew up in Edwardian comfort and they reacted against the prevailing conventions of the poetry of the time. The best-known of the three was probably Edith, although if she is remembered now it is less on account of her writings and more for the calculated staginess of her appearance.

PRETENTIOUSNESS INDEX *!*

SMILESIAN

in the style or with the message of Samuel Smiles (1812–1904);

'relentlessly upbeat', 'self-improving':

> *She went to see the doctor at Uplyme, a nice old man, but he could give her only nice-old-man advice about outside interests and social work; this 'take up social work' is the modern equivalent of some Smilesian exhortation: rise with a smile.* (John Fowles, quoted in the Guardian)

Samuel Smiles, in some ways an archetypal Victorian, wrote the lives of other archetypal Victorians like George Stephenson, but he is chiefly known for his book *Self-help* (1859). Smiles promoted an energetic individualism and achievement through hard work (other books are titled *Thrift* and *Duty*). If Smiles is remembered at all now, it is largely in a mocking or satirical context. Contemporary therapeutic books are just as optimistic and aspirational, but they tend to be vapid rather than rigorous.

PRETENTIOUSNESS INDEX *!*

SOCRATIC

connected to the methods or beliefs of the Athenian philosopher Socrates (469–399 BC);

'going against conventional beliefs', 'seeking to establish truth through questioning':

> *But who could have guessed that the final confrontation between the last surviving Timelord and the only remaining Dalek would turn into a sci-fi Socratic dialogue?* (Guardian)

Socrates never wrote a word himself and his reputation and teachings have come down to us principally through his follower Plato. *Socratic* is identified not so much with the philosopher's own beliefs, which are hard to establish, as with the sceptical, questioning attitude by which he took on conventional thinking in the attempt to discover the nature of good. Socrates, according to Plato, was a master of cross-examination, exposing those who believed in their own wisdom. *Socratic* may also refer to the philosopher's famous execution by poison – he drank hemlock after being accused of 'corrupting' the young – and the term could carry implications of martyrdom and self-sacrifice in the disinterested pursuit of the truth.

PRETENTIOUSNESS INDEX **Nil**

(see also *Platonic*)

SOLOMON-LIKE

like Solomon (c.970–c.930 BC), the king of the Israelites;

'impartial', 'just', 'wise':

> *These were among the many delicate questions on which the duke, a figure of Solomon-like wisdom, was required to adjudicate.* (Daily Telegraph)

King Solomon's reputation for wisdom seems to be built on the famous story, found in the Old Testament book of Kings, in which two women living in the same house had both borne children, one of which died. They appeared before him, each claiming to be the mother of the surviving baby. Solomon ordered a sword to be produced so that the baby might be divided. One cried out that the child should be spared and given to the other mother, while the second agreed to the killing. Solomon awarded the baby to the first mother.

PRETENTIOUSNESS INDEX **Nil**

SOVIET-STYLE

of or relating to the former USSR (Union of Soviet Socialist Republics);

'authoritarian', 'oppressive', 'excessively bureaucratic', 'centralised', 'dreary':

> *The cheerful thing about all this prodigal plenty is that nobody need go around in rags or stand in dreary Soviet-style queues for every pair of ill-fitting knickers.* (The Times)

It is interesting to note that *Soviet-style* tends to refer less to the authoritarian Communist governments of the former USSR or their brutal methods of treating dissent (for that sense, *Stalinist* is frequently used) than to the uniformity and dreariness of life in that country. The monolithic buildings, the food shortages, the ever-present queues to buy dull products – all of this may be conjured up by *Soviet-style*. The word is also employed as a term of abuse against any system that is regarded as very bureaucratic and where control is kept tightly in the hands of a few people at the top.

PRETENTIOUSNESS INDEX **Nil**

SPARTAN

typical of the ancient Greek city of Sparta;

'tough', 'unadorned', 'plain':

> *Downstairs, it was a quiet, old-fashioned, elegant place; upstairs, where the bathrooms and showers were shared, it turned out to be rather more spartan.* (Jonathan Coe, *The Closed Circle*)

Sparta, the capital of the state of Laconia, attached more significance to military matters than the other Greek city-states and had a reputation for efficient action and no-frills speech (*laconic* comes from *Laconia*). In current use *spartan* is generally applied to physical conditions, indicating a lack of comfort, and far from being a compliment to austerity and simple living there may be an implicit criticism in the term.

PRETENTIOUSNESS INDEX **Nil**

SPARTIST

like the fictional columnist Dave Spart in the satirical magazine *Private Eye*;

'rantingly left-wing', 'expressing formulaic left-wing attitudes':

> *Or, as the* Weekly Worker *put the question in more typically Spartist form: 'Is it possible for working-class politicians to utilise an establishment cultural form, designed for a completely different purpose, in order to bolster an oppositional message?'* (The Times)

Dave Spart is one of several satirical and imaginary figures who have strayed outside the pages of *Private Eye* and become comic archetypes (others are the legendary journalist Lunchtime O'Booze and female columnists Glenda Slagg and Polly Filler). Known for his dreary rants, Spart satirises the knee-jerk reaction that blames the bosses/police/government for everything. The 'columns' are cut off after a few lines, usually with the tag 'continued on page 94'. Spart's heyday was the 1970s and 1980s, but the reference still raises a smile for those in the know.

PRETENTIOUSNESS INDEX **!**

SPHINX-LIKE

in the manner of the Sphinx, a mythological creature with the body of a lion and the head of a woman;

'riddling', 'enigmatic':

Almost invariably, any direct inquiry will be met with a sphinx-like response, as enigmatic as it is evasive. For example: 'Let's just say we got a good deal', or 'Pretty close to our asking price, actually'. (Daily Telegraph)

The Sphinx was a hybrid creature that lived outside the city of Thebes in eastern Greece. In the manner of mythological monsters, it stopped travellers to the city and asked them a riddle. Those who could not give the correct answer were strangled (*sphinx* means 'strangler'). The riddle was 'What animal walks on four legs at dawn, two legs at noon, and three by evening?' The answer to the riddle was man, who crawls as a baby, walks on two legs for most of his life but who needs the support of a stick in old age. Oedipus was the first to answer correctly and, in response, the Sphinx killed itself, while Oedipus was invited to become king of Thebes – where his troubles were only just beginning (see *Oedipal*). *Sphinx-like* has therefore come to mean 'riddling' or, in facial expressions, 'impassive'. This second sense is reinforced by the stony, unreadable look on the face of the statue of the Sphinx that sits near the great pyramids in Giza on the edge of Cairo.

PRETENTIOUSNESS INDEX **Nil**

SPIELBERGIAN

characteristic of the style or themes favoured by US film director Steven Spielberg (1947–);

'calculating', 'sentimental', 'upbeat', 'visually dazzling':

Though publicised as the truth about the brutality of battle, the movie [Saving Private Ryan] – after the half-hour bloodbath at its start – concentrates on a sentimental and unrepresentative episode which achieves the inevitable Spielbergian happy ending. (Guardian)

It's a measure of the ambivalent attitude of some people – all right, then, of some critics – towards Steven Spielberg's unparalleled cinematic success that his name and the term *Spielbergian* should stand for things that are both positive and negative. Generally, references seem slightly pejorative, focusing on the director's calculating approach to an audience and his sentimentality, especially in relation to childhood, as well as his taste for happy endings. But Spielberg is hardly unique in Hollywood in any of these. The more positive references stress his love of spectacle, his ability to suggest child-like wonder on screen, etc.

<small>PRETENTIOUSNESS INDEX **!**</small>

SPOCKISH

in the style of US paediatrician Dr Benjamin Spock (1903–98);

'child-centred', 'gentle', 'liberal':

> *It may also be a sign that Blair, an expert on wayward adolescents and infant innocents alike, has a Dr Spockish urge to treat the nation's children as his own.* (Guardian)

Dr Spock's *The Common Sense Book of Baby and Child Care* was first published in America in 1946. During the next half-century it sold more than 50 million copies and was credited with bringing about a revolution in the way parents treated their young children. Telling mothers that they should trust their instincts because 'you know more than you think you do', Spock encouraged a greater responsiveness to a child's needs. For example, parents ought to pick up crying babies and generally show affection rather than trying to instil independence by ignoring them, which had been the advice of previous experts. Spock was sometimes seen – and blamed – as a trailblazer of the permissive society of the 1960s when his babies came of age, since that generation had grown up apparently accustomed to instant gratification and impatient with any restraints. And, indeed, in his old age Dr Spock became an increasingly liberal figure by US standards, campaigning against the Vietnam war and in favour of abortion rights, the legalisation of marijuana, etc.

<small>PRETENTIOUSNESS INDEX **!**</small>

SPOCK-LIKE

in the style of Mr Spock, iconic alien in the television and film series *Star Trek*;

'unemotional', 'logical':

> *Tim Allen is their leader, Alan Rickman is the English thesp who sacrificed his stage career by playing a Spock-like alien, Sigourney Weaver the female interest.* (Guardian)

Mr Spock – half Vulcan, half human, and all played by Leonard Nimoy – shouldn't be confused with Dr Benjamin Spock (see previous entry), though he sometimes is. Gene Roddenberry, creator of *Star Trek*, always denied any connection, saying that he was simply searching for an alien-sounding name when he lighted on Mr Spock. But the benevolent influence of Dr Spock, the real-life paediatrician, on child development is perhaps not so far removed from Mr Spock's attitude towards his fellow crew members on the Starship Enterprise. Science fiction aliens tend to fall under three headings, the cute, the nasty and the wise, and there is little doubt that Spock fits into the latter category. *Spock-like* tends to refer to an alien's superior logic and wisdom unless, of course, it is merely an allusion to those pointy ears.

PRETENTIOUSNESS INDEX **Nil**

STAKHANOVITE

following the pattern set by Soviet miner Aleksei Stakhanov in the mid-1930s;

'dedicated to work', 'fiercely industrious':

From now on, those Stakhanovite types who turn up to all their shifts for six months will be entered in a draw to win a new Ford Focus. (Daily Telegraph)

In the rapidly industrialising USSR of the 1930s, Aleksei Stakhanov supposedly mined more than a hundred tons of coal in less than six hours, exceeding his quota many times over. The Soviet Communist Party established a *Stakhanovite* movement and encouraged its spread to other industries so as to increase production. Stakhanov's actual achievements were highly questionable – he received unacknowledged help and the statistics were exaggerated or fiddled – but he was a useful propaganda tool, part of the process of transforming the Soviet worker into a heroic, idealised figure. *Stakhanovite*, not such an obscure reference as one might think, can be applied to any person who keeps up an unremitting work-rate, not just in manual labour.

PRETENTIOUSNESS INDEX **!**

STALINIST

reminiscent of the style, policies or personality of Soviet leader Joseph Stalin (1879–1953);

1) (of politics) 'not tolerating opposition', 'dictatorial', 'brutal', 'ruthless':

In the name of 'efficiency' [...] the Department of Education and Science,
as it was then called, embarked on a purge of Stalinist ferocity.

(Guardian)

2) (of buildings, etc.) 'utilitarian', 'plain to the point of ugliness':

They strode quickly through Senate House Passage and across the river to
the looming Stalinist facade of Cambridge University Library.

(David Wolstencroft, *Good News, Bad News*)

Stalin, born Iosif Vissarionovich Dzhugashvili, adopted his new
surname from the Russian word for 'steel' some years before the
Communists came to power in the 1917 revolution. Assuming
absolute power after the death of Lenin, Stalin became increasingly
ruthless in his rule and was responsible for the deaths of millions
during the forced collectivisation of land and the mass purges of his
supposed enemies. *Stalinist* therefore connotes an absolutist style of
rule, which stamps on opposition, which may employ terror as a
method of internal control and which has a strongly centralising tendency. Rather like *Soviet-style* (see entry), the term may also be used to
characterise anything that seems to the user to combine bureaucracy
with a brutal rigour, and this can extend even to public architecture,
organised demonstrations, etc. It's hardly necessary to say that use of
the term is rarely justified.

PRETENTIOUSNESS INDEX **Nil**

STEINBECKIAN

typical of the style or themes favoured by US novelist John
Steinbeck (1902–68);

'realistic', 'poignant', 'concerned with the lives of ordinary people':

The outward appearance of his life seems pretty simple: standing on a
corner, pointing people in the direction of an English school. Underneath it
all, however, lurks the stuff of Steinbeckian pathos, transported from the
prewar dust bowl to the newly expanded EU.   (Guardian)

Steinbeck turned himself into the chronicler of the lives of the poor
and dispossessed in the American West, most famously in *Of Mice and*
Men (1937) and *The Grapes of Wrath* (1939). *Steinbeckian* tends to suggest sympathy for the underdog, although there may be a trace of
sentimentality in the response.

PRETENTIOUSNESS INDEX *!*

STEPFORDIAN

in the manner of one of the title characters in the book and film *The Stepford Wives*;

'submissively feminine', 'unthinking', 'robotic':

> *So, why am I currently enjoying [daytime TV] so much? What can that possibly mean? I've just turned 36 – is there something that happens that my mother neglected to tell me? Does one undergo a sort of Stepfordian lobotomy, perhaps?* (Observer)

Originally a novel by Ira Levin (author of *Rosemary's Baby*) and then a film (1974, remade 2004), *The Stepford Wives* has perhaps achieved more success as a phrase or an idea than it ever did on page or screen. The reason the wives in the beautiful Connecticut town of Stepford behave like programmed dummies is that they are programmed dummies – or robots. Whether this was an early 1970s male fantasy or a feminist satire on male fantasy, or both at once, was never entirely clear. But *Stepfordian* can describe a mindless feminine conformity to what males want, or just mindlessness.

PRETENTIOUSNESS INDEX *!*

STOIC

connected to the philosophy originally propounded by the Stoics of ancient Greece;

'uncomplaining', 'detached', 'making oneself indifferent to pain or suffering':

> *So it is that we arrive at a particularly important question. How much do his stoic, frozen, hard-working board guys get paid?* (Guardian)

The Stoics derive their name from the 'porch' (*stoa*) in Athens marketplace where Zeno, their founder, used to deliver his lectures. They preached, among other things, the universal brotherhood of man. But *stoic(al)* now simply refers to that part of their philosophy which claimed that, by self-control, a person could reduce his or her dependence on or vulnerability to the outside world. It's the cultivation of a stiff upper lip.

PRETENTIOUSNESS INDEX **Nil**

STOPPARDIAN

typical of the style or themes favoured by Czech-born playwright Tom Stoppard (1937–);

'intellectual', 'witty', 'games-playing':

> *As Stoppard himself has cheerfully admitted, he is not much interested in writing about people. No, it is ideas that fire Tom's foolery – that exquisite blend of seriousness and custard pies that is as uniquely Stoppardian as the menacing pause is Pinteresque.* (Guardian)

Stoppard achieved international success with *Rosencrantz and Guildenstern are Dead* (1966), a witty combination of *Hamlet* and *Waiting for Godot*, which focused on two minor figures in Shakespeare's drama who didn't have a clue what they were doing. The play contains several of the features now seen as quintessentially *Stoppardian*: a love of puns and other verbal jokes, elements of slapstick, lightly garnished philosophical discussion and an awareness of the great figures of history and literature always at your shoulder. Stoppard's other plays include *Jumpers* (1972), combining philosophy and acrobatics, *Travesties* (1975), which brings together Lenin and James Joyce in wartime Zurich, and *Arcadia* (1993), a time-hopping drama set in a country house. *Stoppardian* is almost always a term of approval though it sometimes suggests an excessive liking for ideas, the 'head' at the expense of the 'heart' (see quote above).

PRETENTIOUSNESS INDEX *!*

STYGIAN

like the river Styx in the classical underworld;

'dark', 'hellish':

> *There's a certain frisson to wading underneath the city's main sights, and the dark, dank passages have an authentically Stygian feel.* (Independent)

The Styx was one of the rivers that marked the boundary between the upper world and Hades in Greek mythology. An oath taken by its waters was supposed to be especially binding. Darkness is routinely described as *Stygian* but there should be a sinister aspect to the context.

PRETENTIOUSNESS INDEX **Nil**

SVENGALI-LIKE

in the style of Svengali, a character in the novel *Trilby* (1894) by George du Maurier (1834–96);

'dangerously manipulative', 'mesmerising':

> *It has taken 18 months and £2.5m to investigate, prosecute, and defend. But the Svengali-like character who charmed women, spinning wild yarns about his bogus MI5 career while extracting hundreds of thousands of pounds from their bank accounts, has finally been brought to book.*   (Guardian)

Trilby, now a largely forgotten novel, was an enormous best-seller in its day. Its success was at least partly attributable to the sinister character of Svengali, a musician and mesmerist, who turns Trilby, an artist's model, into a great singer before marrying her. When he dies, her talent fades and she dies too. *Svengali-like* is always used in a negative sense, describing the way in which a man sets out to tutor and control another person, usually young and female, through manipulation and mind-games.

PRETENTIOUSNESS INDEX **Nil**

SVEN-LIKE

typical of the style of Swedish-born football manager Sven-Goran Eriksson (1948–);

'understated', 'enigmatic', 'imperturbable', 'ordinary-seeming':

> *'At the moment, the South Koreans kick everyone's butt,' says Young, with a Sven-like acceptance that there's a lot of work to be done before our boys and girls can compete at the very top level – in robot football, at least.*   (Guardian)

Sven-Goran Eriksson was the first foreign manager of the English national team and, predictably, his appointment in 2001 drew flak from the standard press quarters. Early success when England beat Germany stilled most of the criticism and Eriksson became a figure of some curiosity, even intrigue. His affairs became the stuff of the tabloids with the implicit question as to how such an ordinary-looking man – bland, spectacle-wearing, soft-spoken – could attract the likes of fellow Swede Ulrika Jonsson and other attractive women. Perhaps Sven's wealth and status have something to do with it. But Eriksson possesses his own magnetism. He generally exudes an air of meditative calm and his careful use of English gives weight to his utterances. There may also be an echo of *Zen-like* in *Sven-like*, which is not inappropriate.

PRETENTIOUSNESS INDEX **Nil**

SWIFTIAN

typical of the work or attitudes of clergyman and writer Jonathan Swift (1667–1745);

'satirical', 'misanthropic':

Endowed by nature with more than their fair share of ugliness, and completely lacking in dignity or self-respect, let alone respect for others, they contrive to arouse a Swiftian disgust in any impartial observer.

(Daily Telegraph)

Swift wrote a great deal, from poetry to political pamphlets, but he is largely remembered for the classic *Gulliver's Travels* (1726), a parody of the travellers' tales then growing in popularity with the public. The hapless Lemuel Gulliver is shipwrecked and cast up on one strange land after another, from Lilliput to Brobdingnag to the flying-saucer-like Laputa. Swift's satire develops from the mockery of political parties in Lilliput to something more like wholesale condemnation of the human race in the final part: in the land of the Houyhnhnms, which is ruled by rational, talking horses, humanity is depicted as the filthy and ape-like Yahoo. Gulliver is at first reluctant to recognise his similarity with these Yahoos and when he eventually returns home he prefers the company of his horses to his fellow humans. It is debatable whether this is Swift's final joke or whether it reflects a genuine disgust with humankind on the author's part – probably a bit of both. Jonathan Swift can still bite: his pamphlet 'A Modest Proposal' (1729) suggests that the children of the poor should be fattened up and fed to the rich, whether 'stewed, roasted, baked or boiled'. It's an ironic joke, isn't it? So *Swiftian* usually characterises an extreme and savage form of satire or outlook.

PRETENTIOUSNESS INDEX *!*

(see also *Lilliputian* and *Brobdingnagian*)

T

TARANTINO-ESQUE

in the style of film director and screenwriter Quentin Tarantino (1963–);

'exuberant and violent', 'eloquent and flip':

> *The rest of the movie is brimful of audience-pleasing gangsters, hit men and hoodlums, plus a wealth of knowing crime-flick nods, all of which contribute to a viewing experience which can best be described as Tarantino-esque.* (The Times)

It's hard to summarise the essence of Quentin Tarantino, the director of *Reservoir Dogs* (1993), *Pulp Fiction* (1995) and *Kill Bill* (2004), who famously began his working life as a clerk in a video store. His films – witty but flip; ultra-violent and excusing it all with the veneer of comedy; very much of the moment although aware of film history – are highly influential. *Tarantino-esque* perhaps best describes his imitators rather than anything he does himself.

Pretentiousness Index *!*

TARDIS-LIKE

similar to the time machine/spaceship in the TV programme *Doctor Who*;

'deceptively small', 'bigger than it looks on the outside':

> *My house has Tardis-like qualities. From the outside, it is in a perfectly ordinary London terrace; inside it is a farmhouse with Hunter wellies piled in the hallway and vestiges of hay strewn everywhere.* (Daily Telegraph)

Budgetary constraints allegedly led the BBC designers to plump for a police phone box when searching for a machine to whisk Doctor Who and his assistants through time and space when the series was conceived in the early 1960s – if this is so, shortage of money prompted a brilliant choice. At once familiar (because a one-time fixture of urban streets) and unfamiliar (because their interior remained a mystery to the civilian public), the Tardis captured viewers' imaginations and affections in a way only equalled by the Daleks. The result is that Tardis – an acronym for 'Time And Relative Dimensions In Space' – can now be used as a half-humorous benchmark for anything that is larger on the inside than it looks from the exterior.

PRETENTIOUSNESS INDEX **Nil**

TATI-LIKE

in the style of the films starring Jacques Tati (1908–82);

'slapstick', 'accident-prone':

> *At this point it is necessary to imagine yourself wandering Jacques Tati-like (or Mr Bean for younger readers) from basin to basin, looking for signs of a knob or a hidden foot switch or a helpful diagram, your hands cupped full of soap, thrusting them tentatively under this tap and that, puzzled that everyone else's tap is gushing away while yours isn't ...* (Observer)

Jacques Tati developed the character of Monsieur Hulot across several films in the 1950s and 1960s as a figure at odds with the modern world and its appliances. The humour was visual, mostly silent and carefully planned – a sort of rueful slapstick.

PRETENTIOUSNESS INDEX *!*

TEBBIT

typical of the style or approach of Conservative politician Norman Tebbit (1931–) or describing his political beliefs or his followers;

'forthright', 'confrontational', 'assertively right-wing', 'unashamedly patriotic':

> *And despite its producers' insistence that members are carefully chosen to represent a cross-section of Britain today, the audience often seems selected for their value as agents provocateurs – religious extremists, Tebbit Tories, loony lefties.* (Observer)

There are many individuals, and not all of them on the left or centre of politics, for whom Norman Tebbit is something of a bogey-man – and one senses that this exactly as he likes it. Throughout a long career Tebbit has specialised in speaking his mind and, without going out of his way to offend, he has nevertheless been unconcerned when people have duly taken offence. He has neither hidden nor capitalised on his working-class background, even if he did famously say of his own father, unemployed during the 1930s, that 'he got on his bike and looked for work, and he went on looking until he found it.' As MP for the Essex constituency of Chingford, Tebbit was a staunch ally of Margaret Thatcher and, though never holding any of the most senior Cabinet positions, he had an influence not usually associated with the posts he did occupy, such as Secretary for Trade and Industry. Tebbit could, and still can, be relied on for quotes that are anti-BBC, the 1960s ('that third-rate decade'), the European Union, large-scale immigration, and so on. If Tebbit can dish it out, he is also required to take it, as is suggested by descriptions of him such as 'Chingford skinhead' or 'semi-house-trained polecat'.

PRETENTIOUSNESS INDEX **Nil**

TENNYSONIAN

relating to the style or subject matter of poet Alfred Tennyson (1809–92);

'musical', 'elegiac', 'lush':

Shallots have everything going for them. The name is soft and specific, cushioned by the romantic association of a Tennysonian 'lady of'. (Observer)

Tennyson was the most celebrated poet of the Victorian era. He became Poet Laureate in 1850 and in what is probably his best-known poem, 'The Charge of the Light Brigade', he celebrated imperial grit and guts. However, Tennyson's output is really more notable for its softer and more melancholic strain. Whether in a long poem like *In Memoriam*, written as an elegy to a dead friend, or in the Arthurian lyric 'The Lady of Shalott' (the reference in the *Observer* quote above), Tennyson expresses a sense of yearning or regret, embodied in flowing verse.

PRETENTIOUSNESS INDEX *!*

TERMINATOR-LIKE

in the style of the character played by Arnold Schwarzenegger in the three *Terminator* films;

'violently efficient', 'robotic and indestructible', 'remorseless':

So, when leaves get so pock-marked that they start to resemble Swiss cheese, and flower buds become home to colonies of insects, we tend to over-react – out come the spray canisters, weed pencils and watering cans full of noxious milky fluids as we stride, Terminator-like, through the garden. (Guardian)

The Terminator is not exclusively a figure of destruction, it only seems that way. In the first film, titled simply *The Terminator* (1984), Arnie plays a straightforward killing machine, relentless in his pursuit of targets. In the second, *Terminator 2: Judgement Day* (1991), Schwarzenegger the cyborg develops human feelings, perhaps not unrelated to the fact that at the time Schwarzenegger the actor was trying to broaden his range. In the third and least successful of the films, *Terminator 3: Rise of the Machines* (2003), he makes rueful references to obsolescence. But, however many humanising touches there may be, *Terminator-like* still conjures up images of gleeful, high-tech mayhem.

PRETENTIOUSNESS INDEX **Nil**

TEUTONIC

connected to the ancient Germanic tribe of Teutons in Jutland;

'Germanic', 'ordered', 'disciplined':

The mainstream media then were so in awe of the White House's vindictiveness and Teutonic discipline that few dared step out of line. (Observer)

Although *Teutonic* may appear in a neutral context, simply describing one of the origins of the Germanic and Scandinavian peoples, it tends to crop up in more pejorative senses. Some of the attributes traditionally associated with Germany – order, discipline, seriousness – are embodied in the word. And, in fact, *Teutonic* can appear as an alternative to Nazi where that term would either be unhistorical or offensive. (The *Observer* quote above refers to the White House during the time of Richard Nixon, two of whose key advisors were Bob Haldeman and John Erlichman. Their fiercely protective attitude towards the President and *Teutonic*-sounding names led to their being called the Berlin Wall.)

PRETENTIOUSNESS INDEX **Nil**

THATCHERITE

typical of the style or political ideas espoused by Margaret Thatcher (1925–), British politician and Prime Minister (1979–90);

'radical', 'no-nonsense', 'strident':

An Iberian Thatcherite, Jose Manuel Barroso, has taken charge of the Commission, promising a war on red tape and market barriers, and awarding the top economic slots to free-market champions. (Daily Telegraph)

Where to start? Love her or loathe her – and there seemed and seems to be no middle way – Margaret Thatcher was one of the most influential politicians of the 20th century. Some of her policies are hinted at in the *Telegraph* quote above: she was anti-bureaucratic, anti-protectionist, fervently pro-free-market. She was also credited with a large role in the downfall of Communism and, almost single-handed, with the restoration of Britain's place in the world. From a critical standpoint she tends to be regarded as abrasive, divisive and (as far as her long-term influence on the Conservative Party was concerned) ruinous. The term *Thatcherite* is truly a mirror in which each person sees more or less what they want to see.

PRETENTIOUSNESS INDEX **Nil**

THESPIAN

connected to Thespis, the legendary Greek poet in the sixth century BC who is supposed to have been the first to introduce actors to the stage;

(as noun) 'self-aware actor'; (as adjective) 'stagy':

> *At the whimsical end of the spectrum a sensitive Canadian thesp has spiritual intercourse with his Canadian landlady.* (The Times)

Whether *thespian* (with or without a capital *T*) was ever used entirely seriously, it is now employed only in self-mockery or to poke fun at others. A *thesp* – the abbreviation says it all – is a luvvie who probably hasn't made it far beyond the level of am-dram, while the adjectival application of *thespian* is more derisive than descriptive. As far as I know, the term 'actorish' does not exist but if it did it would define *thespian* neatly.

PRETENTIOUSNESS INDEX **!!**

THOREAUESQUE

typical of the life or work of US writer Henry David Thoreau (1817–62);

'reclusive', 'individualist', 'visionary', 'ecological', 'environmentally aware':

> *Thus what outsiders call 'extreme sports' and regard as a symptom of peculiarly modern thrill-seeking are more like an updated version of Thoreauesque self-reliance.* (Guardian)

Thoreau was one of the group of transcendentalist writers and thinkers who came to prominence in early 19th-century New England. His best-known work is *Walden* (1854), an account of a two-year period that the author spent by himself in a self-built cabin in the woods outside his birthplace, the town of Concord, Massachusetts. The book is a mixture of practical observation – he includes a list of the cost of the materials of his house – and a near-mystical appreciation of nature. Thoreau preached self-reliance and is seen as an early advocate of the ties that link human beings to the natural world. As well as keeping voluminous journals, Thoreau also wrote the tract 'On the Duty of Civil Disobedience', which influenced later campaigners for civil rights.

PRETENTIOUSNESS INDEX *!*

THURBERESQUE

recalling the style or subject matter of US cartoonist and humorous writer James Thurber (1894–1961);

'wry', 'wistful', 'quirky':

> ... *there is no reason to suppose they [gay couples] will not, in due course, observe all the other traditions associated with modern marriage, from the early snoring/map-reading disputes to less Thurberesque money resentments, wrangling over cleaning and cooking, and the never-to-be-resolved question of whose work-life imbalance is causing the greater degree of martyrdom.*

(Guardian)

James Thurber produced essays, stories and cartoons for the *New Yorker* magazine. His work often combines elements of fantasy with a wry treatment of relations between men and women, particularly in marriage. *Thurberesque* (also *Thurberish*) may refer to this or to the hapless look of the characters in his economical line drawings.

PRETENTIOUSNESS INDEX *!*

(see also *Walter Mittyish*)

TIGGERISH

like the character of Tigger in the children's book *The House at Pooh Corner* (1928) by A.A. Milne (1882–1956);

'confident', 'bouncy':

> *His great gift was his contagious enthusiasm. He could seem Tiggerish, but his students came to know a sharp intellect ...* (The Times)

A.A. Milne remains famous for his Winnie-the-Pooh books and Tigger is one of his best-loved creations. Tigger is a resilient, optimistic animal, with his saying that 'Bouncing is what Tiggers do best', so *Tiggerish* suggests an endearing enthusiasm.

PRETENTIOUSNESS INDEX **Nil**

(see also *Eeyorish*)

TOLKIENESQUE

connected to the writings of J(ohn) R(onald) R(euel) Tolkien (1892–1973), and particularly to *The Lord of the Rings*;

'epic', 'magical', 'creating a fictional world':

> *Across the road, the Crystal Quest is a spooky cave trail past Tolkienesque fantasy figures – fire-breathing dragons, evil sorcerers, goblins and strobe lights.* (Independent)

J.R.R. Tolkien's creation of Middle Earth grew out of his love for the early languages of northern Europe such as old Norse. (The term Middle Earth is a direct translation of the Anglo-Saxon *middan-geard*, the 'middle dwelling' between heaven and hell.) And out of this passion for ancient tribes and cultures grew the world of hobbits, ents, orcs and all the rest. *The Hobbit* appeared in 1937 and the trilogy *The Lord of the Rings* between 1954 and 1955, but it was another decade or so before Tolkien became internationally famous. It is no coincidence that it was the hippy period of the late 1960s that embraced Tolkien's vision and that the magical, hallucinatory and dangerous pilgrimage that is the subject of *The Lord of the Rings* became blurred with psychedelic trips. The global reach of the books was reinforced by the extraordinary success of Peter Jackson's films of the trilogy, released between 2001 and 2003, which not only encouraged a whole new readership but devotedly reproduced the minutiae of Tolkien's fictional worlds.

PRETENTIOUSNESS INDEX *!*

TOLSTOYAN

relating to the work or life of Russian writer Count Leo Nikolayevich Tolstoy (1828–1910);

'epic', 'panoramic', 'unorthodox', 'idealistic':

> *The founders included a bank manager, a philosopher, an auctioneer and a governess, and their intention was to build a Tolstoyan community free from restraint and injustice, where everyone would share work, love and comradeship.* (Daily Telegraph)

Tolstoy was the most influential of the 19th-century Russian novelists, and his writing and beliefs had a profound effect on his contemporaries as well as on later political leaders such as Mahatma Gandhi. If *Tolstoyan* is used in a literary context it tends to suggest something epic, since Tolstoy's novels, in particular *War and Peace*, are unequalled in their range of characters and historical sweep. But Tolstoy's thinking also led him to adopt a pacifist outlook and to reject organised government and institutional religion, so *Tolstoyan* could also allude to this idealistic, anarchist side of his beliefs.

PRETENTIOUSNESS INDEX *!*

TRANSYLVANIAN

connected to the region of Transylvania in Romania;

'sinister', 'vampire-like':

> *On stage one towering performance dominates. John Tomlinson's Claggart is a Hammer horror creation: an immense, baleful voice matched by the sort of make-up they favour in Transylvanian coffins.* (The Times)

Transylvania is not a figment of *Dracula*-author Bram Stoker's imagination but a remote, mountainous area of central Romania. Stoker fixed on it – 'one of the wildest and least known portions of Europe' – as the site of Dracula's castle, and *Transylvanian* has been synonymous with 'vampire' ever since.

PRETENTIOUSNESS INDEX **Nil**

TROLLOPIAN

typical of the style or themes favoured by Victorian novelist Anthony Trollope (1815–82);

'industrious', 'highly productive', 'connected to the church or politics':

> *He was much involved with the cathedral and the close: he raised money for the spire and enjoyed the Trollopian gossip.* (Observer)

Trollope was famously disciplined as an author. With a full-time job at the Post Office (where he is credited with the introduction of the pillar box), he wrote a specified number of words each morning before going off to work. As soon as he had finished writing one book he would begin another. So *Trollopian* (also *Trollopean*) may indicate a ferocious work-rate, but the term is more likely to refer to one of his two great sequences of novels. The Barsetshire series is centred on the cathedral town of Barchester and the surrounding country, while the Palliser series focuses more on politics and high society. Trollope's interest was not in issues but in character. Any person who takes pleasure in the intricate worlds of politics or the church, and regards the men and women engaged in them with affection and amusement, could be described as having a *Trollopian* attitude.

PRETENTIOUSNESS INDEX *!*

TURNERESQUE

connected to the style or subject matter of artist Joseph Mallord William Turner (1775–1851);

'dramatically coloured', 'swirling', 'impressionistic':

> A *Turneresque* sunset is being mixed. Gunsmoke clouds mass over Mull and march westwards, where they burst into flames.   (Daily Telegraph)

It is interesting that nature has to borrow from art when it comes to describing a certain kind of sunset: one that is multi-hued and highly dramatic. Turner's pictures are characterised by their fluid use of strong colours like reds and yellows, and a composition in which natural and man-made objects seem to blend with or dissolve into the air. *Turneresque* might be applied to any painter following in his footsteps, or it might be used to describe nature's attempt to imitate art, as in the *Telegraph* quote.

PRETENTIOUSNESS INDEX *!*

U, V

UNCLE TOM-LIKE

similar to the title character in *Uncle Tom's Cabin* (1852) by US author Harriet Beecher Stowe;

'co-operative', 'disloyal':

> *It wasn't long before he [Steven Spielberg] was talking down* Jaws *to anyone who would listen, in an Uncle Tom-like ingestion of the standard critical line on the film.* (Tom Shone, *Blockbuster*)

Although the Beecher Stowe novel helped in the campaign to end slavery in America, its principal legacy as far as language is concerned is the pejorative use of the term *Uncle Tom* or *Uncle Tom-like* to describe a black person who is too accommodating to white people and who therefore shows disloyalty to his own race. The expression is a sensitive one, not to say downright insulting, but it can be used to describe a person who turns on something which, by instinct, he ought to be defending.

PRETENTIOUSNESS INDEX *!*

UTOPIAN

from *Utopia*, literally 'no-place' and originally the title of a book by Sir Thomas More (1478–1535);

1) 'perfect', 'idealised':

> *It is socialist, but libertarian socialism of a utopian kind which sits more easily with his long commitment to freedoms of expression and lifestyle than with his abiding respect for trade-union restrictive practices and closed shops.* (Guardian)

2) 'hopelessly unrealistic':

> *Conservatives will always – and rightly – favour realism over utopian dreaming.* (Daily Telegraph)

Utopia (1516) is a political essay presented in the guise of a traveller's tale. In Thomas More's imaginary country a kind of communism prevails and there is complete freedom of religion and so on. The application of *utopian* depends almost entirely on the user's political and cultural slant. For those on the left, the notion represents a high ideal towards which governments and societies can aspire even though they will probably never reach it. For those on the right, *utopian* is a handy way of dismissing ideas that are absurd because they are impractical, unrealistic, take no account of the realities of human nature, etc. Overall, the term is more often used dismissively than positively.

PRETENTIOUSNESS INDEX **Nil**

VICTORIAN

characteristic of Queen Victoria (1819–1901) or of the period of her reign (1837–1901);

'imperial', 'confident and expansive', 'repressed', 'old-fashioned', 'respectable', 'industrious':

Claiming that European hours would wreck the economy is no more enlightened than Victorian industrialists predicting ruin if factories lost their child labour. (Observer)

The days when the term *Victorian* was equated with a severe, unenlightened attitude to everything from sexuality to child labour are mostly gone (though traces of this remain, as shown by the *Observer* quote). Now the *Victorian* era is more likely to be celebrated, or at least commended, as a period of growing prosperity and national confidence and achievement.

PRETENTIOUSNESS INDEX **Nil**

VOLTAIREAN

connected to the life, work or sayings of the French writer Voltaire, pseudonym of François-Marie Arouet (1694–1778);

'satirical', 'rational', 'sceptical':

His defence is not only the old Voltairean one about fighting for the right of others to hold views even when they are violently opposed to your own.
(Observer)

In speaking out against religious superstition and obscurantism, Voltaire became a byword for radicalism in pre-Revolutionary France and, for his pains, was variously imprisoned and exiled (to England). His best-known work is *Candide* (see *Candide-like*), the tale of an innocent let loose in the world. But Voltaire is as celebrated for his waspish wit – 'If God did not exist, it would be necessary to invent him', he wrote – and his support of tolerance. The reference in the *Observer* quote is to one of his most famous sayings, 'I disapprove of what you say, but I will defend to the death your right to say it', and even though he may not have uttered those precise words they are a fair reflection of his outlook.

PRETENTIOUSNESS INDEX *!*

W, Y, Z

WAGNERIAN

relating to the musical style or beliefs of composer and dramatist Richard Wagner (1813–83);

'large-scale', 'titanic', 'controversial', 'using myth and legend', 'mystic', 'Germanic or Teutonic':

> *The bonking sessions, on the other hand, are almost Wagnerian in their portentousness and will shortly be leaving this desk for the welcoming embrace of the* Literary Review *Bad Sex award.* (Spectator)

Wagnerian is a loaded adjective and is quite often found in a negative or mocking context, as in the *Spectator* quote. It may be that the English have never been quite sure what to do with Wagner – Oscar Wilde was making jokes about him more than a hundred years ago – and *Wagnerian* is sometimes equated with a heavy-handed, quintessentially Germanic attitude to art and life. But, positively applied, *Wagnerian* suggests music or drama conceived on the largest and most passionate scale.

PRETENTIOUSNESS INDEX **Nil**

WALTER MITTYISH

in the style of Walter Mitty, a fictional character created by US writer and cartoonist James Thurber (1894–1961);

'highly imaginative', 'leading a fantasy life':

> *She excelled at school, received her first kiss from a teacher and travelled the world with her dad, whose Walter Mittyish career path as an international hustler sounds as though it might rate a book of its own.* (Observer)

Thurber's comic story 'The Secret Life of Walter Mitty' runs to less than six pages but the title character has given his name to any male who leads an energetic but innocent fantasy life. Mitty – a middle-aged man sent on errands by his wife in between being rebuked for driving too fast – retreats into heroic daydreams in which he imagines himself commanding a ship in a storm, conducting a tricky surgical operation, facing a firing squad, etc. The term *Walter Mittyish* isn't particularly critical, since there is usually no attempt to deceive other people, but it may suggest an almost obsessive taste for creating imaginary selves and an unwillingness to face the real world.

PRETENTIOUSNESS INDEX **Nil**

(see also *Thurberesque*)

WARHOLIAN

relating to the style or work of pop artist Andy Warhol (1928–87); 'mass-produced', 'impersonal', 'camp', 'detached':

> *Great pop moments […] are very often the work of Holy Fools brave enough to barge to the front of the queue, confront the world with their own ludicrousness, and rejoice in their Warholian quarter of an hour.* (Guardian)

Warhol advocated a new type of American art, one that not merely depicted objects of mass production like soup cans but, by using silkscreen prints, mass-produced the images themselves, which then acquired an iconic quality. He was famous for his extraordinary looks, his studio called the Factory, his gayness – and, long before his death, famous just for being Warhol. The *Guardian* quote above refers to his well-known observation, 'In the future everyone will be world-famous for 15 minutes.' In its way, it's an oddly democratic remark, of a piece with his elevation of the most familiar items of US (and therefore world) culture: Coke cans, Marilyn Monroe, etc.

PRETENTIOUSNESS INDEX *!*

WASHINGTONIAN

describing either the first US President, George Washington (1732–99), or the city of that name, capital of the United States;

(of the person) 'honest', 'inspirational'; (of the city) 'neo-classical', 'imperial':

> *A little later came the proconsuls, men of imperial gravitas, stately courtesy and crisp, regulation haircuts. All wore the Washingtonian toga: sober, dark suit and white shirt.* (Guardian)

Washingtonian is more frequently used to refer to the city than the President who gave the place its name. If describing the man, then the term is most likely to refer either to his leadership or to his reputation for honesty (the childhood story of Washington cutting down the cherry tree and not being able to lie about it to his father). If *Washingtonian* is used about the US capital itself, rather than one of its inhabitants, the term frequently carries some 'imperial' connotations. This is a city whose public buildings are not merely modelled on classical originals but whose predominance in world affairs inevitably recalls the Roman Empire. The writer of the *Guardian* piece above wittily develops the idea so that plain suits become the equivalent of senatorial togas.

PRETENTIOUSNESS INDEX **Nil**

WAUGHISH

typical of the style, work or personality of writer Evelyn Waugh (1903–66);

'satirical', 'deadpan', 'unsentimental', 'curmudgeonly':

> *I loved Logan's Waugh-ish moment with his baby son: 'Lionel has croup. He seems a sickly baby. I sat him on my knee the other day and he stared at me with a baleful, sullen, and unknowing eye.'* (Daily Telegraph)

In the 1920s and 1930s Evelyn Waugh was at the heart of fashionable society and wrote a series of stylish novels, such as *Decline and Fall* (1928) and *A Handful of Dust* (1934), that treated the world in which he moved with a mixture of affection and satirical disdain. Conversion to Catholicism and service in World War Two brought out the serious strain that had always lurked in Waugh, and he later turned himself into the caricature of a crusty country squire: reactionary, prematurely aged and bored with life. *Waugh-ish* may refer to his literary style, notable for its spare elegance, or to his later public persona – which, as his diaries show, wasn't far removed from the private reality. In particular, Waugh could be very detached in his attitude to his own children, as the parody referred to in the *Telegraph* quote shows.

PRETENTIOUSNESS INDEX *!*

WELLESIAN

in the style of actor and film director Orson Welles (1915–85);

'maverick', 'wildly talented', 'self-destructive', 'zestful':

> *There's ample video footage of Troy proclaiming his own Wellesian skills, but little suggesting any inkling of actual talent.* (Observer)

There were many sides to Orson Welles, and the term *Wellesian* might mean any or all of them. There was the prodigious success of his first film, *Citizen Kane* (1941), which he directed, starred in and co-wrote before the age of 30, and which is regularly cited by critics as one of the greatest films of all time. There was his screen presence: he dominates *The Third Man* (1949) yet features on screen for only a few minutes of it. Then there was his habit of embarking on grand film projects and leaving them unfinished, and his habit of alienating the big Hollywood studios. There was the way his career seemed to follow a great descending arc so that, starting at the top, he finished up making sherry commercials and appearing in a Muppet movie. And there was the larger than life character of Welles: his size, his charisma, his ability to inspire others.

PRETENTIOUSNESS INDEX *!*

(see also *Kane-like*)

WELLINGTONIAN

in the style of Arthur Wellesley, first Duke of Wellington (1769–1852);

'resolute', 'disciplined', 'ingenious':

Clearly some simple, Wellingtonian solution is required to cope with the problem of pigeons in Trafalgar Square, the swarms of 'rats with wings', as Ken Livingstone, the Mayor of London has called them ... (Daily Telegraph)

The reference above is to do with the Iron Duke's reply to a query from Queen Victoria about the problem of what to do with the sparrows that were threatening to overrun the Crystal Palace at the Great Exhibition of 1851. 'Sparrowhawks, ma'am,' said the one-time Prime Minister and commander-for-life of British forces. But Wellington was distinguished for more than robust good sense. Tactically brilliant, his command was said by one of his soldiers to guarantee two things: a constant supply of rations and a 'd—d good thrashing' to the enemy.

PRETENTIOUSNESS INDEX *!*

WELLSIAN

typical of the style or themes favoured by novelist H(erbert) G(eorge) Wells (1866–1946);

'visionary', 'futuristic':

That 'terrible ghost' is the Seventies, and no matter how awful things appear to be, nothing is more devastating than a return to that hideous decade. What signals this Wellsian journey through time? (Independent)

Although H.G. Wells was a very prolific writer, producing a range of work from social comedies to children's histories, he is largely remembered now for a handful of science-fiction stories such as *The Time Machine* (1895), *The Island of Doctor Moreau* (1896) and *The War of the Worlds* (1898). Oddly, given the rather bleak quality of these tales, Wells is identified with a progressive, generally optimistic view of human progress. His views darkened as he grew older, but *Wellsian* recalls the sense of broadening horizons in science and society towards the end of the 19th century.

PRETENTIOUSNESS INDEX *!*

WILDEAN

typical of the style, work or life of dramatist and writer Oscar Wilde (1854–1900);

'scandalous', 'witty', 'paradoxical', 'aesthetic', 'elegant':

George Dubya's sense of humour could never be described as Wildean but, thanks to former British ambassador Sir Christopher Meyer, we now know what makes the world's most powerful man laugh. (Observer)

Oscar Wilde's life was brought to a tragic and premature climax by his imprisonment for homosexual offences for two years from 1895. Prison did not break him, quite, but he died in Paris at the turn of the 19th century. For a long time afterwards Wilde's name was synonymous with scandal and sexual practices that couldn't be decently discussed. Now *Wildean* is more likely to refer to the elegance of his phrasing and wit – whether in person or through the mouths of his characters in plays such as *The Importance of Being Earnest* (1895) – as well as to an aesthetic doctrine that made beauty rather than any moral consideration the supreme aim of art.

PRETENTIOUSNESS INDEX *!*

WILDERISH

in the style of a film directed by Billy Wilder (1906–2002);

'waspish', 'witty', 'acutely observed':

A spruce-looking Dennis Quaid plays that most Wilderish of figures, an advertising executive, immersed in one mother of a midlife crisis. (Guardian)

Billy Wilder was born in Vienna and worked as a scriptwriter in the German film industry in the early 1930s. Escaping Nazism, he made his way to America and Hollywood where he directed a string of classics such as *Sunset Boulevard* (1951) and *Some Like It Hot* (1960). Wilder's European background, though not unusual in post-war Hollywood, was sometimes given as the reason why he made films that were unusually witty and often acerbic as well as 'literary' in their approach. The adjective *Wilderish* might mean any of these things, or more simply be applied to one of the neurotic, middle-aged and urban men who are frequent characters in his work and whose best-known film incarnations were Jack Lemmon and Walter Matthau.

PRETENTIOUSNESS INDEX *!*

WILSONIAN

characteristic of Harold Wilson (1916–95), Labour politician and Prime Minister;

'wily', 'pragmatic', 'devious':

> *The price of power is messy compromise: he used that Wilsonian word, pragmatism.* (Guardian)

Harold Wilson was Prime Minister twice (1964–70 and 1974–76). Both of his premierships were marked by union troubles and economic misfortune that verged on the disastrous. He was seen, unfairly or not, as a leader who was more interested in fiddling with the levers of power than applying principles to government. So *Wilsonian* has come to mean 'pragmatic' or 'opportunist', although now that the 30th anniversary of his resigning as Prime Minister has passed there is a revaluation of his period in office.

PRETENTIOUSNESS INDEX **Nil**

WODEHOUSIAN

typical of the style or subject matter of comic novelist P(elham) G(renville) Wodehouse (1881–1975);

'witty', 'affectionately mocking', 'stylish', 'amiable', 'creating a self-enclosed world':

> *Years ago, when we all knew our place thanks to drama such as* Brideshead Revisited *and* To the Manor Born, *television treated posh eccentrics with a gentle, Wodehousian humour.* (The Times)

Wodehouse enjoyed a remarkably long and successful career as a writer, although the latter part of his life was dogged by controversy over wartime broadcasts he had made from Germany (he and his wife had been taken prisoner in France and then interned in Germany). Wodehouse never returned to England but spent the rest of his life in the US. This dark interlude is at odds with the sunny nature of his fiction, which deals with a world of upper-class twits and eccentrics attended by shrewd servants, most famously Jeeves and Bertie Wooster. *Wodehousian* may describe this universe, as complete as anything created by Dickens or Tolkien, or it may refer to his unique comic style which can, accurately for once, be called inimitable.

PRETENTIOUSNESS INDEX **Nil**

(see also *Jeevesian* and *Woosterish*)

WOOSTERISH

typical of the character of Bertie Wooster, created by P.G. Wodehouse;

'amiable', 'upper-class but dim', 'accident-prone':

Or Harry Andrews, author of Training, dispensing charmingly Woosterish advice: 'I find champagne is practically the only wine of genuine use to the athlete' – well, absolutely, old chap. (Independent on Sunday)

P.G. Wodehouse's most famous characters, Wooster and Jeeves, are, like Holmes and Watson, one of the great double acts of English literature. The agreeable but buffoonish Bertie Wooster requires the subtle hand of his manservant to steer him away from trouble. Applied to someone who is well-meaning but dim and bumbling, *Woosterish* conveys a mixture of exasperation and affection.

PRETENTIOUSNESS INDEX **Nil**

(see also *Jeevesian* and *Wodehousian*)

WORDSWORTHIAN

typical of the style or subject matter of poet William Wordsworth (1770–1850);

'transcendental', 'serious', 'nature-loving':

They are wary at first but when they get in the water and realise they are up a mountain [...] and the only noise is the echo of their friends shrieking about how amazing it is, they love it, or get all Wordsworthian. (Observer)

Wordsworth may not be much read these days but he is forever associated with the Lake District, where he spent most of his life and which forms the backdrop to much of his work. He had an almost pantheistic belief in the natural world, sometimes seeing it as embodying a moral force. But the complex emotions that nature inspired in him are narrowed to a clichéd rapture, and it's in this sense that *Wordsworthian* is frequently used.

PRETENTIOUSNESS INDEX **Nil**

YEATSIAN

typical of the style or subject matter of Irish poet W(illiam) B(utler) Yeats (1865–1939);

'lyrical', 'quintessentially Irish', 'mystical':

She saw herself not as Australian but as displaced from Ireland – her father's country – and longed to 'return' to its Yeatsian mists and myth.

(Daily Telegraph)

Yeats is Ireland's national poet and he was highly influential in the movement that came to be known as the Celtic Revival, a celebration of his country's roots in culture, myth and folklore. Yeats enjoyed a public career in the arts and politics – he was involved in the setting up of the famous Abbey Theatre and he became an Irish senator in 1922 – but *Yeatsian* tends to be used in a fairly restricted way. It may describe the lyrical quality of his verse but it is as likely to be used to evoke a vague and clichéd image of 'Oirish' life.

PRETENTIOUSNESS INDEX *!*

ZOLA-ESQUE

typical of the style or themes of the French novelist Émile Zola (1840–1902);

'realistic', 'factual', 'squalid', 'panoramic':

It was a surprise to find the opera set in the late 1940s, amid this Zola-esque grimness, but it worked well. (Daily Telegraph)

By the standards of his day Émile Zola was an explicit writer. One of his earliest works, the thriller-like *Thérèse Raquin* (1867), was called pornographic, and much of his writing explores the power of the sexual instinct. His focus on daily life among the middle and working classes was underpinned by a naturalistic style, and the term *Zola-esque* has come to be equated with a realism that doesn't turn away from squalid or grim subject matter.

PRETENTIOUSNESS INDEX *!*

INDEX

Othello-like
Ozymandian
Pandarus-like
Panglossian
Paxmanesque
Pecksniffian
Pepysian
Pickwickian
Pinteresque
Pirandellian
Piranesian
Poirot-esque
Pollyanna-ish
Polonius-like
Pooterish
Potterish
Prospero-like
Proustian
Prufrockian
Puckish
Pythonesque
Quixotic
Rabelaisian
Ramboesque
Rebecca-like
Reithian
Rembrandtesque
Renoiresque
Rimbaudian
Rubenesque
Runyonesque
Ruritanian
Scrooge-like
Shakespearean
Shandyesque
Shangri-la-like
Shavian
Shelleyan
Sitwellian
Spielbergian
Spock-like

Steinbeckian
Stepfordian
Stoppardian
Svengali-like
Swiftian
Tarantino-esque
Tardis-like
Tati-like
Tennysonian
Terminator-like
Thoreauesque
Thurberesque
Tiggerish
Tolkienesque
Tolstoyan
Transylvanian
Trollopian
Turneresque
Uncle Tom-like
Voltairean
Wagnerian
Walter Mittyish
Warholian
Waughish
Wellesian
Wellsian
Wildean
Wilderish
Wodehousian
Woosterish
Wordsworthian
Yeatsian
Zolaesque

*Biblical &
    religious*
Babylonian
Buddhist-style
Calvinist
Herodian
Judas-like

Lazarus-like
Manichaean
Methuselan
Philistine
Pilate-like
Protestant
Samsonesque
Solomon-like

*Classical &
    legendary*
Adonis-like
Amazonian
Apollonian
Arcadian
Arthurian
Augean
Augustan
Bacchanalian
Caligulan
Cassandra-like
Ciceronian
Circean
Colosseum-style
Croesus-like
Cyclopean
Damoclean
Delphic
Dionysian
Draconian
Elysian
Epicurean
Erotic
Gordian (knot)
Herculean
Homeric
Hydra-like
Janus-like
Junoesque
Lucullan
Midas-like

Narcissistic
Nero-esque
Odyssean
Oedipal
Olympian
Orphic
Pandora's (box)
Parnassian
Parthian (shot)
Periclean
Philippic
Priapic
Procrustean
Promethean
Protean
Pyrrhic (victory)
Sapphic
Sibylline
Sisyphean
Spartan
Sphinx-like
Stygian
Thespian

Miscellaneous
Alamo-like
Balkan
Barbie-doll
Beckhamesque
Blimpish
Bothamesque
Bransonesque
Brummellesque
Byzantine
Canute-like
Chauvinist
Cinderella
Damascene
Diana-like
Edwardian
Gazza-like

Gettyesque
Gothic
Hampstead
Houdini-like
Howard
  Hughes-like
Islingtonian
Jordanesque
Lewinsky-like
Lucan-like
Luddite
Mandarin
Mansonesque
Masochistic
Maxwellian
Murdochian
Oates-like
Oxbridge
Oxonian
Potemkin-style
Rachmanite
Rooneyesque
Sadistic
Scott-like
Sven-like
Teutonic

Victorian

*Philosophy,
  psychology,
  science &
  economics*
Confucian
Darwinian
Einsteinian
Freudian
Hobbesian
Jungian
Keynesian
Laingian
Machiavellian
Malthusian
Nietzschean
Pavlovian
Platonic
Rousseauesque
Sartrean
Smilesian
Spockish
Socratic
Stoic
Utopian

*Politics, war &
  leadership*
Attleean
Bevanite
Blairite
Boadicean
Brownite
Bushite
Butskellite
Cameronian
Carteresque
Churchillian
Clarkeite
Clintonian
Cromwellian
Disraelian
Gaitskellite
Gandhian
Gladstonian
Goebbels-like
Heathite
Hitlerian
Jeffersonian
Kennedyesque
Majorish
Mandela-like

Mandelsonian
Maoist
McCarthyite
Mosleyite
Mussolini-like
Napoleonic
Nelsonian
Nixonian
Palmerstonian
Poujadist
Powellite
Prescottian
Profumo-like
Reaganite
Rumsfeldian
Soviet-style
Spartist
Stakhanovite
Stalinist
Tebbit
Thatcherite
Washingtonian
Wellingtonian
Wilsonian